Ezekiel Watch

Then They Shall Know...

Chris Hambleton

Ezekiel Watch – Then They Shall Know
Copyright © 2011, 2014, 2018 by Chris Hambleton
www.cwhambleton.com

Scripture taken from the New King James Version. Copyright © 1982 by
Thomas Nelson, Inc. Used by permission. All rights reserved.

Connect with Me Online:
Website: http://www.cwhambleton.com
Blog: http://fictionsoftware.wordpress.com
Facebook: http://facebook.com/cwhambleton
Twitter: http://twitter.com/chris_hambleton

Discover Other Titles by the Author

Speculative Fiction Titles
"Out of the Whirlwind"
"The Exchange"
"The Castors of Giza"
"The Cell"
"Endeavor in Time"

The Time of Jacob's Trouble Trilogy
"The Last Aliyah" (Book 1)
"The Son of Shinar" (Book 2)
"The Siege of Zion" (Book 3)

The Sons of Liberty Trilogy
"The Convention" (Book 1)
"The Green Zone" (Book 2)
"The Declaration" (Book 3)

The HaZikaron Series
"The Seed of Haman" (Book 1)

Non-Fiction Titles
"Walks with Rich"
"Our American Awakening"
"The American Tyrant"
"Ezekiel Watch"
"On the Precipice"

To learn more about Chris Hambleton and his other books, please visit his author website at http://www.cwhambleton.com..

Table of Contents

Foreword

NOTE: *The first edition of this book was written in 2010 and later updated in 2014 and then again in 2018 to include the most recent developments in the Middle East, Europe, Russia, and the United States.*

When the Cold War ended with the collapse of the Soviet Union in 1991, much of the Western world breathed a collective sigh of relief. I remember it vividly because that was the year I graduated from high school. The "peace in our time" that so many had yearned for since the 1950's had finally become a reality. Our prayers in the West were answered – we no longer had to fear waking up to a "Red Dawn".

However, quickly following on the heels of the fall of global communism, a new enemy arose – a much more determined, much deadlier enemy: radical Islam. Only a few years after the Cold War ended, we found our embassies, battleships, and even cities attacked by Islamic terrorists. But rather than take the attacks seriously, we refused to mount any adequate response to their acts of terrorism. Radical Islam had declared war upon us, and it was often shrugged off as a tragedy but not a real threat.

But then came the horrendous attacks of September 11th, 2001, and the West finally woke up to the new enemy rising against us. America invaded Afghanistan in order to destroy the al Qaeda terrorist-network and their state-sponsor, the Taliban. Two years later, the United States invaded Iraq under the premise of removing the WMDs (Weapons of Mass Destruction), and America was soon bogged down in a war against foreign terrorists and insurgents. It wasn't until nearly five years later that stability began to return to Iraq – but it wasn't to last.

The next significant event after 9/11 was the financial crisis in late 2008 and the subsequent election of Barack Obama, who's foreign policies in the Middle East further destabilized the region, particularly the withdrawal of nearly all US forces from Iraq, pulling support from our allies, and supporting various revolutionary organizations with deep ties to Islamic terrorism.

Obama's policies upended decades of US foreign policy and precipitated revolutions in at least three separate countries, leading to several Western allies being deposed, as well as triggering the ongoing Syrian Civil War which has claimed over half a million lives and displaced more than 11 million people.

As the stability in the Middle East continues to deteriorate, many people are fearful for the future and wondering, "What's going to happen next?" Many have been examining the End Times and Israel, especially with the looming threat of Iran's nuclear weapons program, the civil war in Syria, and the increasing presence of Russia in the Middle East. While the recent election of Donald Trump and the relocation of the American embassy to Jerusalem initially triggered another round of flare-ups, it remains to be seen how long before the next large-scale upheaval occurs. This book will examine in detail the prophetic events of Ezekiel 38-39, the apparent precursor to those events (Psalm 83), and analyze many of the recent events which have already transpired.

As more time has passed since first diving into Middle Eastern events and Bible prophecy (2003-2010), I've noticed that while various modern events seem to indicate that the fulfillment of prophetic events are at hand, often the events pass and what we thought could be prophetic fulfillment turns out not to be. In fact, as history has demonstrated (particularly recent history), it's nearly impossible to accurately identify a modern event as the prophetic fulfillment beforehand – as God intended. Because of this observation, only trends are given in this book, not near-term dates/predictions. If the Lord wills to delay the events of Ezekiel 38-39 or anything else in His Word, that's His business – not ours. Our responsibility is to be faithful and watchful (Matt 24:42, 25:21, Romans 8).

Many world events which are occurring today can be viewed as the moving of pieces on a chessboard, with pawns on either side being maneuvered, conquered, and removed, as the major players are inching into position. And though there are wars, revolutions, and upheavals break out across the world, the first of the major End Times events has yet to occur: Ezekiel 38-39. The sobering aspect of this particular prophecy is that it appears to be on our very-near horizon, and could be literally fulfilled within our lifetimes.

Since the advent of the Industrial Age, but especially since the dawn of the Nuclear Age, many people have been dusting off their Bibles and have been taking another look at what it says about the End Times events, particularly the Book of Revelation. However, what many fail to realize is that the Book of Revelation is primarily a coagulation of thousands of detailed prophecies described in the Old Testament. Revelation sequences many of the Old Testament prophecies which can often seem disjointed or even contradictory at times. As Bible students and scholars of the last century or so reexamined the Old Testament prophecies more carefully, they encountered many surprises, with one of the foremost being the prophecies within Ezekiel 38-39.

The Ezekiel 38-39 prophecies describe in detail a massive attack (frequently termed the "Magog Invasion") on Israel by Russia, Iran, Turkey, and the other Islamic nations of the Middle East and God's supernatural intervention on Israel's behalf. This attack occurs after Israel has been regathered to her native homeland, which was unimaginable before the Twentieth Century. In fact, when Ezekiel wrote these prophecies, Israel and Judah had just been carried off to Captivity and the Jewish nation had essentially died.

But then came the rebirth of the nation of Israel in 1948, and has since been experiencing the incredible regathering of her people from every corner of the globe as described in Ezekiel 36-37. When that process began, scholars began examining the surrounding passages, which of course led them to the two chapters that followed the Regathering: Ezekiel 38-39. And since the Regathering closely followed the birth of the Nuclear Age, some realized that the strange descriptions of the aftermath of the Magog Invasion appear to parallel the basic procedures involved in the cleanup when ABC (Atomic, Biological, and Chemical) weapons are involved.

With the discovery of a modern doomsday scenario described in detail more than 2500 years ago, the Ezekiel 38-39 prophecies suddenly began being heavily scrutinized, since they could very well involve the use of tactical nuclear weapons. And given the demand for oil and the current circumstances, such a war could have devastating global repercussions.

In 1999, I was given an MP3 CD entitled "Learn the Bible in 24 Hours" by Koinonia House, and it had a huge impact on my views of the Bible, Israel, and also America. While I had been a Christian for more than ten years at that point, I had failed to fully comprehend the supernatural, integrated message of the Scriptures, in that every word in the Bible (in the original languages, of course) was put there by Divine design. Suddenly, the Living Word became very "alive" to me and took on an entirely new meaning.

Soon after going through that study, I set out to do my own thorough examination of the Bible, which ended up lasting nearly two years. About the time my study was finished, the War in Iraq began and I felt led to create a website to describe the events of Ezekiel 36-39 and track the current events in the Middle East through the lens of Scripture (EzekielWatch.com).

Several years later in 2010, I went on a study-tour of Israel with Koinonia House and visited the land of Israel for myself. Next to the "Bible in 24 Hours" study, that trip has had the single most important impact on my faith and perception of the world. The brief tour of the Holy Land had a deep impact on my perspectives of Israel, the United States of America, and the other nations involved in the lasting Middle East conflict. The guide for our group was phenomenal and constantly taught us both Israel's Biblical history and her recent history over the past century.

Upon my return to the States, I began reading the modern story of Israel and joined several online Israeli pages/groups. I have found that the Israeli people have several characteristics that seem to be sorely lacking in many parts of the Western world today: a strong national identity and a clear sense of purpose. Though they are hard-pressed on every side, they are determined to not only survive, but thrive in a very hostile world.

In the months following the tour, I came to feel a strong connection with the Jewish people along with a deep longing to return to Israel. As a Christian, just being in the very place where so much of the Scriptures took place – and where so much of our future will center around – I could not help but desire to go back to the place often referred to as the Lord's Inheritance.

At the time I first created the EzekielWatch.com website, I did not fully understand many of the complexities involved with the Palestinians, Israel, the Arabs, and Jordan. It's not as simple as "the Jews should just annex the West Bank and Gaza and make it part of Israel" as many American evangelicals (along with many Orthodox Jews) proclaim. If it was, I am certain that Israel would have done so after 1967 in the aftermath of the Six Day War.

My first excursion into writing began in 2006 and my first book, "The Time of Jacob's Trouble" was released in 2008. After I returned from Israel in 2010, I rewrote the book into a trilogy based upon all I had learned about the people, the land, and the political situation. With the completion of "The Time of Jacob's Trouble" trilogy, I noticed that the EzekielWatch.com website badly needed updating, which then led to the conclusion that the material on the site could better be utilized in the form of a book.

And with that realization, the "Ezekiel Watch" book was born. It's my sincerest desire that this study will bolster your faith, give you a greater understanding of the Scriptures and Israel, and give you a greater appreciation for the truly miraculous times we are living in and the challenges we face. Though we face days of rising turbulence and uncertainty, we can rely upon the Lord just as He has promised Israel: "He who keeps us shall not slumber nor sleep." (Psalm 121:4)

I. The Worst of Times, the Best of Times

Today in the West, we are often living in the Worst of Times, yet also the Best of Times. Our world is filled with increasing uncertainty, from widespread famines to global unrest to devastating wars and horrific acts of terrorism. At the same time, we have access to greater knowledge, incredible technology, and vast resources which were unimaginable only a matter of years ago. Our world is changing faster than ever before, and these changes continue to increase in speed and volatility.

In the ten years that have passed since the Financial Crisis of 2008, the US economy has not only stabilized, but boomed over the past several years, particularly since the lame-duck period of Barack Obama's presidency and the election of Donald Trump. However, such economic booms are fraught with risk and volatility, and often the bigger the boom, the bigger the crash. Household spending as well as the national debt continues to rise out of control and there seems to be little concern about returning to financial solvency in America.

While the economies of the European Union have also stabilized, another recession could quickly throw them into financial and civil chaos very quickly. As with the United States, many of the same problems haven't been solved over the last decade, they've simply been papered over and ignored. Meanwhile, across much of Europe the liberal democracies are slowly but steadily being taken over by Islam, but not by the sword as in the Middle Ages – they are simply being out-bred and then one day, out-voted. In democracies where every person gets a vote, it's the number of people in each people-group and their accompanying values that determine the course of the society. And if one group is producing only one child for every four or five children of another group, then it's only a matter of years before the society is permanently altered.

After World War II, Europe was devastated and needed to be rebuilt. With millions of her men slaughtered in the preceding Great War, she was in critical need of more laborers, yet had little resources. The two World Wars had bled Europe dry of capital, resources, and labor classes. So she turned to the only source of cheap labor available nearby: the Muslims of North Africa and the Middle East. Mass immigration was instituted and Europe began being rebuilt. However, the new immigrants did not assimilate nor in most cases adopt Western values and beliefs – they held to their own, which are inherently incompatible.

Over the decades of the Cold War, the primary concern of Europe was the constant threat of communism due to the aggressive policies of the Soviet Union. Meanwhile, the Muslim immigration continued unabated, but many of them did not integrate into the Western society. They not only retained their religion, but their languages, their ways of thinking, and their cultures and traditions. Now Europe is faced with millions of her own citizens who not only have an entirely different way of looking at the world, but their values are often the exact opposite of those of the West, especially in the areas of liberalism, tolerance, race, and equality.

After World War II ended, Europe and Great Britain rushed headlong into socialism, which has the cumulative effect of robbing societies of their souls. Under socialism, immorality and debauchery always take root and then the population of the society steadily declines because it breaks down the family structures. After all, why look out for your family if the government will take care of them, and why have children if the State will take care of you in your old age? Why have children if they are more of an expense than a benefit, an interference with your life rather than a benefit? The socialist state wants productive members of society, and the elderly and the young are more of a burden than a benefit.

While the traditional Europeans began having fewer and fewer children, the Muslims within their borders had more and more. The effects of such differences in birthrates aren't felt for several generations, but when they finally are, they become practically insurmountable. By 2050, Muslims will make up one-fourth of the entire population of Europe – that's less than two more generations away. Thirty years ago, they were but a fraction of a percent, and they haven't assimilated in the decades since. Such shifts in population are very difficult, if not impossible to reverse, much less overcome – particularly under socialism. What can Europe do when they're being out-born five to one?

During the Cold War, Europe was trapped between America and the Soviet Union, between capitalism and communism. Today, Europe is trapped between insolvent socialism and growing Islam. In many ways, Europe's days of greatness ended in World War II – she just doesn't seem to acknowledge it yet. The European Union was the last opportunity for them to right the sinking ship of their continent, but now they are all headed down the same path together: into the dark abyss of history. While radical Islam grows in their midst, much of Europe and the United Kingdom seems to lack the basic will to preserve their own cultures, laws, and way of life, let alone repel the creeping tyranny of Sharia law.

How will the rise of Islam change Europe over the course of the next fifty years? If the Middle East is any example, Europe will become a very dark and bloody place. Already, numerous European courts now allow their Muslims to be tried by Sharia law rather than their own legal system of justice and equal rights. Sharia law is a brutal, barbaric legal system which often involves beating, stoning, lashing, mutilation, and even death by beheading. The very nations that outlawed capital punishment as inhumane may soon allow beheadings as prescribed by Sharia law. And what of slavery, which has been abolished in Europe for centuries but is legal in various forms under Sharia law? Meanwhile, it seems that enforcing political correctness and combating hate-speech has become more of a priority in Great Britain than fighting real crimes such as child sex-trafficking and youth violence. Much of London and the British Isles are increasingly unrecognizable to her native citizens.

The Book of Revelation speaks of beheading for those who don't take the "mark of the Beast," but beheading hasn't been done on a large scale in Europe since the guillotines of the French Revolution over two hundred years ago. Yet beheading today is one of the preferred forms of capital punishment in Islam. Could it be that the beheadings spoken of in Revelation are merely the tenants of a world run by Islam in the End Times? As the picture of the End Times becomes clearer, it is becoming increasingly likely that Islamic law and culture will be widespread at that time.

Across the Atlantic, we in America face the long-term decline of the United States of America, both as an economic superpower and as a military superpower. America is also infected with the wasting disease of socialism, which has already decaying much of Europe and Great Britain. Our people are faced with crushing amounts of debt, debilitating federal regulations, and declining means of production and sources of income. The fate of the West lies with America, and with our decline goes the bulk of our remaining Western values, traditions, and heritage.

Strangely enough, there are numerous alliances being formed between Islam and radical leftists/socialists to hasten the collapse of the West. After all, they both have the same enemies: capitalists, Christians, and Jews. Even the previous president of the United States seemed to go out of his way to embrace Islam and put down Judeo-Christian traditions while in office (Barack Obama). As each day goes by, we march closer and closer to the death of the West. These truly are the Worst of Times, and the days ahead only seem to be darkening.

But from another perspective, we are living in the Best of Times. Our generation is the only one to be able to watch Biblical prophecy being fulfilled before our very eyes. For the last sixty-odd years, we've been able to pick up a Bible and daily read about its fulfillment in the newspaper and the nightly news. Next to the Coming of the Messiah, the Rebirth of Israel is the most significant prophetic fulfillment in history, and it's been happening in our time.

Every day, we can turn on the television, read the newspaper, or browse the Internet and see firsthand the faithfulness of God in restoring, preserving, and prospering Israel, in spite of the massive forces gathered against her. Every day, we can literally watch Israel being regathered from the nations after their two-thousand year Diaspora. Every day, we can watch Jerusalem becoming a greater stone-of-contention as God described thousands of years ago. Only the Gospel-period could rival this time in history!

In the days to come, there will likely be more and more chaos and strange weather and earthquakes throughout the world and it will seem that everything is coming apart. Nation will rise against nation, there will be wars and rumors of war, and many earthquakes will occur in diverse places (Matthew 24:7). The nations will plot and rage against Israel and while she may falter,

God will watch over her and preserve her (Psalm 121, Zechariah 12).

But in the midst of these turbulent times, Jesus told us emphatically to watch and not fear, for such things would certainly indeed transpire as the End approaches (Matt 24:4-8). Of all the peoples on the earth, we Christians should recognize these times and prepare ourselves to be called Home.

Let none of us be found with idle hands and slumbering as that Day approaches.

II. A Brief History of Ancient Israel

The best place to begin every story is at the beginning, and
the primary focus of the Old Testament is about a specific group
of people that God chose for Himself, the people of Israel. The
first six books of the Old Testament concern how that nation
began with one man and one family, the enslavement and
liberation of that new nation in Egypt, and then the establishment
of the nation in the land of Canaan. The rest of the books of the
Old Testament describe God's interactions with the Twelve
Tribes of Israel.

Starting in the Book of Genesis, the nation of Israel first
began with God calling a man named Abram out of Ur of the
Chaldeans in roughly 2100 BC. Abram migrated to the land of
Canaan (one of Noah's grandsons) and became a nomad or
sojourner in the land. His son Isaac had two sons, Esau and
Jacob, through which came two nations: Edom and Israel.
Jacob's name was changed to Israel after he returned to the land
from Haran, where he had fled from his brother after stealing his
birthright and his blessing.

While in Haran, Jacob had eleven sons, with the twelfth son
being born in Canaan (Benjamin). Ten of his older sons sold
their brother Joseph into slavery in Egypt, and then soon began
having children of their own. When a severe famine struck the
land of Canaan, Jacob moved his entire family – now seventy in
all – down to the land of Egypt and settled there.

In the four centuries that followed, the Israelites quickly grew
in number and were subsequently enslaved by the Egyptians.
The Book of Exodus tells how God raised up Moses and then
delivered the Israelites out of bondage by a series of devastating
plagues upon the land of Egypt. When Israel left Egypt, they had
a population of 603,550 men ready for war (Numbers 1:46), with
a total estimated population of about 2.5 million. At Mount Sinai
where God gave Israel His laws, He entered into a conditional
covenant with Israel, in that they could remain in the land He
would give them if they obeyed His laws. But due to their lack of
faith and disobedience, the children of Israel were forced to

wander in the wilderness for forty years before God took them into the Promised Land, the land of Canaan.

After Israel settled in the land following the days of Joshua, she had a very erratic relationship with God which usually involved them falling into idolatry, being punished by their enemies, then repenting before being delivered from her oppressors. This four-hundred year period is described in the Book of Judges and the early chapters of 1 Samuel. At the end of the time of the Judges, the people demanded a king, and God granted their request by first giving them King Saul, and then King David.

King Saul and King David united the Twelve Tribes under one banner, and Israel achieved great wealth and power under David's son Solomon. After Solomon's kingdom ended in roughly 950 BC, the northern tribes of Israel broke away and formed the Northern Kingdom, commonly referred to as the House of Israel, while the Southern Kingdom formed the House of Judah. (The Northern Kingdom was made up of the nine northern tribes of Israel: Zebulon, Issachar, Asher, Naphtali, Dan, Manasseh, Ephraim, Reuben, and Gad; the Southern Kingdom was made up of the tribes of Judah, Simeon, Benjamin, and Levi, the tribe of the priesthood.) However, while the Southern Kingdom remained faithful to God (at least at first), the Northern Kingdom abandoned His covenant and pursued the terrible gods of the Canaanites and her other neighbors like the Moabites, Assyrians, and the Ammonites.

Many of the books of the Old Testament are God's warnings to the Divided Kingdom which had broken their covenant with God and were about to be cast out of the land. This event occurred in 722 BC when the Assyrian Empire invaded the land and disbursed the Northern Kingdom throughout the empire – just as God had promised to do centuries earlier in Deuteronomy 28. Tragically, the Southern Kingdom failed to learn from Israel's punishment and was subsequently exiled to Babylon in 586 BC, with both Jerusalem and the Temple completely destroyed.

A common misconception in extra-Biblical literature is the idea of the Ten Lost Tribes of Israel. However, there is no Biblical basis for such an idea, since there were only nine tribes of the Northern Kingdom that were scattered throughout the

Assyrian Empire, which later became the Babylonian Empire, the Persian Empire, the Greek Empire, and then lastly the Roman Empire and the Parthenon Empire. Not only that, but none of them were ever actually "lost," just widely scattered. There may be several offshoots of the Twelve Tribes that could be considered "lost", but their numbers are not really significant. In fact, the New Testament book of James was written specifically to the Twelve Tribes scattered abroad (James 1:1). Various families and groups were scattered further, but none of the entire tribes were lost in the way such fictional literature describes.

Seventy years after the Southern Kingdom was taken away to Babylon, the Medo-Persian Empire conquered the Babylonian Empire and restored many of the ancient peoples to their original homelands. Judah was one such nation, and various remnants of the Twelve Tribes returned back to the land of Israel, just as God had foretold through several prophets like Daniel, Ezekiel, and Jeremiah. However, the bulk of the Twelve Tribes remained scattered throughout the Persian Empire and the subsequent empires, kingdoms, and nations that followed.

The times and locations of the scattered people of Israel is what is commonly referred to as the Diaspora. And so the tribes remained – outside of the land of Israel – until the last century when they began to be awakened and called to return to their native homeland.

III. The Promise to Abraham

Genesis 12:1-3

1 Now the LORD had said to Abram:
"Get out of your country,
From your family
And from your father's house,
To a land that I will show you.

2 I will make you a great nation;
I will bless you
And make your name great;
And you shall be a blessing.

3 I will bless those who bless you,
And I will curse him who curses you;
And in you all the families of the earth shall be blessed."

Soon after God called Abraham out of the land of the Chaldeans, He made several promises to him, which were later repeated to his son Isaac and then to his grandson Jacob. The first promise was the promise that "Those who bless you, I will bless, and those who curse you, I will curse." (Genesis 12:3)

After Abraham went down to Egypt to escape a terrible famine and then returned to the land, God made another promise to him and his descendants which involved a huge land grant that spanned from the Nile River to the Euphrates River. (Genesis 15:18)

However, soon after making this promise, God had Abraham do something strange: He instructed Abraham to take some sacrificial animals and cut them in half and place them on two altars. But then He put Abraham into a deep sleep and then passed as a burning lantern between the pieces uttering the promise, which became known as the Abrahamic Covenant. Included in the covenant was also a prophecy uttered by God that Abraham's descendants would be enslaved for four hundred years but then He would deliver them and return them to the land. (Genesis 15:9-21)

While this occurrence seems very strange to us at first glance, this was the traditional way of making a covenant at that time. We still have that figure of speech in our language: "cut a covenant." The way the process would work is that both parties would bring their sacrifices, divide them in half, and then walk between the two piles in a figure-eight fashion while reciting the terms of the covenant. Then they would partake of the sacrifice together.

So why did God put Abraham into a deep sleep before making the covenant binding? He did that to make the agreement entirely up to Him. Abraham had no conditions placed upon him – the land grant was an eternal promise that could not be broken even if Abraham tried, because he had nothing to do with it. God promised to give Abraham and his descendants the land of Canaan simply because of His grace. Since the covenant was one-sided, the only one who could break the covenant was God Himself, and God never breaks His promises. Israel cannot violate the covenant even if they wanted to, and from their subsequent history in the Old Testament, it certainly seemed as if they often were trying!

Did you know there are some things that God cannot do? It's true: God cannot sin, and God cannot lie. It's simply impossible for Him to do either one of those, because it would violate His Divine Nature. For us who have fallen because of Adam, we cannot grasp that concept of perfect holiness and all that entails, but the basic idea is that One who is utterly perfect and consistent cannot become imperfect or inconsistent.

Therefore, since God is the one who made the covenant in the first place, the Abrahamic Covenant is eternal, even though it has yet to be fulfilled. God has yet to give the Jews the entire expanse of land He promised to Abraham, and even during the pinnacle of Israel's Kingdom under King Solomon, the Israelites only controlled one-third of the territory God had promised them.

In its most basic definition, a covenant is a binding agreement – or a promise – between two or more parties. Typically, the terms of the covenant would be listed and the restitutions or compensations would also be detailed in the event that one or more parties failed to uphold to their portion of the agreement, which would essentially "break" the covenant and free both from their obligations under the agreement.

The first covenant mentioned in the Bible was that of marriage, namely the marriage between Adam and Eve. In a marriage covenant, there is usually no "exit-clause," implying that the covenant is to be a permanent agreement between both the man and the woman – until death do them part. In the original marriage covenant, there were no conditions such as abuse, adultery, or even death mentioned as being able to end or alter the covenant because sin had not yet entered the world. It was only afterwards that such conditions were added as a result of our fallen nature and the hardness of our hearts (Matt 19:8).

The next covenant recorded in the Bible was between God and Noah (and Noah's sons and descendants) in His promise to never again destroy the earth and all life with a flood. Like the Abrahamic Covenant, this covenant was also one-sided in that all life and death is in God's hands, and He promised to never wipe out all life on earth again (with water). It's understandable how fearful Noah's descendants would be after seeing God destroy the world, and God wanted to provide some reassurance that He would not do that again. And while that promise was given to every living creature on the earth, the next set of covenants – namely the Abrahamic Covenant – was made exclusively with Abraham, Isaac, and Jacob, as well as their descendants.

All the covenants given by God in the Book of Genesis were everlasting covenants which God had made TO the patriarchs, not WITH them, since there were no terms or conditions placed upon the patriarchs. God simply made a promise to them that He swore by Himself to uphold, and nothing the patriarchs (or their descendants) could do would nullify that agreement. In fact, God often restated the promise to "Bless those who bless you, and curse those who curse you," in times of their disobedience and uncertainty (Genesis 12:2-3, 26:3, 28:13-15). Unlike us, God cannot and does not break His promises. Ever.

After the times of the patriarchs passed and Jacob's family went down to Egypt to escape another terrible famine in Canaan, there was a four hundred-year "silent period" between the Book of Genesis and the Book of Exodus. During this silent period, the simple family of Jacob and his sons that when down to Egypt became a great nation of millions of people, who were subsequently enslaved by the Egyptians and pressed into bitter, hard-labor.

If it hadn't been for God intervening on their behalf, it's likely that Israel would have remained oppressed in slavery and then eventually be either scattered within Egypt or simply vanish into history like most enslaved peoples. But God remembered His covenant with Abraham, Isaac, and Jacob and delivered His people out of bondage – because He had made a promise to them and He had to keep it.

IV. The Wedding at Sinai

After the deliverance of the Israelites from their bondage in Egypt, the next major covenant that God made with the descendants of Abraham, Isaac, and Jacob was at Mount Sinai, but this covenant was not one-sided and unconditional as the others had been.

When the Tablets of Stone and the Law were given to Moses and the Twelve Tribes in the wilderness, there were certain conditions that the Israelites had to abide by if they wanted to remain in the Promised Land. This was essentially a marriage-covenant between God and the nation of Israel in a fallen world, with both promising to be faithful to one another or the conditions of the broken covenant would go into effect.

God's covenant with the tribes of Israel at Mount Sinai can be summarized as follows: "If Israel followed the laws and precepts that God had set before her (i.e., the Ten Commandments), then she would dwell in His Land and prosper. But if she forsook those laws – breaking the marriage covenant – she would be cursed, punished, and cast out of His Land. There were no conditions that God placed upon Himself because He's incapable of breaking any covenant.

However, there was always an underlying promise that Israel would one day be brought back to the land and after that time be faithful to God, which would still allow Him to fulfill His promises to Abraham, Isaac, and Jacob (Leviticus 26:40-45, Deuteronomy 4:29-31, Isaiah 43:5-6). Essentially, the Abrahamic Covenant supersedes the Mosaic Covenant just as a marriage covenant supersedes a "living covenant" with one's children. And while Israel is back in the land today after thousands of years, the Abrahamic Covenant still has yet to be fulfilled, but will be after the Messiah returns (Ezekiel 40-48).

Approximately two years after the agreement at Sinai, God instructed Israel to go up and enter into the Promised Land, but because of their fear of the Anakim (the giants) Israel refused to obey – they wanted to go back to Egypt, even if that meant being enslaved again. After all they had seen in Egypt from the Plagues to Passing through the Red Sea to being given manna and water in the desert, Israel was still filled with unbelief. Therefore, God punished them by forcing the Israelites to remain in the wilderness for the next thirty-eight years until the entire generation of unfaithful adults died off (except for Moses, Caleb, and Joshua).

It's been appropriately observed that it only took forty hours for Israel to get out of Egypt, but it took forty years to get "Egypt" out of Israel. But after the generation of unbelievers had died off, the younger Israelites had been living "by faith" for most of their lives and they were finally ready to go in and possess the land that God had given them. The story of the Israelites and their inheritance parallels the gift of salvation that God offers to us: He has given us an incredible promise that's available to all, but it's up to us to first accept it by faith and then possess it.

When the time finally came for the new generation of Israel to go up into the Promised Land, Moses repeated the terms of the marriage-covenant from Sinai (Horeb) to all the people, wrote them down, and then bound the people to it. This has become known as the "Blessings and Cursings" passage in the Torah, which is found in Deuteronomy 28:

Deut 28:1 "Now it shall come to pass, if you diligently obey the voice of the LORD your God, to observe carefully all His commandments which I command you today, that the LORD your God will set you high above all nations of the earth. 2 And all these blessings shall come upon you and overtake you, because you obey the voice of the LORD your God:

3 "Blessed shall you be in the city, and blessed shall you be in the country.

4 "Blessed shall be the fruit of your body, the produce of your ground and the increase of your herds, the increase of your cattle and the offspring of your flocks.

5 "Blessed shall be your basket and your kneading bowl.

6 "Blessed shall you be when you come in, and blessed shall you be when you go out.

7 "The LORD will cause your enemies who rise against you to be defeated before your face; they shall come out against you one way and flee before you seven ways.

8 *"The LORD will command the blessing on you in your storehouses and in all to which you set your hand, and He will bless you in the land which the LORD your God is giving you.*

9 *"The LORD will establish you as a holy people to Himself, just as He has sworn to you, if you keep the commandments of the LORD your God and walk in His ways. 10 Then all peoples of the earth shall see that you are called by the name of the LORD, and they shall be afraid of you. 11 And the LORD will grant you plenty of goods, in the fruit of your body, in the increase of your livestock, and in the produce of your ground, in the land of which the LORD swore to your fathers to give you. 12 The LORD will open to you His good treasure, the heavens, to give the rain to your land in its season, and to bless all the work of your hand. You shall lend to many nations, but you shall not borrow. 13 And the LORD will make you the head and not the tail; you shall be above only, and not be beneath, if you heed the commandments of the LORD your God, which I command you today, and are careful to observe them. 14 So you shall not turn aside from any of the words which I command you this day, to the right or the left, to go after other gods to serve them.*

15 *"But it shall come to pass, if you do not obey the voice of the LORD your God, to observe carefully all His commandments and His statutes which I command you today, that all these curses will come upon you and overtake you:*

16 *"Cursed shall you be in the city, and cursed shall you be in the country.*

17 *"Cursed shall be your basket and your kneading bowl.*

18 *"Cursed shall be the fruit of your body and the produce of your land, the increase of your cattle and the offspring of your flocks.*

19 *"Cursed shall you be when you come in, and cursed shall you be when you go out.*

20 *"The LORD will send on you cursing, confusion, and rebuke in all that you set your hand to do, until you are destroyed and until you perish quickly, because of the wickedness of your doings in which you have forsaken Me. 21 The LORD will make the plague cling to you until He has consumed you from the land which you are going to possess. 22 The LORD will strike you with consumption, with fever, with inflammation, with severe burning fever, with the sword, with*

scorching, and with mildew; they shall pursue you until you perish. *23* And your heavens which are over your head shall be bronze, and the earth which is under you shall be iron. *24* The LORD will change the rain of your land to powder and dust; from the heaven it shall come down on you until you are destroyed.

25 "The LORD will cause you to be defeated before your enemies; you shall go out one way against them and flee seven ways before them; and you shall become troublesome to all the kingdoms of the earth. *26* Your carcasses shall be food for all the birds of the air and the beasts of the earth, and no one shall frighten them away. *27* The LORD will strike you with the boils of Egypt, with tumors, with the scab, and with the itch, from which you cannot be healed. *28* The LORD will strike you with madness and blindness and confusion of heart. *29* And you shall grope at noonday, as a blind man gropes in darkness; you shall not prosper in your ways; you shall be only oppressed and plundered continually, and no one shall save you.

30 "You shall betroth a wife, but another man shall lie with her; you shall build a house, but you shall not dwell in it; you shall plant a vineyard, but shall not gather its grapes. *31* Your ox shall be slaughtered before your eyes, but you shall not eat of it; your donkey shall be violently taken away from before you, and shall not be restored to you; your sheep shall be given to your enemies, and you shall have no one to rescue them. *32* Your sons and your daughters shall be given to another people, and your eyes shall look and fail with longing for them all day long; and there shall be no strength in your hand. *33* A nation whom you have not known shall eat the fruit of your land and the produce of your labor, and you shall be only oppressed and crushed continually. *34* So you shall be driven mad because of the sight which your eyes see. *35* The LORD will strike you in the knees and on the legs with severe boils which cannot be healed, and from the sole of your foot to the top of your head.

36 "The LORD will bring you and the king whom you set over you to a nation which neither you nor your fathers have known, and there you shall serve other gods—wood and stone. *37* And you shall become an astonishment, a proverb, and a byword among all nations where the LORD will drive you.

38 "You shall carry much seed out to the field but gather little in, for the locust shall consume it. 39 You shall plant vineyards and tend them, but you shall neither drink of the wine nor gather the grapes; for the worms shall eat them. 40 You shall have olive trees throughout all your territory, but you shall not anoint yourself with the oil; for your olives shall drop off. 41 You shall beget sons and daughters, but they shall not be yours; for they shall go into captivity. 42 Locusts shall consume all your trees and the produce of your land.

43 "The alien who is among you shall rise higher and higher above you, and you shall come down lower and lower. 44 He shall lend to you, but you shall not lend to him; he shall be the head, and you shall be the tail.

45 "Moreover all these curses shall come upon you and pursue and overtake you, until you are destroyed, because you did not obey the voice of the LORD your God, to keep His commandments and His statutes which He commanded you. 46 And they shall be upon you for a sign and a wonder, and on your descendants forever.

47 "Because you did not serve the LORD your God with joy and gladness of heart, for the abundance of everything, 48 therefore you shall serve your enemies, whom the LORD will send against you, in hunger, in thirst, in nakedness, and in need of everything; and He will put a yoke of iron on your neck until He has destroyed you. 49 The LORD will bring a nation against you from afar, from the end of the earth, as swift as the eagle flies, a nation whose language you will not understand, 50 a nation of fierce countenance, which does not respect the elderly nor show favor to the young. 51 And they shall eat the increase of your livestock and the produce of your land, until you are destroyed; they shall not leave you grain or new wine or oil, or the increase of your cattle or the offspring of your flocks, until they have destroyed you.

52 "They shall besiege you at all your gates until your high and fortified walls, in which you trust, come down throughout all your land; and they shall besiege you at all your gates throughout all your land which the LORD your God has given you. 53 You shall eat the fruit of your own body, the flesh of your sons and your daughters whom the LORD your God has given you, in the siege and desperate straits in which your enemy shall distress you. 54 The sensitive and very refined man among you will be hostile toward his brother, toward the wife of his bosom, and toward the rest of his children whom he leaves behind, 55 so that he will not give any of them the flesh of his children whom he will eat, because he has nothing left in the siege and desperate straits in which your enemy shall distress you at all your gates. 56 The tender and delicate woman among you, who would not venture to set the sole of her foot on the ground because of her delicateness and sensitivity, will refuse to the husband of her bosom, and to her son and her daughter, 57 her placenta which comes out from between her feet and her children whom she bears; for she will eat them secretly for lack of everything in the siege and desperate straits in which your enemy shall distress you at all your gates.

58 "If you do not carefully observe all the words of this law that are written in this book, that you may fear this glorious and awesome name, THE LORD YOUR GOD, 59 then the LORD will bring upon you and your descendants extraordinary plagues— great and prolonged plagues—and serious and prolonged sicknesses. 60 Moreover He will bring back on you all the diseases of Egypt, of which you were afraid, and they shall cling to you. 61 Also every sickness and every plague, which is not written in this Book of the Law, will the LORD bring upon you until you are destroyed. 62 You shall be left few in number, whereas you were as the stars of heaven in multitude, because you would not obey the voice of the LORD your God. 63 And it shall be, that just as the LORD rejoiced over you to do you good and multiply you, so the LORD will rejoice over you to destroy you and bring you to nothing; and you shall be plucked from off the land which you go to possess.

64 "Then the LORD will scatter you among all peoples, from one end of the earth to the other, and there you shall serve other gods, which neither you nor your fathers have known—wood and stone. 65 And among those nations you shall find no rest, nor shall the sole of your foot have a resting place; but there the LORD will give you a trembling heart, failing eyes, and anguish of soul. 66 Your life shall hang in doubt before you; you shall fear day and night, and have no assurance of life. 67 In the morning you shall say, 'Oh, that it were evening!' And at evening you shall say, 'Oh, that it were morning!' because of the fear which terrifies your heart, and because of the sight which your eyes see.

68 "And the LORD will take you back to Egypt in ships, by the way of which I said to you, 'You shall never see it again.' And there you shall be offered for sale to your enemies as male and female slaves, but no one will buy you."

Deut 29:1 These are the words of the covenant which the LORD commanded Moses to make with the children of Israel in the land of Moab, besides the covenant which He made with them in Horeb.

The Blessings portion of the agreement is from verses 1-15, while the Cursings are from verses 16-68 and described in vivid detail. Remarkably, the Cursings foretell that one day, Israel will set a king over themselves – one not chosen by the Lord – who will also go into captivity with them (v 36) which can be applied to Hoshea, Jehoiakim, Jehoiachin, and Zedekiah, the last kings of Israel and Judah. The Cursings also describe a time of inhabitation by foreigners or becoming a vassal state as occurred with the Assyrian Empire and the Babylonian Empire (vv 49-51). The horrible sieges of their fortified cities are described in verses 52-57, which mirror various passages in Jeremiah and Lamentations. Lastly, the Diaspora, enslavements, and the terrible times of the pogroms and the Holocaust are foretold in verses 64-68.

In the proceeding passage of Deuteronomy 29, Moses then recounts for the Israelites all that God had done for them, from the Plagues in Egypt to the conquering of the eastern tribes of the Amorite giants (Sihon and Og). By reminding them of how God kept His promises in the past, he shows how God can be trusted to fulfill His promise to bring them into the land and that He will keep His promises in the future. Moses then admonishes them to keep the covenant and pass them onto their descendants.

However, halfway through the passage, Moses begins to prophesy that in the future, Israel will grow prideful and violate the terms of the covenant and eventually be cast out of the land. When foreigners look at the land of Israel which has been laid waste and made barren, they'll ask why this happened and others will respond that it was because of Israel's disobedience and their breaking of the covenant:

Deut 29:14 "I make this covenant and this oath, not with you alone, 15 but with him who stands here with us today before the LORD our God, as well as with him who is not here with us today 16 (for you know that we dwelt in the land of Egypt and that we came through the nations which you passed by, 17 and you saw their abominations and their idols which were among them—wood and stone and silver and gold); 18 so that there may not be among you man or woman or family or tribe, whose heart turns away today from the LORD our God, to go and serve the gods of these nations, and that there may not be among you a root bearing bitterness or wormwood; 19 and so it may not happen, when he hears the words of this curse, that he blesses himself in his heart, saying, 'I shall have peace, even though I follow the dictates of my heart'—as though the drunkard could be included with the sober.

20 "The LORD would not spare him; for then the anger of the LORD and His jealousy would burn against that man, and every curse that is written in this book would settle on him, and the LORD would blot out his name from under heaven. 21 And the LORD would separate him from all the tribes of Israel for adversity, according to all the curses of the covenant that are written in this Book of the Law, 22 so that the coming generation of your children who rise up after you, and the foreigner who comes from a far land, would say, when they see the plagues of that land and the sicknesses which the LORD has laid on it:

23 'The whole land is brimstone, salt, and burning; it is not sown, nor does it bear, nor does any grass grow there, like the overthrow of Sodom and Gomorrah, Admah, and Zeboiim, which the LORD overthrew in His anger and His wrath.' 24 All nations would say, 'Why has the LORD done so to this land? What does the heat of this great anger mean?' 25 Then people would say: 'Because they have forsaken the covenant of the LORD God of their fathers, which He made with them when He brought them out of the land of Egypt; 26 for they went and served other gods and worshiped them, gods that they did not know and that He had not given to them. 27 Then the anger of the LORD was aroused against this land, to bring on it every curse that is written in this book. *28 And the LORD uprooted them from their land in anger, in wrath, and in great indignation, and cast them into another land, as it is this day.'*

29 "The secret things belong to the LORD our God, but those things which are revealed belong to us and to our children forever, that we may do all the words of this law.

Soon after Israel entered into the land and took possession of it, they began to prosper and take the covenant for granted – they forgot about God and all He had done for them. By the time the Book of Judges opens only a century or so later, it says that, *"When all that generation had been gathered to their fathers, another generation arose after them who did not know the LORD nor the work which He had done for Israel. Then the children of Israel did evil in the sight of the LORD, and served the Baals." (Judges 2:10-11)*

As so often happens, the first generation which had lived by faith failed to pass it on to their children, grandchildren, and great-grandchildren, and Israel began breaking the marriage-covenant with God through spiritual adultery: idolatry. For the next four hundred years, the Israelites would fall away from God, be punished/enslaved, repent and cry out to God, and then He would send a deliverer to restore them.

This cycle would continue until the time of the Kings when Israel refused to be ruled by God any longer, but by kings like all the other nations (1 Samuel 8). And though hurt by their refusal, God granted their request and gave them King Saul and then later King David. But once Israel had their kings, they began looking to them for deliverance, and they soon followed and obeyed their kings rather the Lord.

Two hundred years after the House of Israel (the nine Northern tribes) had separated from House of Judah (the three Southern tribes) under Solomon's son Rehoboam, God declared that Israel (through Amos and Hosea) had broken the covenant and sent them into captivity by the Assyrians. The Assyrians had a policy of obliterating entire nations not by genocide or extermination, but by breaking up tribes, clans, and families and then scattering them throughout the empire, along with resettling their land with other groups from other lands.

By wrenching the tribes from one another and separating them from their land, the people would lose their history, heritage, and national/tribal identity and thus be unable to mount much of a rebellion against the Empire. After all, it's hard to rally your people to take back your land when you're no longer dwelling in it. The Samaritans in the New Testament were made up of the descendants of the half-Jews and the other foreigners who were resettled in the land by the Assyrians and later empires.

A century after Israel had been dispersed by the Assyrians, Judah was similarly punished and taken into captivity by the Babylonians (as described in Jeremiah and Lamentations). However, the Babylonians did not enforce their policies of national obliteration and scattering quite as rigorously as the Assyrians, and the nation of Judah and the Jewish people maintained more of their history and cohesion than the nation of Israel did, with much of Judah being settled around the capital city of Babylon.

V. The Diaspora

The Diaspora, the scattering of the Chosen People throughout the nations, is one of the more tragic events in the history of Israel. The time of Israel's Diaspora has occupied over half their history as a people, spanning from 722 BC and 586 BC to the Twentieth Century (over 2600 years), when Israel began to be called back to their ancient homeland. By all accounts, the Jews should have lost their national identity after only a century or two in captivity like all the other nations taken away by the Assyrians and Babylonians.

An interesting study to conduct is to make a list of all the nations that the Bible foretold would be removed from history in contrast to those who would remain. When was the last time you heard of an Ammonite, Moabite, Babylonian, Canaanite, Amalekite, Edomite, or a Philistine? Those peoples and nations were foretold to be removed and exist no more as nations or peoples. However, the Egyptians, the Israelites, the Ethiopians, and the Syrians were predicted to remain as nations and peoples, even after thousands of years. But of all the nations which remained, their people always remained in their own lands: except Israel.

When God gave Moses the Law at Mount Sinai, it didn't merely consist of the Ten Commandments we're familiar with, but 613 specific commandments and ordinances that governed Jewish life. The Ten Commandments that Moses brought down from the mountain comprised the broad, general moral laws of conduct between the people and God and the people with one another. The first Four Commandments are "vertical" in nature (our relationship with God), while the next Six are "horizontal" (our relationships with other people).

The first half of the Book of Leviticus specifies all the details of the Levitical priestly system concerning the offerings and sacrifices and the procedures for the priests. The second half specifies the moral/religious code for the nation, along with their weekly Sabbaths, their holy-days, their Sabbatical years and Jubilee years. The book ends with a set of Blessings and Cursings which are paralleled later in Deuteronomy 28.

In Leviticus 26, the passage opens with two specific commands for the nation: they are not to worship any form of idol or image, and they are to keep the Lord's Sabbaths. There was the weekly Sabbath that most people are familiar with, but there was also a Sabbatical year decreed for the land which would occur every seventh year. After six years of sowing and reaping, they were to let the land rest to provide for the poor and for the wild animals (Exodus 23:10-11). Today, we know from agriculture that in order to keep the soil from becoming depleted of minerals and nutrients, we need to rotate the types of crops grown and also let it rest (leave it fallow) every few years.

The next ten verses describe the Blessings that Israel would have if she kept those commandments, while the rest of the chapter describes the Cursings that would come upon them if they disobeyed. However, the passage is worded so vividly (and accurately) that it's very clear that God knew from the beginning that their descendants would disobey Him. In fact, in v35 God foretells that when Israel will dwell in the land, they will not keep those Sabbatical years: "As long as it lies desolate it shall rest – for the time it did not rest on your Sabbaths when you dwelt in it."

God then goes on in the same passage to declare that if Israel doesn't repent after being sent into captivity the first time, He will punish them seven-times more for their sin. And He doesn't just mention that once, but four times in the same passage, presumably so they would know that He was very serious. Therefore, there are two distinct periods of captivity alluded to in this passage of the Blessings and Cursings of Leviticus, as a consequence for their idolatry and not keeping His Sabbaths.

In Jeremiah 17 which was written while Judah was being threatened by the Babylonian Empire, God holds Judah accountable for not keeping the Sabbath and decrees captivity for them if they don't repent. Needless to say, Judah didn't turn from their idols and they were made into a vassal state by Babylon, subsequently rebelled, and were deported from the land in three waves: 605 BC, 597 BC and 586 BC. The Siege of Jerusalem lasted thirty months before it fell in 586 BC, which is recorded in detail by Jeremiah in the Book of Lamentations. The aftermath of the siege in the land is recorded in the latter part of the Book of Jeremiah. The people refused to listen and believe

God again, even after all they had heard and seen and experienced.

Years before Jerusalem fell, Jeremiah foretold that Judah and the entire land would go into captivity and be removed from the land, which would last a full seventy years. Once those seventy years were completed, the Babylonians themselves would be punished (Jeremiah 25:11-12). The fall of the Babylonian Empire is recorded in Daniel 5, though the city of Babylon itself never fell – it just changed ownership; first to the Persians, then to the Greeks. Alexander the Great had even made Babylon the eastern capital of his empire.

During the Babylonian Captivity, God raised up a number of prophets to minister to His broken people: Daniel (and his friends), Jeremiah, and Ezekiel, and then later Ezra and Nehemiah who would help the captives return to the land and rebuild Jerusalem and the Temple. The miracles of the captivity (Shadrach, Meshach, and Abednego in the Fiery Furnace, Daniel in the Lion's Den, etc.) were given to bolster the faith of the people, most of which had turned away from God long before. When Israel had been in the land, they had abandoned God and pushed Him away – but there in captivity, they finally repented and sought Him again.

The primary sin of Israel wasn't merely worshipping idols and not keeping the Sabbaths, but their unbelief in the Lord. God had given them His Word and the promises of the Blessings and Cursings, but over and over, Israel consistently refused to believe Him.

Unbelief and pride are the two "root sins" behind all others, and they often go hand-in-hand. Before Jerusalem was destroyed in 586 BC, Judah was filled with pride and refused to believe the prophets that God would cast them out of the land – after all, would God really destroy His own Holy City, His Temple, and even His Chosen People? (Jeremiah 7) But He did, because He had to remain true to His Righteous Nature and punish them for their sin which had become worse than the Canaanite nations He had expelled from the land over a thousand years earlier (2 Kings 21:9-11).

One of the more peculiar visions that God gave during the Babylonian Captivity was the "430 Days of Iniquity" of Ezekiel 4, in which God instructed the prophet to lie on his left side for

390 days to represent the 390 years of Israel's sin. After those days were completed, he was told to lie on his right side for 40 more days to represent the 40 years of Judah's sin. However, the context of the passage concerns the punishment of Jerusalem.

There remains some debate about exactly where these two numbers really "fit" into Scripture and history, since there isn't much interpretation given. The interpretation that seems to be the most adequate is that those are the amounts of time in which both nations were unfaithful to Jerusalem or abandoned the Temple. Removing the Sabbatical years from those figures brings them to be about when each nation permanently turned away from God. Israel fell away in about 950 BC when Solomon's son Rehoboam became king and they appointed their own king Jeroboam in the north. Judah fell away from God after the death of their beloved king Josiah in 624 BC (2 Kings 23).

After the Seventy Years of Captivity in Babylon ended, King Cyrus of the Persian Empire allowed most of the captives to return to their native lands (Ezra 1, 2 Chronicles 36:21-23). His career and even his very name was prophesied nearly three centuries earlier by the prophet Isaiah (Isaiah 44:24:28, 45:1-14). The Jewish Talmud records that when Cyrus entered Babylon, the prophet Daniel showed him the scroll of Isaiah, and the king was so moved that he elevated Daniel and followed that passage. He soon freed the captives and even gave the Jews incentives to return to their native lands and rebuild the Temple.

However, though they were now free, only a few thousand Jews returned to Judea – most remained in the lands where they had been scattered. After all, they were comfortable for the most part and had their families, friends, and community. The shepherds and farmers had become merchants and city-dwellers in the rich cities of the East and didn't want to return to that hard, primitive lifestyle. Those who did return to the land found it to be very difficult to rebuild and were often harassed by their neighbors who had moved into the land (like the Edomites). The Book of Ezra and Nehemiah tell of their difficulties in rebuilding the walls of Jerusalem and resettling the land. But they did eventually secure the land and rebuilt many of the towns and cities which had been destroyed by the Assyrians and the Babylonians.

During this time, the land of Israel always remained under the control of a greater empire or kingdom. The Assyrians and Babylonians had been the first to capture the land and completely remove the sovereignty of the Jews. The empires that followed simply transferred the land from one to the other, from the Babylonians to the Persians, the Greeks, and then to the Romans. In Daniel 2 and Daniel 7, the progression of world power moved from one empire to the next, until the last one (the Roman Empire) which broke into pieces.

Jesus in the Book of Luke refers to this era of history as "the Times of the Gentiles" (Luke 21:24) which would continue for many years, until the "days of the end" drew close. Except for very brief periods of time when the Jews rebelled against their Gentile rulers, they were never able to fully reclaim their sovereignty.

In 66 AD, the Jews rebelled against the Roman Empire and successfully cast them off, but Titus Vespasian returned with the 10th, 12th, 15th, and 5th Legions and besieged Jerusalem (recorded by Josephus and others). The city fell after six months in 70 AD on the 9th of Av and decimated the Jewish people. Josephus records that over one million Jews died, with many by crucifixion.

Tragically, the Temple was also destroyed during the siege, much to the dismay of both the Jews and the Romans. The Roman commander had given explicit instructions to not harm the Temple so they could strip it of its gold and other valuable furnishings and give it as a gift to the emperor. But when a fire broke out and consumed the Temple, the gold which had overlaid the inside of the Temple melted and sank between the cracks of the stones. The commander then ordered that all the Temple stones be torn apart so they could remove the gold. This fulfilled the prophecy of the Temple that Jesus had given His disciples thirty-eight years earlier that "not one stone would be left upon another." (Matthew 24:2)

Many of the survivors of Jerusalem were disbursed throughout the Roman Empire, but in 132 AD, another rebellion by Simon Bar Kochba temporarily succeeded before it was crushed by Emperor Hadrian. By that time, the Romans were so tired of dealing with the rebellious Jews that they leveled the entire city of Jerusalem, renamed it to Aelia Capitolina, and built their own temple to Jupiter over the ruins of the Jewish Temple. The renamed the region to "Palestine" after the Philistines, the ancient enemy of the Jews. They also made it illegal for any Jews to live in Jerusalem and expelled most from the land entirely, dispersing them throughout the Mediterranean and the Empire.

The land of Israel remained barren and unsettled for the next eighteen centuries, except for small pockets of Jews in villages and various Arab nomads and traders that passed though the land. Jerusalem has been completely destroyed twice, besieged twenty-three times, attacked fifty-two times, and captured and recaptured forty-four times over its long history. Since the Bar Kochba Revolt, Jerusalem has changed hands from one group to another, but was never again under Jewish control until June 7, 1967.

The Diaspora of the Jews lasted nearly 2700 years and officially ended when Israel became a sovereign nation again on May 14, 1948. Though the Diaspora ended over seventy years ago, over half the Jews still live outside their native homeland. However, renewed persecution, anti-Semitism, and other circumstances have been steadily pressing many to return – so many that there are only tiny fractions remaining outside Israel today. The only exception is that there are nearly as many Jews living in America as in Israel, though they may soon be called to return also.

The first time Israel went into captivity, it was to punish her for embracing horrible forms of idol-worship, regularly performing child-sacrifice and vile fertility rituals, and for repeatedly violating the Sabbath days and the Sabbatical years. But the question that few seem to ever ask – especially in the Jewish community – is why did they have to go into captivity the second time?

After all, the Levitical system was rigorously maintained from the days of Ezra to the destruction of the Jewish Temple in 70 AD. There was no idol-worship to speak of and they were careful to keep the Sabbaths (perhaps too careful!) – they hadn't sinned against God as they had the first time. So why did God punish them again and send Israel into the Diaspora for nearly two thousand years? What had they done to warrant that second judgement that in many ways was worse than the first?

From a spiritual perspective, Israel had persisted in their unbelief that God would do what He said if they didn't obey Him, and He removed them from the land after their idolatry. The cause for Israel's second (and last) Diaspora was also due to unbelief, though of a different sort than their first punishment. However, that reason cannot be found in the Old Testament, but in the New Testament. The last and greatest of the prophets to be sent to Israel was John the Baptist, but the Jewish religious leaders all but ignored him. Then Jesus came on the scene and He wasn't just ignored, but rejected as the Jewish Messiah and then executed.

There were numerous reasons why the Jewish leaders should have recognized Jesus as the Messiah, not only by the power and authority with which He spoke and taught, but also by the miracles He performed time and time again for them. He gave them sign after sign – even raising the dead to life – but it didn't matter. The main reason He was rejected was because the religious leaders wanted to keep their power, authority, and wealth; if the Messiah would've been enthroned, all those trappings would've been taken away from them (again, unbelief, pride, and arrogance). After His Resurrection when the Church Age began, many Jewish people (and priests) did place their faith in him, but the religious leadership did not (Acts 6-7).

At least twice in the Gospels, the people tried to make Jesus their king, but each time He refused; sometimes He even had to escape from them so they wouldn't forcibly crown Him (John 6:14-15). However, at the end of His ministry as the Passover approached, He went up to Jerusalem and presented Himself as the Messiah. On this special day the Christians call "Palm Sunday," Jesus had a donkey brought to Him and began fulfilling several Old Testament prophecies (Zechariah 9:9, Daniel 9:25-26). This time, there was no way they would miss Him and not realize who He really was.

However, then Jesus does something very peculiar – He begins weeping over the city of Jerusalem and says, "O Jerusalem, Jerusalem, if you had known this day that your king has come…but now these things have been hidden from your eyes until you say 'blessed is he who comes in the name of the Lord'." (Luke 13:34-35) This wasn't just an arbitrary day that He had chosen to enter the city in this fashion; this was the Day that the Messiah was foretold to present Himself to the people – the Day that everyone in Israel should've been watching for – especially the Jewish scribes and scholars. They all should have known.

So why was Israel punished with the Diaspora a second time? Because God held Israel accountable for recognizing her Messiah and for knowing the passage of Daniel 9:24-27, in which the entire prophetic future of Israel is foretold from the time of Daniel to the End.

This passage is known as "Daniel's 70 Weeks," in which the angel Gabriel told Daniel that Israel's future is comprised of seventy "sevens" (or weeks) of years, 490 years in all. After sixty-nine of those weeks of years passed, the Messiah would come, be executed, and then there would be an indeterminate time of wars and destruction, followed by the desolations of an evil-ruler during the last week of years (the Seventieth Week).

Daniel 9:24-27

"Seventy weeks are determined
For your people and for your holy city,
To finish the transgression,
To make an end of sins,
To make reconciliation for iniquity,
To bring in everlasting righteousness,
To seal up vision and prophecy,
And to anoint the Most Holy."

"Know therefore and understand,
That from the going forth of the command
To restore and build Jerusalem
Until Messiah the Prince,
There shall be seven weeks and sixty-two weeks;
The street shall be built again, and the wall,
Even in troublesome times.

"And after the sixty-two weeks
Messiah shall be cut off, but not for Himself;
And the people of the prince who is to come

Shall destroy the city and the sanctuary.
The end of it shall be with a flood,
    And till the end of the war
Desolations are determined.

"Then he shall confirm a covenant
    With many for one week;
But in the middle of the week
    He shall bring an end to sacrifice and offering.
And on the wing of abominations
    Shall be one who makes desolate,
Even until the consummation, which is determined,
Is poured out on the desolate."

Dr. Chuck Missler (working from Sir Robert Anderson's writings) has written an excellent analysis of this passage in which the precise day of the Messiah's arrival can be calculated. Excerpts of his article "Daniel's 70 Weeks" (http://www.khouse.org/articles/2004/552/) are as follows:

This includes a mathematical prophecy. As we have noted in previous articles, the Jewish (and Babylonian) calendars used a 360-day year; four 69 weeks of 360-day years totals 173,880 days. In effect, Gabriel told Daniel that the interval between the commandment to rebuild Jerusalem until the presentation of the Messiah as King would be 173,880 days.

...

The commandment to restore and build Jerusalem was given by Artaxerxes Longimanus on March 14, 445 B.C. (The emphasis in the verse on "the street" and "the wall" was to avoid confusion with other earlier mandates confined to rebuilding the Temple.)

...

This is the only occasion that Jesus presented Himself as King. It occurred on April 6, 32 A.D.

When we examine the period between March 14, 445 B.C. and April 6, 32 A.D., and correct for leap years, we discover that it is 173,880 days exactly, to the very day!

On this day – April 6, 32 AD – the ultimate Passover Lamb was sacrificed for the sins of the world, just as John the Baptist had identified Him when he declared, *"Behold! The Lamb of God which takes away the sin of the world!"* when He was baptized (John 1:29). Then three days later, He arose from the tomb, forever conquering death and the grave.

The Day of Pentecost (or Feast of Weeks) in which the Church began in Acts 2 happens to be the same feast-day as when the Law was given to Moses (Exodus 34:22, Deuteronomy 16:9). Jeremiah 31:31-34 declares that one day God would make a new covenant with Israel and take away their hearts of stone (the Tablets) and give them a heart of flesh (Law of Spirit), which Paul explains in 2 Corinthians 3.

Paul also says in Colossians 2:17 that Israel's feasts are merely shadows of the greater events to be fulfilled in the future, with the Passover (or Sacrifice of the Firstborn) looking forward to the Sacrifice of the Messiah (God's Firstborn), the Feast of First Fruits celebrating His Resurrection, and the Feast of Weeks celebrating the New Covenant. The last three Feasts have yet to be fulfilled, but will be upon the Messiah's return.

In Stephen's famous address to the Sanhedrin in Acts 17, he gives the Jewish leaders a history lesson from Abraham onward about how they always disobey God the first time, but then they obey after that. He ends with accusing them of killing the Messiah just as had been foretold, which so enrages the Sanhedrin that they haul Stephen outside and stone him to death. Again, He's holding them accountable for rejecting the Messiah and pressing them to repent before He punishes them with another Diaspora.

Interestingly enough, after Israel rejected Jesus as their Messiah, they were given thirty-eight years (from 32 AD to 70 AD) to become a part of the Church before the next Diaspora began. This thirty-eight year interval turns out to be the same amount of time as their forefathers had wandered in the desert after they too had refused to enter the Promised Land the first time. Coincidence? I don't think so. Could it be that this same interval was given in order to give that unbelieving generation (or their children's generation) the opportunity to repent and turn to Him by faith before the second Diaspora?

After the Romans expelled the Jews from Jerusalem in 70 AD and much of Palestine, they were disbursed throughout the Roman Empire, moving from place to place wherever persecution or opportunity drove them. Tiny remnants of Jews still lived in Palestine, but the vast majority were scattered throughout that hemisphere and would be driven from country to country over the centuries that followed. And though they longed to return to Jerusalem and the land of Israel, it was never more than a wistful pipe-dream.

When the New World was discovered by the Europeans, many Jews fled to America to start new lives. For decades, the largest number of Jews in the world was found in the United States of America. The rest remained scattered throughout Europe, Russia, the Middle East, Central Asia, and even Africa.

But then late in the Nineteenth Century, God began stirring the hearts of His people to return home.

VI. The First of Many Sons

Most people in the West are familiar with the Parable of the Prodigal Son, even those who don't hold to Christianity or regularly attend church. This parable that Jesus gave is a beautiful portrayal of how each of us have wandered from God, how He yearns for us to repent and turn to Him, and how He will unconditionally accept us into His Family after we repent. But though millions have heard the parable and multitudes have preached and taught the passage over the centuries, very few have ever applied it to the Ultimate Prodigal Son: the nation of Israel.

The basic elements of the Parable of the Prodigal Son are: a loving father, a rebellious son, an accusing brother, a misuse of the father's inheritance, and an extended time living in a foreign land that end in deplorable conditions. After becoming utterly destitute, the son comes to his senses and realizes that it was better for him in his father's house/land and returns to him, where he humbles himself and is immediately accepted and exalted by the father. However, upon the prodigal son's return, the older brother is embittered and becomes his brother's accuser, who is then reprimanded by his father.

Like the prodigal son, Israel also misused the Father's inheritance by committing idolatry and disobeying while in His land. Because of their behavior, disbelief, and love of other gods, they were scattered among the Gentile nations where they soon became destitute. In their plight, the Jews realized that things were better for them in their ancient homeland, and then they began to return. To their surprise, the land – and the Father – received them and the land began to prosper. However, their brothers (the remnants of Moab, Ammon, Edom, Syria, etc.) became jealous and have bitterly opposed them.

During most of the Diaspora, the land of Israel was "cursed" and became filled with deserts and swamps and was almost unusable. When Mark Twain visited the land in 1867, he remarked that he could go for miles without seeing another living soul. The Ottoman Empire had also made the condition of the land worse because they had a policy of taxing property owners by the number of trees on their land. Since most were so poor, the landowners reduced their taxes by cutting down all the trees, which led to soil erosion and the condition of the land became even worse.

However, this should have been no surprise to anyone, as the conditions of the land during the Diaspora were foretold in Deuteronomy 29 as a sign to both Israel and the nations around her:

23 'The whole land is brimstone, salt, and burning; it is not sown, nor does it bear, nor does any grass grow there, like the overthrow of Sodom and Gomorrah, Admah, and Zeboiim, which the LORD overthrew in His anger and His wrath.' 24 All nations would say, 'Why has the LORD done so to this land? What does the heat of this great anger mean?' 25 Then people would say: 'Because they have forsaken the covenant of the LORD God of their fathers, which He made with them when He brought them out of the land of Egypt; 26 for they went and served other gods and worshiped them, gods that they did not know and that He had not given to them. 27 Then the anger of the LORD was aroused against this land, to bring on it every curse that is written in this book. 28 And the LORD uprooted them from their land in anger, in wrath, and in great indignation, and cast them into another land, as it is this day.'

In building any nation or culture, three elements are primarily needed: a common language, a common belief system or religion, and a common location, or land. However, for nearly two thousand years, the Jewish people had neither language nor location, only their religion – yet they survived as a distinct culture group wherever they went. They had no common language, nor a common location or land to bind them together, yet they were still inherently "Jewish". They had their traditions and holidays and their religious writings which they diligently preserved, but very little other than that. Every other culture or group is typically absorbed and loses most of their identity within a generation or two, but not the Jewish people.

The First Aliyah (return to Israel) began in 1881 when several thousand Jews fled Eastern Europe to escape the persecution (pogroms) and settled in Palestine. Soon the rumblings of a new idea called "Zionism" began, in which the Jews began to yearn to establish their own political state in their native homeland rather than live under others as they had throughout their exile. Societies in Russia and Romania called "Hovevei Zion" (lovers of Zion) began to spread, which promoted agricultural settlement in Palestine. Land began to be purchased in Palestine and small pockets of Jews began to immigrate back to the land, though largely for utopian, religious reasons.

During this time, a man named Eliezar Ben Yehuda decided that the Jews across the world could be united if they had a common, modernized form of the Hebrew language. For centuries, Hebrew had only been used for scholarly or religious reasons, but rarely for common, everyday use. Ironically, the religious leaders initially opposed the idea because they didn't want to see the sacred Hebrew language be used so commonly.

Regardless of the obstacles, Ben Yehuda set out to modernize the ancient language and formed the Hebrew Language Committee, which still exists today. Through his tireless efforts, he almost single-handedly caused the ancient Biblical language of Hebrew to be reborn. Today, Hebrew is the official language of the Jewish State, and is consistent enough with the earlier forms of Hebrew that any of the ancient prophets could go into a modern Jewish restaurant and order from the menu. And thus was fulfilled the first of many recent prophecies: in the latter years, the Jews would return to speaking a pure language: Hebrew. (Zephaniah 3:9)

In 1895, a Hungarian Jew named Theodor Herzl became shocked at a mass outbreak of anti-Semitism in France concerning the Dreyfus Affair, in which a French Jewish army officer was falsely convicted of spying for Germany. The multitudes of marchers with their signs and shouts of "Death to the Jews!" convinced Herzl that it was a losing battle to continue fighting anti-Semitism in the Diaspora. After all, many had been in the same areas for centuries and they were still not accepted, though they had contributed much to their host nations and cultures! Later that year, he wrote "Der Judenstaat," ("The Jewish State") in which he outlined the reasons why Jews should leave Europe and move to either Argentina or Palestine. The book immediately received enormous attention throughout

Europe, and word of the Zionist movement spread: to resettle the Jews in their own political state and become a free people.

The First Zionist Congress was convened in 1897 and called for the establishment of a national home for the Jews in Palestine, which at that time was under the control of the Ottoman Empire (Turkey). Several more Zionist Congresses followed, and the movement turned into action with more land in Palestine being purchased and settled. The Second Aliyah began in 1904 with nearly 40,000 Jews migrating to Palestine, but later half left and returned to the Diaspora. Agriculture was very difficult for the first settlers because much of the land was either arid deserts or disease-filled, malaria-ridden swamps. It seemed that the Promised Land was anything but that.

Yet the hardy Jewish settlers persisted, and the wealthy Rothschilds of Europe used their enormous wealth to buy up large tracts of land (at inflated prices from the Arabs no-less), and various reforestry projects began. As more Jews began to settle the land and build, nearby Arabs moved in due to the increased employment opportunities and the modern Israeli-Arab dispute over the land took root.

In 1914, World War I began and by 1917, the British defeated the Ottoman Empire and took control of much of the Middle East. In that same year, the Balfour Declaration was issued in Great Britain, which pledged the British government's support for the establishment of a Jewish national home in Palestine. In 1919, the Third Aliyah began, along with much larger resistance from the Arabs in the region.

However, by 1922, the Balfour Declaration was heavily revised by Britain and the League of Nations so the Jewish Homeland would only encompass one-fourth of the land they had been originally promised, the territory west of the Jordan River. All the land east of the Jordan would be given to the Arabs, and became known as the Trans-Jordan, which today mostly comprises the nation of Jordan. In the past, this area was known as Moab, Ammon, and Edom. Later that same year, Winston Churchill published "The White Paper" which severely restricted Jewish immigration to Palestine.

Meanwhile the Zionist movement continued to grow and the Jews in Palestine began to organize themselves both for defense and for permanent settlement, mostly against the Arabs who had become increasingly violent. However, the Zionist movement did not go unnoticed by Israel's enemies, particularly their spiritual Adversary.

As previously mentioned, Leviticus 26 emphatically declares that if Israel didn't repent of their sin (unbelief) and obey God after their first exile from the land, they would be punished seven times over. Like the Arrival Date of the Messiah in Daniel 9, this is a prophecy with a mathematical component, though it was incomplete (or rather, not revealed) when first written in Leviticus. At that time, no one knew how long the second exile would be because the length of the first one hadn't been given yet.

Nine hundred years later, the length of the first exile was given to Jeremiah: 70 years, though this punishment was specific to Judah for their refusal to observe the Sabbatical years (Jeremiah 25). The "430 Days" prophecy of Ezekiel 4 gives a more precise number for both the iniquity of Judah and Israel. If 70 of those years were served in the Babylonian Captivity, then there were 360 years left for Israel to be punished. However, there doesn't appear to be any time in history where that number seems to fit – unless it's multiplied by 7 which produces a figure of 2520 years, the approximate length of the Diaspora.

Once again, Dr. Chuck Missler has written an excellent article entitled "A Peculiar Calculation" (http://www.khouse.org/articles/2000/276/) which examines "Ezekiel's 430 Days" in detail and found that it can be used to calculate both the rebirth of Israel as a Jewish State on May 14, 1948 and also the reclaiming of Jerusalem on June 7, 1967. Portions of the article are as follows:

The Prophet Ezekiel was called upon to undertake a number of strange performances, one of which was to lie on his side for a total of 430 days. Each day was expressly to represent a year of judgment against the nation.

A number of commentators acknowledge a difficulty which appears when one attempts to apply this specifically to Israel's history. Seventy of the years would seem to be accounted for in the Babylonian Captivity, but that leaves 360 years (430 minus 70) unaccounted for. The 360 years do not seem to fit any period of their history.

...

It has been suggested that multiplying the "problem" 360 years by seven [from Leviticus 26] yields 2520 years, which is "approximately" the duration of time from the exile through the Diaspora.

...

Sir Robert Anderson, in his classic work "The Coming Prince", noted that the Bible uses 360-day years in both Genesis and Revelation. However, I noticed that no one seemed to try to apply this insight to the 2520 years potentially suggested in Ezekiel Chapter 4.

In attempting to reconcile the 2520 360-day years to our Roman calendar, one is faced with the discrepancies between the sidereal year and the solar year. (The Julian year is 11 minutes and 10.46 seconds longer than the mean solar year.)

In 1572, it was recognized that errors had accumulated to 11 days too many, and adjustments were required. In the Gregorian Reform, September 4th was declared September 14th, and the formula for leap years was changed to exclude centuries unless divisible by four (and millennia by 400). Thus, 2520 360-day years contain 907,200 days, which are accounted for on our current calendar as 2483 years, 9 months and 21 days.

...

Another problem occurs when we examine more closely the "Babylonian Captivity." There are two different periods that are candidates: "the Servitude of the Nation," and the "Desolations of Jerusalem." Each of these was prophesied to be seventy years in duration and many assume they are synonymous of each other; however, they are not.

There were actually three sieges of Nebuchadnezzar upon Jerusalem. The first siege began the "Servitude of the Nation" and was prophesied to last 70 years. (And it did, to the very day. When Cyrus conquered Babylon he encountered the amazing letter written to him by Isaiah a century and a half earlier, which addressed him by name, highlighted his meteoric career, and predicted that he would free the captives. His astonishment resulted in his releasing the Hebrew captives to return to Judea to rebuild their temple.)

The vassal king that Nebuchadnezzar left later rebelled; a second siege resulted in his uncle, Zedekiah, being appointed to the throne. The prophets Jeremiah and Ezekiel both went on to warn that if they persisted in rebelling against Nebuchadnezzar the city of Jerusalem would be destroyed. Yet Zedekiah ultimately yielded to the false prophets and rebelled.

A third siege resulted in the destruction and desolation of the city of Jerusalem. The "Desolations of Jerusalem" also lasted 70 years, until Nehemiah ultimately succeeded in getting the authority to rebuild the city of Jerusalem. This, too, was precisely 70 years. To which of these two periods should we apply the 2520 years?

The 70 years of servitude, to be consistent, should be reckoned as 25,200 days, or two days short of 69 years on our Roman calendar. The first siege of Nebuchadnezzar, in 606 B.C., began the "Servitude of the Nation," which lasted until the summer of 537 B.C. If July 23, 537 B.C. was the time of their release [the ending date of their captivity can be calculated to be May 14, 1948]

On May 14, 1948, the nation Israel was reestablished on the world scene. A remarkable coincidence.

...

Yet, there is another alternative application of the 2520 years: the "Desolations of Jerusalem"?

The third siege of Nebuchadnezzar, in 587 B.C., began the "Desolations of Jerusalem," which lasted until 518 B.C. If August 16, 518 B.C. was the completion of the walls of Jerusalem, then [the ending date of the Desolations of Jerusalem can be calculated by applying the 907,200 days]

On June 7, 1967, as a result of the Six Day War, the Biblical city of Old Jerusalem was restored to the nation. Another remarkable coincidence!

It should be borne in mind that the "starting" dates are not known precisely to the day. More research needs to be done. But this certainly seems provocative enough to ponder.

Is it possible that somehow the dates and times were being manipulated behind the scenes to restore Israel on the precise day of May 14, 1948? Was it possible that there was some sort of Jewish conspiracy to re-establish the nation of Israel on a particular day or year? Hardly – the only reason why the Israelis chose to declare their statehood on May 14, 1948 was because the British Mandate ended on May 15th and they were essentially forced to. Israel had been trying to drive the British out of Palestine for years following World War II but they really weren't ready to be independent when they declared their statehood, having little infrastructure and little military resources. And as far as the recapture of Jerusalem on June 7, 1967, Israel didn't start the Six Day War – her enemies did!

However, behind both events, many (like myself) contend that the times and events were being directed by God. In the Bible, the Seventy Year Babylonian captivity ended exactly seventy years after it began – to the day. If God is completely just (like the Bible declares He is), if He says the punishment of Israel or Jerusalem is going to last for X-years, wouldn't He be accurate to the exact day as before? If the punishment ended a day later (or earlier) than the amount of time He had declared, couldn't His justice be called into question? For example, if you tell your child that you'll punish them justly and you're giving them a ten-minute timeout, couldn't your justice be called into question if you ended their punishment a minute or two early or extended it a minute or two longer?

Regardless of whether the exact starting dates are known, the rough time period of Israel's reestablishment can be estimated at the mid-Twentieth Century. Also, it's quite interesting that the Desolations of Jerusalem began nineteen years after the Servitude of the Nation, and then nineteen years after Israel became a nation in 1948, they recaptured Jerusalem for the first time in nearly two thousand years. Again, that's quite a "coincidence," which isn't exactly a kosher word.

An unsettling thought to consider is that if God (and Israel) has an Enemy who actively seeks to thwart God's plans and prevent Scripture from being fulfilled, and this Enemy sees Israel start to be regathered as a nation, what will he do? The Enemy will set out to ensure that either the land is closed to the Jews – or that there are no Jews alive to settle the land. Better yet, why not do both simultaneously?

In 1939, the British published and began enforcing another White Paper which severely restricted Jewish immigration into Palestine. The Enemy then resorted to implementing the second option to deal with his own "Jewish Problem": the Holocaust.

51

VII. The Holocaust

The Ghettos. The trains to Auschwitz. The concentration camps. The Final Solution. The Holocaust. Ha Shoah.

Throughout the long centuries of the Diaspora, while there were mass expulsions and persecutions of Jews, none can be compared to the horrible years of the Holocaust. Most historians generally cite January 30, 1933 as the date the Holocaust began, though the actual events that most associate with the Holocaust didn't occur until a few years later. The extermination effort began in June, 1941 with the Einsatzgruppen, the four mobile killing groups which terrorized and murdered German Jews.

While there's some debate about whether Adolph Hitler wanted to exterminate all the Jews or simply expel them from Germany, there is documentation that in 1933 he wanted to send all the Jews to Palestine. However, the costs of such a deportation would be quite expensive, so the Nazis established the ghettos instead. From the time he took office and became the German dictator, Hitler and the Nazi Party began restricting and then persecuting the Jews through segregation from society, then confinement to the ghettos, and then outright extermination.

When the restrictive policies of the Nazis first began and many Jews began to flee Germany, only to find that most of the nations around them were closing their doors for immigration, the United States included. By the time World War II broke out, there were very few places the Jews could flee to. Even those fortunate enough to escape from Hitler soon found themselves under Nazi rule as Germany quickly took over most of Europe.

At the very time the Jews desperately needed the land of Palestine to be opened to them, the British slammed the door in their face by passing the White Paper of 1939, which severely restricted Jewish immigration into Palestine. A year later in 1940, the Blitz – the strategic bombing of Great Britain and London – began. An uncomfortable question to consider is whether the Blitz was a Divine punishment upon the British for their terrible policies towards the Jews, particularly during that time. After all, God had promised to bless those who blessed the

Jews and curse those who cursed them, and has kept His word throughout history. (Genesis 12:3)

The region of Palestine needed her people as much as the Jews needed a land – but the British adamantly refused, effectively condemning millions of Jews to their fate under Hitler and the Nazis. But by this time, millions of Jews were confined to the ghettos, horrible slums where starvation and disease were rampant. But the worst was yet to come.

The Cursings of Deuteronomy 28:65-67 foretell a picture of this terrible time in Israel's history:

And among those nations you shall find no rest, nor shall the sole of your foot have a resting place; but there the LORD will give you a trembling heart, failing eyes, and anguish of soul. Your life shall hang in doubt before you; you shall fear day and night, and have no assurance of life. In the morning you shall say, 'Oh, that it were evening!' And at evening you shall say, 'Oh, that it were morning!' because of the fear which terrifies your heart, and because of the sight which your eyes see.

While the Jews were being confined in the ghettos and the concentration/labor camps, mass-killings throughout the Axis-controlled areas began. Hundreds of thousands of Jews, Gypsies, and other "undesirables" were soon killed, but the extermination effort wasn't going fast enough for Hitler. The Final Solution to the "Jewish Question" was implemented in 1942, which set out to exterminate all the Jews of Europe in a highly-efficient, industrialized fashion with trains, concentration camps, and poison-gas chambers.

Once the death-camps were set up, the Germans began liquidating the ghettos – systematically shipping all the Jews to the death-camps via mass transportation. The extermination effort would last nearly three years and claim approximately six million Jews, along with several million others like the Gypsies, Soviet POWs, and other enemies of the Nazis. Over ten million Slavs were also exterminated by the Nazis.

By the time World War II finally ended and the horror of what the Nazis had done was revealed, almost twenty-one million people had been systematically murdered by the Nazis. Hitler and the Nazis also killed at least half a million of their fellow native Germans. In the end, World War II itself claimed the lives of over twenty-eight million Europeans (including soldiers).

Despite the extensive testimonies, documentation, and evidence, Holocaust Denial is on the rise, particularly in the Middle East among the Islamic nations. Even in some Western universities and on the political fringes, there are Deniers who question whether the Holocaust actually happened, if not outright deny it as a Jewish fabrication or conspiracy.

But the Holocaust did indeed occur, and even eighty years later, the global Jewish population still has not recovered to the numbers it had before the Holocaust began, being approximately 2 million short of the 16.6 million Jews in 1939.

VIII. From the Ashes of Auschwitz

After World War II ended and the Allies realized what the
Nazis had been doing, they were not equipped to deal with the
tens of thousands of Jews and others confined to the
concentration camps. In most of the camps, the management
simply changed hands after the war, though the extermination
effort did cease. Lack of food and basic medical supplies only
prolonged the victims' suffering. Even though the war had
ended, the prisoners (newly reclassified as "Displaced Persons")
were not allowed to go free and remained in their horrible
conditions for weeks that soon turned into months.

President Truman ordered widespread changes in the
internment camps and conditions slowly improved, but not
nearly enough. In Poland and other parts of Eastern Europe, the
Jews continued to undergo persecution, which only intensified as
they began to be released from the internment camps in 1946.
Truman pressed the British to open Palestine for mass
immigration to the Jews from Europe, but again as before,
Britain stubbornly refused. Other DP camps were soon set up
throughout Europe and the Jews were segregated from the
general population, with many being sent to the island of Cyprus.

In Palestine, the Jews were outraged at the British
immigration stance and their pro-Arab policies and began to
rebel in any and every way they could. They formed
underground defense organizations such as the Irgun and the
Haganah to harass the British, arm and protect themselves
against the Arabs, and smuggle in as many of their fellow Jews
as possible. While for the British it was a nuisance, for the Jews
it was life and death. For the next four years, the Israelis
manufactured bullets, guns, and smuggled in as much weaponry
as they could, sometimes even entire airplanes in boxes.

Pressure continued to mount and the British and Jews became
bitter enemies, with neither side backing down. Finally in 1948,
the British had enough of the problems in Palestine and declared
that the British Mandate of Palestine would end on May 15,
1948. David Ben-Gurion, the head of the World Zionist
Organization, citing the "two sticks" passage of Ezekiel 37,

declared the founding of the new State of Israel on May 14,
1948.

The rebirth of Israel as a nation is declared in several places
in the Scriptures, but none more elegantly as in Isaiah 66:7-9:

"Before she was in labor, she gave birth;
  Before her pain came,
She delivered a male child."

Who has heard such a thing?
  Who has seen such things?
Shall the earth be made to give birth in one day?
  Or shall a nation be born at once?
For as soon as Zion was in labor,
  She gave birth to her children.

"Shall I bring to the time of birth, and not cause delivery?"
says the LORD.
  Shall I who cause delivery shut up the womb?" says your
God.

The day after the Jewish declaration on May 14th, Egypt,
Syria, Iraq, Lebanon, Jordan, and Saudi Arabia declared war on
Israel and the invasion by the Egyptian, Syrian and Jordanian
armies commenced. Israel was outnumbered at least 100-to-1 by
her enemies and had no tanks, no ships, no armored vehicles, and
only eleven light civilian aircraft. However, in the months that
followed, Israel not only survived, but prevailed against the
invaders and ended up capturing about 50% more territory than
they had been allotted in the U.N. Partition plan.

The Israeli War of Independence lasted for roughly a year and
a half, with many of the Arabs fleeing their homes and cities due
to the ongoing war. Before the war, many of the Arab residents
had been warned by the nearby Arab states to flee because of the
approaching invasion, and that they could then return after the
Israelis were annihilated. Israel pleaded with many of their Arab
neighbors to remain, though most fled voluntarily. The Arab
villages that cooperated with Israel and remained still peaceably
inhabit the land today.

Following the War of Independence, massive Jewish immigration to Israel commenced, and the nation doubled its population in only three years. As if building the new Jewish State wasn't challenging enough, assimilating thousands upon thousands of their downtrodden brothers and sisters presented an even greater challenge – but they adapted and prevailed. Tens of thousands would steadily immigrate to Israel every few years, with the nation of Israel rapidly assimilating them. However, the next huge wave didn't occur until the early 1990's when the Soviet Union collapsed; since 1989, over a million Russian Jews have been absorbed into Israel.

In the years that followed their independence, Israel began building the State as quickly as possible, absorbing tens of thousands of Jewish immigrants, and building up their fledgling military. The Suez Crisis of 1956 showed the world that Israel was building a top-notch civilian military, though they still lacked the more advanced weaponry that other nations had.

Eleven years later in May 1967, the Egyptian, Jordanian and Syrian armies began mobilizing along Israel's borders in preparation for another massive invasion, but Israel launched a pre-emptive strike against Egypt and wiped out their entire air force in less than two hours. On the western side, Jordan and Syria simultaneously invaded Israel but were quickly repulsed by the IDF (the Israeli Defense Force).

Within six days, (hence the name, the Six Day War), Israel had driven the Syrians out of the Golan Heights and the Jordanians across to the eastern side of the Jordan River. More importantly, Israel recaptured Jerusalem and all the land west of the Jordan River. Israel also seized the entire Sinai Peninsula, but later returned it to Egypt in 1982 following the Camp David Peace Accords with Anwar Sadat.

Both the 1948 War of Independence and the 1967 Six Day War speak of one of the Blessings in Leviticus 26 (v8):

Five of you shall chase a hundred, and a hundred of you shall put ten thousand to flight; your enemies shall fall by the sword before you.

Numerous miracles have been documented from the time that Israel began being regathered, and an excellent DVD set called

"Against all Odds – Israel Survives" is now available (and highly recommended).

After 1967, Israel grew somewhat complacent after her incredible victories and ignored the buildup of Egypt and Syria along the borders. In 1973 on Yom Kippur, the holiest day on the Jewish calendar, Egypt and Syria launched a surprise attack on Israel that almost devastated her military. After nearly three weeks of fighting and heavy losses, Israel repulsed the Egyptians and Syrians and struck deep into Syria, coming to within twenty-five miles of Damascus (the capital of Syria). But due to the threats of the Soviet Union and then the United States entering the conflict, a cease-fire came about and tensions soon de-escalated.

Since the Yom Kippur War, there have been various smaller wars and conflicts between Israel and her neighbors, but most haven't been with other nations as much as with terrorist groups and factions. In 1982, Israel invaded Lebanon to fight the Palestinian Liberation Organization which had taken up residence in Southern Lebanon. The last significant war was in 2006, in which Israel again entered Lebanon to disarm Hezbollah. Lebanon had been in a long civil war between the Lebanese Christians and the radical Muslims equipped by Iran, Syria, and the PLO. Lebanon is still greatly divided today, but has been relatively quiet for the past few years (as of 2011).

One of the biggest problems in Israel is a direct result of the Six Day War: the Arab refugees, who soon became known as the Palestinians. After the war had ended, the Israelis allowed the Palestinian Arabs to remain in the land, but did not formally annex the territory. If the roughly three-quarters of a million Palestinian Arabs had become citizens of Israel, the Jewish State would've been greatly divided and would no longer be "Jewish." However, Israel couldn't give up the land of the Golan Heights because that would've also endangered the Jewish State for security reasons, namely the high ground. As a result of the Six Day War, Israel won her capital and security, but at tremendous cost in the decades that followed.

In 2000, the Arabs from the West Bank and the Gaza Strip began attacking Israeli citizens with dozens of terrorist attacks and suicide bombings, which increased tensions throughout the region. Those suicide attacks only stopped after Israel built the

Separation Wall several years later, which divides the West Bank from the rest of Israel (along with Gaza). In 2007, Israel handed over control of the Gaza Strip to the Palestinians, which has been turned into a terrorist state controlled largely by Hamas.

Today, the land of Israel is relatively peaceful in the more inhabited areas (for the moment), though they are still surrounded by enemies like Hezbollah in the north, Hamas in Gaza and the West Bank, Syria in the east, and now Egypt in the south. To further complicate matters, Iran routinely threatens Israel with promises of annihilation as the Iranians continue building their nuclear weapons program.

One of the best defense developments in Israel has been the Iron Dome missile defense system. For decades, Israel has been plagued by thousands of rocket attacks from the West Bank, southern Lebanon, and the Gaza Strip. These attacks are typically indiscriminant, falling upon homes, businesses, and schools. Countless people have been injured or even killed in these attacks, and the attacks would often go unanswered until they became unbearable and the IDF was forced to respond.

However, the rocket attacks have gradually become more sophisticated, with wider ranges and much better accuracy. In 2011, Israel deployed the Iron Dome missile defense system which can intercept and neutralize many of these rockets and missiles, and it has been working rather well. However, the Iron Dome can't stop all the attacks and it appears that Hamas and the other groups may be testing the capabilities of the system to determine its vulnerabilities.

But while Israel not only faces imminent threats from above, they also now face them from below. Over the last decade since Hamas has been in control of the Gaza Strip, it's been estimated that over 2,500 "terror tunnels" have been constructed, some of which cross into Israel. Hamas uses these tunnels for smuggling, hiding missiles, and transporting weapons and militants, as well as thwarting surveillance and anti-terrorism efforts. The IDF actively detects and destroys such tunnels as they find them, especially the cross-border tunnels into Israel.

In the spring of 2018, Israel attacked numerous Iranian military targets in Syria, as well as revealed how Iran is actively ignoring and thwarting the nuclear deal it signed with the Obama administration and the European Union. To the west in Lebanon,

Hezbollah (one of the largest Iranian-backed terrorist organizations) and its allies have been elected to the majority in the parliament. Meanwhile in the south, Hamas and other terrorist groups in Gaza staged massive protests at the southwestern border of Israel with the aims of overwhelming border security under the guise of the "Great March of Return" to take back the land they claim that Israel stole over the last seventy years.

While the nation is relatively secure, the people of Israel are anything but dwelling in peace in the land.

IX. Anti-Semitism Explained

An Ancient Hatred Examined

Anti-Semitism is hostility toward or prejudice against the Jews as a religious, ethnic, or racial group, which can range from individual hatred to institutionalized, violent persecution. The root word "Semite" comes from the name of Noah's son, Shem. Technically, a Semite is anyone who comes from the lineage of Shem, which includes most of the Middle Eastern peoples. However, Semites are typically seen (at least in the eyes of the world) as being only Jews, and not Arabs, Lebanese, Assyrian, Iraqis, Persians, or others.

Where did anti-Semitism originate? Biblically, it originated with Satan, and can be better defined as "hatred for God's Chosen nation/people." Anti-Semitism can be both racist (even though skin color doesn't really play a significant role) and anti-Judaistic in nature. The Jewish people have been more systematically persecuted and exterminated like no other people-group on the face of the earth over the centuries. And it hasn't just happened once or twice in history, but many times in many different countries across all the continents.

One of the clearest proofs that anti-Semitism is Satanic is to study the Bible and take note of how often God makes a promise of someone being in the Messianic line, and then how it's followed by Satan's attempts to wipe out that person or their descendants in that line. These focused persecutions began with Abraham, then Isaac, then Jacob, the children of Israel in Egypt, then David, then Solomon, and all the way through to Jeconiah, in which God Himself cut him off from being the "human" line from which the Messiah would come (though there was still David's second son Nathan's line which led to Mary). Even Jesus as an infant was saved from one of Satan's extermination attempts when his parents were divinely warned to flee to Egypt until Herod had died, and then several more attempts were made on His life before He voluntarily went to the Cross.

However, why does anti-Semitism still exist today? The Messiah (recognized as Jesus Christ by Christians) has come and gone and is waiting to return. Satan failed to prevent His birth two thousand years ago but anti-Semitism continues and even worsens. Tragically, much of the anti-Semitism came from the Church throughout most of the Diaspora, particularly during the Middle Ages. One would think that Satan would now leave the Jews alone and focus on the Church IF they have really replaced Israel as many Western churches teach today. But anti-Semitism not only still exists, but is growing all over the world. Such widespread anti-Semitism itself argues against this very idea of Replacement Theology that runs rampant throughout the churches of Europe and in growing numbers of churches in America. Replacement Theology should've drawn its last gasp on May 14, 1948 when the nation of Israel was re-established, but it didn't – and it's growing, particularly as more churches fall away from the Scriptures.

Some could argue that Satan still persecutes the Jews simply because they are the Chosen People, which could be true to some extent. Because he cannot hurt God directly, he must hurt those whom He loves. In fact, Satan knows he can make the pain even worse if he can cause God's people to rebel against Him to the point in which God Himself is forced to punish His own people (as with the Flood). Ancient Israel didn't just stumble haphazardly into idolatry and then judgment; they were enticed by Satan every step of the way through the false gods of their neighbors.

But there's a deeper reason why anti-Semitism still thrives, and we only need to examine the events surrounding the Holocaust to discover why. In the Cursings of Deuteronomy 28, Israel was told that if they didn't learn from their mistakes the first time they were exiled, they would be punished again, but seven-times over. By combining Ezekiel's 430 Days prophecy (70 of which were fulfilled in the first exile) and the seven-fold multiplication of the curses specified in Deuteronomy, the rough date of Israel's return to the land in the mid-Twentieth Century can be calculated. Dr. Chuck Missler has an excellent paper on that calculation, which he narrows to the exact day of Israel's rebirth as a nation.

If Satan's priority is to prevent Scripture from being fulfilled and he knows that Israel will become a nation sometime within the Twentieth Century, why wouldn't he do everything possible to prevent that? And he did – he raised up monsters such as Adolph Hitler, Karl Marx, Vladimir Lenin, and Joseph Stalin to prevent the Jews from returning to their land. Not only that, but he caused nations which had typically been friendly to the Jews – including the United States of America – to close off Jewish immigration so they were doomed to the pogroms and the Nazi extermination camps. Even ships full of Jews fleeing Europe were not allowed into America and forced to return to the death-camps of Europe.

Satan almost succeeded in his Holocaust, in that one out of every three Jews alive at that time was slaughtered – he wanted to take three out of every three. But he failed again and Israel became a nation just as God had promised, rising from the very ashes of the Holocaust that had nearly destroyed her. Who could have ever imagined a people scattered over the earth for more than two thousand years returning to their ancient homeland and establishing their own nation? And yet it happened – and many of us alive today have been watching the rest of her outcasts be regathered. If you need proof that God exists and that the Bible is trustworthy, simply look on any globe or turn on the news: Israel is there, just as He promised thousands of years ago.

Today, Israel is quite modern and is very similar to most Western nations, having a parliament (the Knesset), free elections, low unemployment, freedom of religion, and all the infrastructure and conveniences of a modern society. So why does anti-Semitism continue, even on a global level? And why is the West increasingly turning their backs on Israel?

The answer lies at the end of Hosea 5 and the first few verses of the next chapter: in order for the Messiah to return and take His place as King in Jerusalem, the Jews must petition Him to first. Then after three days, He will return and save them just as He has promised. When will this be? Near the end of the Great Tribulation after the nation of Israel has been overthrown and the faithful remnant has taken refuge in Petra (Daniel 11:41, Isaiah 26:20-21, Micah 2:12). When the Messiah comes, He returns to Bozrah first, then He goes to Jerusalem and then up to the Valley of Megiddo (Armageddon) to destroy the world's armies. I have been to that valley, and there's no question that millions upon millions of soldiers, tanks, and carriers could fit in that valley.

Just as with the Holocaust, if Satan can wipe out the Jews before they can petition the Messiah to save them, he essentially will win – he will have prevented the Messiah from returning as has been promised. The Holocaust took one out of every three Jews in the world, but Zechariah prophesies that the Great Tribulation will take two out of every three (Zechariah 13:7-9). Anti-Semitism exists today primarily to thwart that petition for the Messiah to return to save them and take his rightful place as King.

For most of the last century, persecution and anti-Semitism throughout Russia, Europe, and the Middle East have driven the Jews back to the land of Israel. Nations that were filled with bustling, vibrant Jewish communities for centuries now only have shadows remaining. In fact, the Regathering has been so extensive that there remains only one nation which has yet to "give up her Jews": the United States of America.

Today, just over 90% of all the Jews in the world are equally divided between America and Israel, with the next largest amount (4%) being in France. The rest are thinly disbursed throughout the rest of the world, with most still in Europe or Russia. But with the rise of Islam in Europe and the accompanying violent anti-Semitism, more European Jews are now migrating to Israel. Next to America, Israel is the only place in the world where they feel secure, even though they are beset by enemies all around.

Will there be a time coming soon when America is also called to "give up her Jews"? I believe there will be. However, America has rarely been anti-Semitic, particularly when compared to most other nations. Could an attack on our coastlands cause millions of Jews to flee to Israel? What about a terrible economic collapse in America, such as the one that appears to be looming before us because of our exploding national debt and inflating currency? What about an extended period of malaise and high unemployment in the United States? It's happened before, and will likely happen again sooner or later.

What about a widespread explosion of anti-Semitism against the "Jewish bankers?" In the Wall Street protests of 2011, there was horrible anti-Semitism throughout the demonstrations, though much of it was covered up by the mainstream media for political purposes. In American politics, the extreme wings of both political parties have high degrees of anti-Semitism. As America continues to fragment, people tend to gravitate toward the extremists.

What if Islam sweeps over America as it has in Europe? It's beginning to grow and thrive in once-great American cities like Detroit, Oakland, Chicago, and even New York.

Anti-Semitism as a Prophetic Alarm-Clock

From the Bible, Satan always seeks to thwart God's plans, regardless of what they are. And since Satan cannot "hurt" God, he has to settle for the next best thing: hurting the people that God loves. From Genesis to Revelation, each time God blesses a person or family (or nation), Satan tries to undo or disrupt that blessing. However, from time to time, Satan uses a king or nation to try to wipe out the entire Jewish people, and he typically raises the levels of anti-Semitism just before prophetic events are about to be fulfilled.

A recent example of this is that Israel was prophesied to be restored as a nation in the mid-Twentieth Century after the long Diaspora. Satan raised up Hitler to power in order to wipe out as much of the Jewish population as he could only a few years before they were due to return. Satan can read the Bible prophecies and run the numbers as well as we can, and he probably figured out that God would begin to restore the nation sometime in the mid- to late-1940s, particularly when he saw the Jews from Europe and Russia begin to return to Palestine. Therefore, he started working quickly and ruthlessly to thwart the restoration of Israel by raising up Hitler and instituting the Holocaust.

Consider all the time, money, and effort Hitler put into "The Final Solution" – he even put the extermination of the Jews ahead of the welfare of his own "Aryan nation!" Towards the end of World War II when the German military and resources were faltering, several of his generals and advisors suggested stopping the relocation and extermination of the Jews and instead putting them to work in factories to help the war effort. But Hitler refused and only increased the activity in the death-camps. Even though the fuel, human resources, and supplies used in the extermination camps could've been used in fighting their enemies, Hitler continued The Final Solution.

But were the Jews ever really a threat to Germany or a problem for Hitler personally? Of course not – the Jews were usually very peaceful in the nations where they were scattered, and were a cultural, economic, and intellectual beneficial to their host nations. Typically, Jews highly value literacy, morality, and are very well-educated. Though globally, the Jews make up only 0.25% of the world's population, they have won 22% of all the Nobel Prizes awarded since 1901.

One way of tracking how close we are to the next Biblically-significant event is to watch whether anti-Semitism is on the rise or on the decrease in the current news events and media. If anti-Semitism appears to be increasing around the world, we should be more watchful for another significant prophetic event to be fulfilled. And the one that many Bible students have been watching for since June of 1967 is the Magog Invasion of Ezekiel 38-39.

Anti-Semitism in our Churches?

One of the most astonishing aspects of Christendom today is the amount of overt anti-Semitism present. Of all the people in the world who should not be anti-Semitic, it's us Christians. After all, we worship the Jewish God, trust in a Jewish Messiah, revere Jewish disciples, and read Jewish Scriptures. Only two books of the sixty-six books of the Bible were written by Gentiles (and by the same man): Luke and Acts. And those two books were likely the trial documents used to defend a Jewish apostle (Paul)!

From the earliest days of Christianity, there was conflict between the religious Jews and Christians, as typified in the New Testament. However, anti-Semitism in the Church didn't really take root until Supersessionism, or Replacement Theology, took hold after Christianity became the state-religion of the fading Roman Empire. This form of theology teaches that because the Jews rejected Jesus as their Messiah and then had him crucified, all the promises that God made to the Jews have been redistributed to the Christians.

In fact, most denominations of the Church today hold anti-Semitic views, and Jewish persecution has been ordered from the highest offices of the Church since the early days of the Roman Catholic Church. Even today with Israel restored as a nation, most churches and denominations teach that the Church has replaced Israel in God's plans, and thus has inherited all the rights and promises that God gave to Israel.

But the Scriptures say no such thing – in fact, God's promises to restore Israel as a nation and make good on His promises usually follows every passage where He has cast them off. Israel and the Church have very different origins, missions, and destinies. In the Bible, God means what He says and says what He means, and when He says "Israel," He means the literal nation or people of Israel!

Such teachings of Replacement Theology are infesting many Western churches and denominations today, though there are growing voices rising to oppose those false doctrines. Replacement Theology is just another form of soft anti-Semitism which denies the Jewish people their rightful inheritance and even God's promises.

Much of Germany and Europe were nominally Christian at the time of the Holocaust, but were infested with similar forms of soft anti-Semitism. "Since the Jews rejected and crucified Jesus, we're justified in punishing them!" or so the thought-process went. When the Nazis began slaughtering the Jews, most of the churches were deafeningly silent. Horribly, some churches even helped the Nazis exterminate the Jews and then provided safe-haven for Nazi leaders after the war ended.

Would the Holocaust have even occurred if anti-Semitism hadn't been so widespread in the churches of Europe? Would more Christians have stood up against the Nazis if their pastors hadn't been teaching that the Christians had replaced the Jews in God's plans?

Churches, pastors, teachers, and even authors teaching that the Church has somehow replaced Israel in the Scriptures need to be confronted and corrected about this false teaching. Romans 9 describes how Israel has been set aside temporarily for the purposes of the Gospel and Jesus building His Church, but that she will also be restored to inherit all the promises given in the Old Testament. In that same passage, Paul explicitly warns against us Gentiles thinking that we are somehow better than Israel or that we have somehow "replaced" the Chosen People.

As Christians, the Jewish people are our spiritual siblings who have been blinded for a time so that we can partake in their blessings and inheritance with them, not disinherit them!

X. Israel Regathered – Ezekiel 36

One of the main passages of the Bible that foretells the return of the Jews to their native homeland is Ezekiel 36-37. The prophet Ezekiel was one of the exiles of the second wave of the Babylonian Captivity who was taken to Babylon in approximately 597 BC. Daniel the prophet and most of the nobility of Jerusalem were taken away in the first exile in 605 BC. The third and final exile occurred in 586 BC when the Babylonians destroyed Jerusalem.

During the time of the Babylonian Captivity, God sought to comfort His People in exile through signs (as through Ezekiel) and wonders (as through Daniel), and also with words of their future restoration. Just as He spoke harshly with them in the decades leading up to their Captivity in order to bring about their repentance, He later spoke words of comfort to give them hope. The Jews desperately needed to know that God had not abandoned them for good and that they hadn't lost the promises He had made to them.

In the ancient world, a nation's gods were often intrinsically linked to their land, so when a people were severed from their land, they would interpret that as their gods had been defeated by the conquering nation's gods. However, God repeatedly demonstrated the fallacy of that premise by showing His People signs and wonders during the Captivity, and also by having several of their Gentile rulers proclaim that the God of the Jews was the One True God (Daniel 4 and 6, and Esther).

The Book of Ezekiel can be basically divided into four sections: Chapters 1-24 concern prophecies about the destruction of Jerusalem, Chapters 25-32 are prophecies of God's judgment on Israel's neighbors, Chapter 33 is a last call for the Jews to repent, and Chapters 34-48 are mostly prophecies concerning the future restoration of Israel. In the last division, Chapters 34-37 concerns the restoration of the people to the land, while Chapters 38-39 describe a confederacy of Israel's enemies who sweep down to plunder Israel after they have been restored. From Chapter 40 to the end of the book, Israel's future glory is described, with the Millennial Temple examined in detail by the prophet.

There are several major highlights of Israel's history in the Bible: the lives of the patriarchs, the enslavement in Egypt, the Sinai wanderings, the entry into the Promised Land and the times of the Judges, the beginning of the monarchy under David and Saul, the division of the kingdom and the subsequent decline of the kingdoms, then the destruction of Jerusalem and the exile to Babylon. After the destruction of Jerusalem, their Biblical history continues with return of the remnant under the Persians, the four-hundred "silent years", the Gospel period, followed by the formation of the early Church before the destruction of the Temple by the Romans.

The future events of Israel described in the Scriptures are the Regathering of the nation and Restoration of the land, followed by the Seventieth Week (commonly known as the Tribulation and the "Time of Jacob's Trouble") and the return of the Messiah. After the Messiah takes the throne in Jerusalem, He restores the world to its pre-Fallen state, fulfills the land-grant to Israel that was made to Abraham, and reigns for one thousand years (the Millennium) from Jerusalem. Once the Millennium has ended, a final rebellion occurs which is promptly put down by God, and then the earth enters into the Eternal Age.

Throughout the Book of Ezekiel, there's a phrase that occurs over and over again: "Then they shall know that I am the LORD." The phrase is repeated forty-eight times throughout the book as God recites the reason why He's allowing or causing a particular event to occur. The idea behind the phrase is that the audience (sometimes Israel, Judah, the nations, or His enemies) does not know that Jehovah – the God of the Jews – is the God of the universe, and those events will cause them to realized that He is Who He says He is and is not to be taken lightly, mocked, or ignored.

In our modern world today, the God of the Bible is routinely mocked and scorned, with His adversaries often brazenly declaring that "God is dead!" Nearly two thousand years have passed from the time that any real miracles have occurred as written in the Scriptures, and the mindset of most of the world is that since there are no miracles or nothing "supernatural" occurs, then God must be a figment of our imagination or simply an invention of an ancient people to explain what they didn't understand.

However, there have been numerous such supernatural incidents occurring over the last century, with many of them being focused on God's people Israel. Widespread, diverse accounts from Israeli soldiers and citizens alike tell of miracles occurring specifically to save or aid them, particularly in times of war and great need. Again, this excellent documentary on such recent miracles in Israel is called "Against All Odds – Israel Survives."

But regardless of whether one believes those eye-witness accounts or not, you only need to look at a globe, turn on the radio or television, or browse the Internet to know that the "supernatural" is real and that the God of the Bible is Who He says He is. There in the center of the Islamic Middle East is a tiny Jewish nation called "Israel" full of exiles who have been regathered from every nation on the earth.

Every year, thousands of Jews "make aliyah" and return to their ancient homeland. Surrounded by millions of Muslims who mostly wish nothing but death and destruction upon them, the Jewish State is growing and thriving in the midst of barbaric cruelty and poverty. And despite attempt after attempt to push the Jews into the Sea, Israel continues to defy all odds and not only survive, but thrive.

In Ezekiel 36, God orders the land of Israel to begin bearing fruit and become fertile again, in preparation for His people to return from all the nations of the earth where He had scattered them. God then tells His people that He is restoring them for His Name and His Reputation, not because of their deeds or merits. Also, God tells the Jews exactly why they were punished and scattered for so long, and then rebukes the nations that surround Israel for their mocking and gloating.

Ezekiel 36 – Full Text

1 "And you, son of man, prophesy to the mountains of Israel, and say, 'O mountains of Israel, hear the word of the LORD! 2 Thus says the Lord GOD: "Because the enemy has said of you, 'Aha! The ancient heights have become our possession,'"' 3

*therefore prophesy, and say, 'Thus says the Lord GOD:
"Because they made you desolate and swallowed you up on
every side, so that you became the possession of the rest of the
nations, and you are taken up by the lips of talkers and
slandered by the people"— 4 therefore, O mountains of Israel,
hear the word of the Lord GOD! Thus says the Lord GOD to the
mountains, the hills, the rivers, the valleys, the desolate wastes,
and the cities that have been forsaken, which became plunder
and mockery to the rest of the nations all around— 5 therefore
thus says the Lord GOD: "Surely I have spoken in My burning
jealousy against the rest of the nations and against all Edom,
who gave My land to themselves as a possession, with
wholehearted joy and spiteful minds, in order to plunder its open
country."'*

*6 "Therefore prophesy concerning the land of Israel, and say
to the mountains, the hills, the rivers, and the valleys, 'Thus says
the Lord GOD: "Behold, I have spoken in My jealousy and My
fury, because you have borne the shame of the nations." 7
Therefore thus says the Lord GOD: "I have raised My hand in
an oath that surely the nations that are around you shall bear
their own shame. 8 But you, O mountains of Israel, you shall
shoot forth your branches and yield your fruit to My people
Israel, for they are about to come. 9 For indeed I am for you,
and I will turn to you, and you shall be tilled and sown. 10 I will
multiply men upon you, all the house of Israel, all of it; and the
cities shall be inhabited and the ruins rebuilt. 11 I will multiply
upon you man and beast; and they shall increase and bear
young; I will make you inhabited as in former times, and do
better for you than at your beginnings. Then you shall know that
I am the LORD. 12 Yes, I will cause men to walk on you, My
people Israel; they shall take possession of you, and you shall be
their inheritance; no more shall you bereave them of children."*

*13 'Thus says the Lord GOD: "Because they say to you, 'You
devour men and bereave your nation of children,' 14 therefore
you shall devour men no more, nor bereave your nation
anymore," says the Lord GOD. 15 "Nor will I let you hear the
taunts of the nations anymore, nor bear the reproach of the
peoples anymore, nor shall you cause your nation to stumble
anymore," says the Lord GOD.'"*

16 Moreover the word of the LORD came to me, saying: 17 "Son of man, when the house of Israel dwelt in their own land, they defiled it by their own ways and deeds; to Me their way was like the uncleanness of a woman in her customary impurity. 18 Therefore I poured out My fury on them for the blood they had shed on the land, and for their idols with which they had defiled it. 19 So I scattered them among the nations, and they were dispersed throughout the countries; I judged them according to their ways and their deeds. 20 When they came to the nations, wherever they went, they profaned My holy name—when they said of them, 'These are the people of the LORD, and yet they have gone out of His land.' 21 But I had concern for My holy name, which the house of Israel had profaned among the nations wherever they went.

22 "Therefore say to the house of Israel, 'Thus says the Lord GOD: "I do not do this for your sake, O house of Israel, but for My holy name's sake, which you have profaned among the nations wherever you went. 23 And I will sanctify My great name, which has been profaned among the nations, which you have profaned in their midst; and the nations shall know that I am the LORD," says the Lord GOD, "when I am hallowed in you before their eyes. 24 For I will take you from among the nations, gather you out of all countries, and bring you into your own land. 25 Then I will sprinkle clean water on you, and you shall be clean; I will cleanse you from all your filthiness and from all your idols. 26 I will give you a new heart and put a new spirit within you; I will take the heart of stone out of your flesh and give you a heart of flesh. 27 I will put My Spirit within you and cause you to walk in My statutes, and you will keep My judgments and do them. 28 Then you shall dwell in the land that I gave to your fathers; you shall be My people, and I will be your God. 29 I will deliver you from all your uncleannesses. I will call for the grain and multiply it, and bring no famine upon you. 30 And I will multiply the fruit of your trees and the increase of your fields, so that you need never again bear the reproach of famine among the nations. 31 Then you will remember your evil ways and your deeds that were not good; and you will loathe yourselves in your own sight, for your iniquities and your abominations. 32 Not for your sake do I do this," says the Lord

GOD, *"let it be known to you. Be ashamed and confounded for
your own ways, O house of Israel!"*

*33 'Thus says the Lord GOD: "On the day that I cleanse you
from all your iniquities, I will also enable you to dwell in the
cities, and the ruins shall be rebuilt. 34 The desolate land shall
be tilled instead of lying desolate in the sight of all who pass by.
35 So they will say, 'This land that was desolate has become like
the garden of Eden; and the wasted, desolate, and ruined cities
are now fortified and inhabited.' 36 Then the nations which are
left all around you shall know that I, the LORD, have rebuilt the
ruined places and planted what was desolate. I, the LORD, have
spoken it, and I will do it."*

*37 'Thus says the Lord GOD: "I will also let the house of
Israel inquire of Me to do this for them: I will increase their men
like a flock. 38 Like a flock offered as holy sacrifices, like the
flock at Jerusalem on its feast days, so shall the ruined cities be
filled with flocks of men. Then they shall know that I am the
LORD."'"*

Ezekiel 36 – Verse by Verse Analysis

Ezekiel 36:1-3 *"And you, son of man, prophesy to the
mountains of Israel, and say, 'O mountains of Israel, hear the
word of the LORD! 2 Thus says the Lord GOD: "Because the
enemy has said of you, 'Aha! The ancient heights have become
our possession,'"' 3 therefore prophesy, and say, 'Thus says the
Lord GOD: "Because they made you desolate and swallowed
you up on every side, so that you became the possession of the
rest of the nations, and you are taken up by the lips of talkers
and slandered by the people"*

This passage begins God's discourse to Ezekiel concerning
the distant, promised restoration of Israel. These prophecies were
given to the prophet Ezekiel during the time of the Babylonian
Captivity, in which the land of Judah would be desolate for 70
years (starting in 605 BC). The Northern Kingdom had already
been taken exiled and scattered by the Assyrian Empire in 722
BC and had been resettled by foreigners, who later became
known as the Samaritans (half-Jews).

In terms of the marriage-covenant outlined in Deuteronomy 28 and Leviticus 26, God detailed His Blessings for Israel's obedience and His Cursings for their disobedience. The Blessings upon Israel were that they would be honored, respected, prosperous, dwell safely in the land, and the Lord would be with them. The Cursings for their disobedience involved Israel being put out of the land and being hated and persecuted by the nations where they were exiled, and God turning His Face away from them.

There's some debate whether the terms of the marriage-covenant at Sinai are still in effect today, because God technically divorced Israel in the Book of Hosea. However, He is currently "wooing" her back to Himself, and has promised that their relationship will one day be fully restored.

From the Leviticus 26 passage, Israel would go through a short exile for idolatry and for not keeping the Sabbaths of the land (v34). Then they would be punished seven times more (or seven times longer) if they didn't obey God after the first exile – and this is precisely what has happened in history. While they may have kept the "letter of the Law" after the Babylonian Captivity, they did not keep the "spirit of the Law", which is what Jesus accused the Jewish leaders of throughout His ministry.

Judah was exiled from the land for 70 years starting about 605 BC and Jerusalem was destroyed 19 years later in 586 BC. After a remnant returned 70 years later, Israel continued to disobey through their unbelief, though they did try extremely hard to keep the Law. Israel pursued a relationship with God based upon their works rather than by their faith (Romans 9:30-32). Legalism always leads to a religion of works rather than faith, which becomes just another form of unbelief. This faithlessness reached its climax in 32 AD, when Jesus of Nazareth entered Jerusalem and presented Himself at the Temple on the exact day as prescribed in Daniel 9, and the Jewish religious leadership rejected Him as their Messiah.

One of the more dramatic phrases uttered by the religious leadership when Jesus was condemned was, "His blood will be upon us and our children!" (Matthew 27:25). Apparently when they made that declaration, God held them accountable for that, along with the blood of all the prophets that had been slain over

the years "from Abel to Zechariah" (Matthew 23:29-36).
Another tragic phrase the leaders uttered was, "We have no king but Caesar!" (John 19:15). Since they declared Caesar to be their king instead of God, they inherently gave up their right to rebel against the king. If and when they rebelled, they would suffer the consequences at the hand of the Romans – and they did.

As described in the Gospels, the Jewish leadership pressured the Romans into executing the Messiah, Who was crucified (as foretold in Isaiah 53 and Psalm 22), was resurrected after three days (Psalm 18), and the Church was born during the Feast of Weeks fifty days later. From that time on, Israel had thirty-eight years in which to repent and believe on the Messiah and join the Church. Many did, but the Jewish leadership continued in their unbelief and rejection of their Messiah and His Church.

In 66 AD, the Jews rebelled and threw off the Roman rule, though only for a very short time. The Romans promptly besieged Jerusalem and in 70 AD, the Jews were completely dispersed again to all the nations in the world, until the time of the long Diaspora had been completed. The last holdouts in the land fled to Masada in 70 AD, the desert fortress built by Herod the Great, where they committed mass-suicide after the Romans finally broke into the fortress in 72 AD.

The mocking of Israel and the inhabitation of their lands by their enemies occurred mostly from 586 BC to the early Middle Ages. The remnants of the Gentile nations surrounding the land of Israel, namely the Moabites, Ammonites, Edomites, and the desert nomads looked at the land of Israel and said, "Israel has been cast off – see, their land is desolate and they are displaced!" Edom, the nation descended from Jacob's brother Esau, had been enemies of Israel from the days of Moses and had helped the Babylonians capture any refugees and delivered them into exile.

The mountains referred to in this passage likely refer to the wilderness southwest of the Dead Sea and also the Golan Heights to the northeast of Jerusalem. The Golan Heights are a major source of contention today because whoever controls the high ground of the Golan can almost control the entire nation, especially the water supply of the Galilee and the Jordan River.

For centuries after the Jews had been dispersed, the land was nearly uninhabitable except for small patches which were used for grazing. The rest of the land was disease-filled swamps or arid desert wilderness. The great forests of the north were no more, especially after the Turks administered the land in the centuries following the Crusades. The deplorable condition of the land reflected directly upon God – when passing through the land, you can almost hear the travelers' mocking words: "This was the Promised Land?"

Again, because the gods were supposedly tied to the land, the Edomites and other nations viewed the God of the Jews as having been defeated because His people had been cast out of the land. It's been observed that demons (who are the true powers behind the gods) seem to be territorial (Daniel 10:12-20) – unseen principalities ruling a particular nation or parcel of land.

Today, that concept of a god's strength being reflected in the size of territory that worship that particular god is still alive one of the largest religions in the world: Islam. In the religion of Mohammed, the world is divided into Dar al-Islam (the land of Islam) and Dar al-Harb (the land of War, or the land not yet conquered).

One of the underlying reasons why the Islamic fundamentalists hate Israel so much is because Islam states that once a land has been made Islamic, it will forever remain Islamic. If that land ever falls out of the hand of Islam, it's viewed as a defeat of Allah and thereby faithlessness on their part, which is utterly blasphemous to them. The Jewish people being back in the land of Israel completely destroys one of the pillars of the Islam and brings shame upon both Allah and his people. Therefore, in order for Muslims to make things right between them and their god, they are obligated to retake that land by whatever means necessary, both to show they are faithful and Allah is supreme.

Ezekiel 36:4-5 *Therefore, O mountains of Israel, hear the word of the Lord GOD! Thus says the Lord GOD to the mountains, the hills, the rivers, the valleys, the desolate wastes, and the cities that have been forsaken, which became plunder and mockery to the rest of the nations all around— 5 therefore thus says the Lord GOD: "Surely I have spoken in My burning jealousy against the rest of the nations and against all Edom, who gave My land to themselves as a possession, with* *wholehearted joy and spiteful minds, in order to plunder its open country."*

The Gentile nations that surround Israel today are Egypt, Jordan, Syria, Lebanon, and an assortment of Arabs and Bedouins that dwell in the land. Those nations attacked Israel in 1948, 1967, and 1973 only to lose land to the new Jewish State. Currently, Israel has peace treaties with Egypt and Jordan, while Lebanon has been a source of conflict between Israel and Syria from the late 1970s onward because it's infested with Islamic terrorist groups like Hezbollah, Islamic Jihad, and other Iranian and Syrian sponsored terror-groups. The Gaza Strip to the southwest near Egypt also remains a continual thorn in Israel's side, though not really much of a national threat (except for forest fires and rocket attacks).

Notice that the nation of Edom in particular is singled out in this passage. After the Babylonian Captivity, the Edomites took the southern regions of Judah for grazing their flocks. Part of the reason was out of spite from being subservient to Judah since the times of King David, but also because they had been pushed out of their native lands by the Nabataeans, who subsequently built up Petra. The Edomites seized a large portion of Judea in the South, and eventually were integrated into the surrounding nomadic peoples.

By the time of the Greek Empire, the remnant of the Edomites were known as the Idumeans, who continued to maintain troubled relations with the Jews. Judas Maccabaeus forcibly converted the Idumeans to Judaism (via mass-circumcision), though the contention persisted. By the time of the Romans, one group of Idumeans in particular rose to power and were given authority by Rome to rule over all Judea: Antipater the Idumaean, who was the forbearer of the Herodian Dynasty. The Jews hated both the Romans and the Herodians, who continually tried to placate them by expanding the Temple, growing Jerusalem, and by many other grand public works.

Though most of us have heard the Christmas Story dozens of times, many don't realize that Herod was extremely afraid of a Jewish king who could unite the Jews and rebel against him and the Roman Empire. Herod was a foreigner, an Edomite king ruling over his ancestors' enemies, which was one reason he tried to kill the One who was "born king of the Jews" as an infant.

Notice how God refers to the land as He accuses Edom: "My land." The land of Israel has been in bitter dispute for centuries, if not thousands of years. Does the land belong to the Arabs, Palestinians, or the Jordanians? No, it does not. Does the land belong to Israel and the Jewish people? Surprisingly, that answer is also "No." The land belongs to God and He has leased it to the Jews, dependent upon their obedience to Him and His Laws as described in the Mosaic Covenant.

When the United States, Great Britain, Russia, Europe, and the United Nations introduce their "peace plans" and speak of dividing the land of Israel in the name of peace, whose land are they really messing with? God's land! Perhaps we'd all be better off if we didn't go about poking our noses in places where it doesn't belong.

Ezekiel 36:6-7 *"Therefore prophesy concerning the land of Israel, and say to the mountains, the hills, the rivers, and the valleys, 'Thus says the Lord GOD: "Behold, I have spoken in My jealousy and My fury, because you have borne the shame of the nations." 7 Therefore thus says the Lord GOD: "I have raised My hand in an oath that surely the nations that are around you shall bear their own shame.*

After centuries of silence, God now rises to defend His land and declares that the days of its shame are over, meaning that the land will no longer be cursed. In the verses which follow, He expounds on that declaration and describes how it will once again be fruitful and inhabited. Notice the emotions He brings into the declaration: jealousy and anger, indicative of intense love and concern for His land.

Not only has His land been scorned and mocked, but His very Name and reputation has been insulted by His people not being in the land. When God's people sin and disobey, they cause His name to be blasphemed. And now that the time of His people's punishment has concluded, He earnestly seeks to restore His reputation and His Name – which is Jehovah, not Allah.

In 1948, 1967, and 1973, God utterly shamed all the nations around Israel by thwarting her neighbors' attacks of annihilation upon Israel, and even caused them to lose some of their land to Israel. Remember, each time Israel takes more land from Dar-al Islam, the more Allah is blasphemed in the eyes of the Muslims. Unfortunately, after each war under the guise of peace, Israel returned much of that land, such as the Sinai Peninsula.

It is utterly shameful to those Gentile nations and the religion of Islam to keep losing both wars and territory to Israel, the cursed nation they have mocked and persecuted for nearly 1400 years. After all, they vastly outnumber the Jews and have huge, established militaries in comparison. By all accounts, Israel should've been wiped out within the first week following their Statehood on May 14, 1948. But they had One who was fighting alongside them against their enemies.

A tongue-in-cheek phrase heard in Israel after 1967 was "Attack us again – we need the land!" But after the Yom Kippur War, the Israelis were humbled and have been more cautious since.

Ezekiel 36:8-9 *But you, O mountains of Israel, you shall shoot forth your branches and yield your fruit to My people Israel, for they are about to come [home]. 9 For indeed I am for you, and I will turn to you, and you shall be tilled and sown.*

As God continues speaking to the mountains, He orders the land itself to become habitable and fertile again, because His people are about to return from the Diaspora. Why is God speaking to the mountains? Because earlier in Ezekiel, He had cursed them after they had become places of idolatry to the other gods (Ezekiel 6). Rather than worship Him in Jerusalem as He had prescribed, the Israelites had taken to worshiping all the other gods on their mountains, hills, and other high places.

From 70 AD to 1948 AD, the land of Israel was an utter wasteland, full of pestilence-ridden marshes and burning deserts. In 1867, Mark Twain remarked in his writings of how desolate the entire land was and how very few people lived there. The land was used for grazing small, scattered flocks but agriculture of any sort was barely even attempted – at least until the first Jewish colonists entered the land.

When the Jewish remnant began to return to the land over the last century, they first made communes called kibbutzim and set out to drain the swamps, replant the forests, and reclaim the desert wastes. Centuries of erosion had all but wiped out much of the topsoil, and few attempts to grow anything on the land were made. Not only that, but some portions of the soil that remained had to be desalinated. Through enormous effort and sacrifice, the Jews have been able to re-invigorate the land, so now it's not only usable for agriculture, but is producing more than was ever thought possible.

The specific mention of fruit in this passage is also curious when taken literally today. While Israel had always been a land of agriculture in her former days, it had never really produced fruit in significant amounts, especially for export. The ancient Jews had grown dates, figs, grapes, and various grains, but never really much fruit. But today, Israel is the second largest exporter of fruit and flowers to Europe and the rest of the Middle East (the United States is the primary supplier).

The feats and accomplishments of modern Israel's agricultural industry are quite remarkable and innovative, as the Israelis have learned how to grow citrus, flowers, and even trees in the deserts of the Negev with a minimal amount of water. The desert has yet to bloom like the rose (Isaiah 35:1), but the Israelis are trying their hardest to make that dream a reality.

In Israel today, there are hundreds of thousands (if not millions) of trees and a large portion of the northern forests have been restored. Yet only sixty years ago, those same areas were barren wastes. Israel is one of the few nations which have successfully reclaimed large portions of the land from centuries of desertification.

An interesting exercise is to look at a satellite map of the Middle East. At first glance, the entire region appears to be nothing but burning sands. However, in the very middle area along the eastern coast of the Mediterranean, there's a dark narrow strip of green completely surrounded by desert wastes. That's the land of Israel today – an oasis in a sea of sand.

Yet while the accomplishments of the Israelis are often astounding, God is responsible for making their land blossom and bloom, as He promised to in this passage. The Israelis may have provided the blood, sweat, and tears, but God provided the spirit, the motivation, and the courage. Strange as it may sound, it's almost as if the land refused to produce for others except the Jewish people, and only when they're living in obedience to the Law.

And rather than hold back these precious secrets of desert agriculture and land reclamation, Israel often shares them with Third World nations which desperately need their own agricultural industries to feed their people. Whether due to their centuries of persecution, their need of allies in an extremely hostile region, or because God has given them a different spirit, Israel is no longer the same nation it was in the pages of the Bible.

The Israelis have been blessed to be a blessing – and they are blessing those nations who are not too proud to accept their assistance.

Ezekiel 36:10-12 I will multiply men upon you, all the house of Israel, all of it; and the cities shall be inhabited and the ruins rebuilt. 11 I will multiply upon you man and beast; and they shall increase and bear young; I will make you inhabited as in former times, and do better for you than at your beginnings. Then you shall know that I am the LORD. 12 Yes, I will cause men to walk on you, My people Israel; they shall take possession of you, and you shall be their inheritance; no more shall you bereave them of children."

Both the Jews and the land have been looking forward to these promises for thousands of years, which until the last sixty years had been little more than a distant, seemingly impossible dream. For centuries, Palestine was a land without a people, while the Jews were a people without a land. But no longer. Today in Israel, many of the same cities and towns named in the Scriptures have been rebuilt and repopulated. Of course, they are quite modern today, but even some of the ancient ruins have been reconstructed by the archaeologists.

Not only have many of the ancient cities been rebuilt, but the land is now filled with people, with thousands more immigrating to Israel every year. After the nightmares of the Holocaust, the pogroms of Europe and Russia, and the harsh persecution in Muslim lands, the Israelis understood that they needed to find a way to quickly assimilate as many of their people into their State as possible. The Law of Return in Israel grants the right of immediate citizenship for any Jew who makes aliyah.

In 1882, there were only 24,000 Jews living in Palestine; by 1948, there were over 650,000. Ten years after their Independence, the population had more than tripled. Now there are nearly six million Jews in Israel (5,874,300, as of September, 2011). However, the immigrants haven't been merely settled in the land and pushed off to the side, they have been absorbed and have become part of the society. Incredible, successful immigration into Israel has occurred in our lifetimes – first from Europe, then Africa/Ethiopia, then Russia/Eastern Europe. But the greatest aliyah in Israel's history may be on the near horizon: the aliyah from America, where more than 40% of all the Jews in the world live today.

Today when Jews make aliyah to Israel, they are immediately granted citizenship and given a temporary residence with other immigrants, along with food, clothing, medical care, and a stipend. In the months that follow, they are taught the language of Israel (Modern Hebrew), how to function in the modern State of Israel, and are also given employment and relocation assistance. Many Jews from very poor nations immigrate to Israel with little more than the clothes they are wearing, and it's often not easy to assimilate Third World people into a modern, industrialized civilization.

The absorption effort has been difficult and challenging, yet Israel has learned how to do it – and do it well. And as this passage foretells, the population of the State has not merely increased over the last century, but has been multiplied time and time again. However, the time of its greatest increase may still be yet to come, when those from the West will return to their homeland.

Notice the phrase "*and do better for you than at your beginnings*" – that is certainly true of Israel today. God has promised to make Israel greater than they were before, and this has held true since the founding of the State. In the days of the Bible (most of her history), Israel had been a small, rather insignificant nation and a minor military power. They were also regularly plagued with famines and droughts, and their exports had not been very significant. Not so today – just read the daily news.

Since the founding of the State and the return of millions of exiles from all over the earth, Israel is disproportionally wealthy compared to the oil-rich nations around her. Israelis have a significantly higher standard of living amidst a sea of poverty. In medicine, technology, agriculture, and industry, Israel is extremely competitive with America, Europe, and most other First World nations. Israel has been referred as the "Startup Nation", and rightly so since they have more new companies per capita than any other nation on earth (jfns.org). Today, Israeli products and innovations are among the best in the world, and they are much more populous and wealthy than they ever were in the past.

Necessity may be the "mother of invention", and this is certainly true for Israel's military. After Israel became a nation in 1948, few nations wanted to even sell them weapons and equipment that they desperately needed for basic self-defense. Due to Arab embargos and threats, it was very difficult for Israel to purchase tanks and planes to quickly build their military. In the 1950's, Israel cobbled together a rudimentary air-force by often purchasing airplane parts and reassembling (and repairing) them the best they could. Several years later, they began building their own planes, tanks, and weaponry to suit their own specific needs, and now they have some of the most advanced military equipment in the world.

The closing phrase of this passage (*"no more shall you bereave them of children"*) is a promise by God to never again exile them after the Diaspora. The days of devastating famines and starvation are over. And while their enemies constantly seek to destroy them, their lands will no longer be overrun by their enemies as they once were. God has kept these promises by defeating Israel's enemies in 1948, 1967, and 1973. The Israelis may have been the ones shooting the bullets and firing the missiles, but God was directing them to their targets, giving the people courage, and defending His land against the invaders.

Ezekiel 36:13-15 *'Thus says the Lord GOD: "Because they say to you, 'You devour men and bereave your nation of children,' 14 therefore you shall devour men no more, nor bereave your nation anymore," says the Lord GOD. 15 "Nor will I let you hear the taunts of the nations anymore, nor bear the reproach of the peoples anymore, nor shall you cause your nation to stumble anymore," says the Lord GOD.'"*

This is similar to v6 earlier in the chapter, where God promised that He will no longer let the land of Israel be mocked by all the nations around her. And indeed today, no one seriously mocks the nation of Israel – the terrible defeats of 1948, 1967, and even 1973 showed them that Israel is a force to be reckoned with. And though Iran, the Arabs, and her other enemies may boast against Israel and vow that they will someday drive the Jews into the Sea, few of them are willing to risk outright war with them.

The phrase "devour men no more" speaks of warfare and plagues in which the population falters and declines in the land. In all her wars, Israel has only lost a small percentage of her soldiers and people, in contrast to the days when tens of thousands were slaughtered in battles and sieges.

Ezekiel 36:16-18 *Moreover the word of the LORD came to me, saying: 17 "Son of man, when the house of Israel dwelt in their own land, they defiled it by their own ways and deeds; to Me their way was like the uncleanness of a woman in her customary impurity. 18 Therefore I poured out My fury on them for the blood they had shed on the land, and for their idols with which they had defiled it.*

The comparison of Israel's misbehavior as being like that of a woman during her menstrual period is rather strange, though it is likely referring not only to Israel's shedding of blood, but shedding blood in an abominable fashion. When Israel and Judah began worshiping the gods of the Canaanites, Ammonites, and Moabites, they would sacrifice their own children – the fruit of their wombs – to the false gods in a number of different horrible ways. The interpretation becomes clearer as to their sin later in v18.

After the Babylonian Captivity, the Jews no longer worshipped idols and false gods, though they erred in going to the other extreme: legalism, or a pursuit of God through works. Their own religious behavior and their own "righteousness" became their gods, rather than God Himself. The references to a woman's customary impurity are quite few in the Scriptures, but one related passage is Isaiah 64:6, in which God says that Israel's righteousness is filthy rags, literally "used menstrual cloths."

After their return to the land, Israel's righteousness became one not by faith but by works (Romans 9:32), which is abhorrent to God. Today, Israel owes everything to God simply because of His grace and promises, and not by their works at all, however considerable their efforts may be. In the upcoming passages of Ezekiel 38-39, God will show Israel very clearly Who is really protecting them. It's not by Israel's great military, cunning, or sheer wits that they survive, but by God's grace.

When the Jews began returning to the land of Israel decades ago, was it by their will or by God's moving in their hearts, minds, and circumstances? When they entered the desolate lands and decided to remain there despite all the terrible hardships, who gave them the fortitude and the courage? God did.

From the Book of Proverbs, there are a number of things that God hates: foremost among them are lying tongues, false witnesses, haughty eyes (pride), and the shedding of innocent blood (Proverbs 6:16-19). Isaiah 6 describes the Six Woes against a nation which involve carnality, adultery, lying, idolatry, corrupt standards, and perverted justice. Idolatry (spiritual adultery) always goes hand-in-hand with adultery and fornication in a nation.

Following closely behind adultery and idolatry is typically a dramatic increase in diseases, social breakdown, and widespread violence. Just before God brings a nation to judgment is the cultural acceptance of perverted sexual practices, an increase in fornication, then homosexuality, and then child sacrifice. Nearly all nations today condemn the killing of children – unless they haven't been born yet. In modern days, our nations sacrifice children in the womb to the gods of self and convenience.

Israel was guilty of all these horrible sins, as are most modern nations today. Evil tends to progress, spread, and grow like cancer until either God sends a revival such as the Great Awakening or brings the land into judgment. But more often, God simply turns away from an evil land and leaves them to self-destruct as a result of their own sin and depravity. As the world grows more and more wicked, the time draws closer to when God will bring the entire world into judgment, the time known as the "Tribulation."

Ezekiel 36:19 So I scattered them among the nations, and they were dispersed throughout the countries; I judged them according to their ways and their deeds.

In both the first exile and the Diaspora when God scattered Israel among the Gentiles, He essentially gave them what they were wanting: to worship false gods and obey Gentile rulers rather than Him. God describes in Hosea, Amos, Ezekiel, and Jeremiah how His judgment upon them would be to give them the desire of their hearts.

Before the Assyrian Exile and the Babylonian Captivity, the Jews had wanted to worship idols, so God sent them into other lands where idolatry was not only encouraged, but enforced. But before the Diaspora under the Romans, the Jews declared at Jesus' trial that "they had no king but Caesar," and God one again gave them what they wanted: to be ruled by the Gentiles. If they obeyed the Romans, they would dwell safely in their land, though they were governed harshly. However, if they rebelled against the Romans, the Empire would crush them without mercy as they did any other rebellious people. Israel had no right to expect God to save them after they rejected His rulership, just as they had no right to rebel against the Roman Empire without bearing the consequences.

Ezekiel 36:20 When they came to the nations, wherever they went, they profaned My holy name—when they said of them, 'These are the people of the LORD, and yet they have gone out of His land.'

How did Israel profane God's name after they had been scattered? By their idolatry and their very exile from the Promised Land. Everywhere they went, the Gentiles mocked them because they were a people without a land, with no place to call their own. When the Jews were mocked, so was the God of the Jews. Again, the idea that a people's gods are tied to the land was prevalent, and there are the Jews who cannot go back to their land, and therefore back to their God.

But today, the Jews are back in their ancient land against all odds and have survived despite all the persecutions and extermination attempts over the centuries. The time for mocking the Jews and Israel has ended – and God is with them.

Ezekiel 36:21 *But I had concern for My holy name, which the house of Israel had profaned among the nations wherever they went.*

God values His Name above everything else, except His Word (Psalm 138:2). Both His Word and His Name constitute most of what He has revealed about Himself to mankind. God's greatness demands reverence for His Name, and when He is profaned among the nations and misrepresented by His people for an extended period of time, He eventually runs out of patience and personally intervenes to set the record straight. When your child misbehaves in church or in school, who's name and reputation do they dishonor? Their parents', in addition to their own. During the Diaspora, God was continually blasphemed among the Gentiles because His own people had been cast out of His land because of their disobedience.

What a comfort it is to know that above all else, God keeps His promises – to break them would be a violation of His very Nature, and is therefore impossible for Him. God is perfect and sinless, and to break a promise is to sin, which He cannot do.

There are a few things that God cannot do, that we humans happen to do very well all the time: He cannot sin and He cannot lie, which includes breaking His promises. From the beginning of Israel's history, God knew they would disobey and be exiled, yet even at that time He promised to bring them back into His land.

Today, Israel is back in the land just as God had promised them time and time again. If any of us ever doubt that God is real, that the Bible is trustworthy, and that God keeps His promises, we simply need to glance at a map of the Middle East. And there we can clearly see that Israel is in the very center of it, just as He promised.

Now, if God can keep His promise to restore millions of people to their native land after thousands of years of exile – a truly incredible promise that we can see with our own eyes everyday – shouldn't we presume that He will keep the rest of His Word? Shouldn't we presume that Jesus is the only Way, Truth, and the Life, and that there really is a literal place called Heaven and a literal place called Hell? The Scriptures really don't grant us the option of picking out the pieces we like or are comfortable with – it's either all or nothing.

Ezekiel 36:22-23 *"Therefore say to the house of Israel, 'Thus says the Lord GOD: "I do not do this for your sake, O house of Israel, but for My holy name's sake, which you have profaned among the nations wherever you went. 23 And I will sanctify My great name, which has been profaned among the nations, which you have profaned in their midst; and the nations shall know that I am the LORD," says the Lord GOD, "when I am hallowed in you before their eyes.*

In this passage, God continues explaining why He is restoring Israel: for His Name's sake alone, His Reputation. He wants to make it perfectly clear that it's by His grace and not by their merit that Israel is back in the land. Pride and self-sufficiency on the part of His people is something that God absolutely hates, because it turns their worship from Him to something else, sometimes even themselves. Israel is ONLY protected because of God's grace and mercy, and not by their works, cleverness, ingenuity, military equipment, or prowess.

After Israel's incredible victories in 1948, 1956, and 1967, they began to grow prideful and placed their faith in themselves, in their own military. Then in 1973, Israel was caught off-guard and suffered tremendous casualties – they almost lost the nation in the first few days of the Yom Kippur attack. Fortunately, they were able to recover, but at a terrible disadvantage and many unnecessarily lost lives. Could it be possible that God allowed the Yom Kippur War to occur in order to humble the Israelis and get their attention, especially on their holiest day of the year? After all, why wouldn't God protect them on the holiest day of the year, the day when practically everyone was praying and worshipping? One observation is that Israel was not nearly as self-confident after 1973 as they were before – perhaps He allowed them to be humbled by their enemies and snuff out pride in themselves.

Do the nations today know that God is the Lord (or Jehovah)? No, they do not – He is known as Allah, Jehovah, and by a variety of other concepts that people have made up about Him, but not as the God of the Bible. Even many of His own people don't recognize Him as God. But they will someday.

When will the nations – including the Jews – know that God is once again with Israel? When the nations described in Ezekiel 38-39 launch a massive, deadly attack on Israel and God wipes them out as Ezekiel wrote 2600 years ago.

Ezekiel 36:24 *For I will take you from among the nations, gather you out of all countries, and bring you into your own land.*

This restoration and regathering of the outcasts of Israel back to the land of Palestine has been occurring since the late Nineteenth Century and continues to this day. The Jews were exiled to every continent on the earth (except Antarctica) and to nearly every nation on the earth. However, persecution and a promise of better lives have been motivating the Jewish people to migrate back to Israel from Russia, Ethiopia, Europe, and many other nations since 1948.

In Isaiah 11:11, God declares that He will regather His people for the second time from all the lands of the earth where He had scattered them, and bring them back to the land of Israel. There have only been two regatherings of Israel in the history of the world: a minor one under Cyrus after the Babylonian Captivity had ended, and the current regathering that's been happening for the last century.

The Isaiah 11:11 prophecy clearly speaks of the regathering from the Diaspora in our times, since the Jews were not dispersed to every nation in the world during the Babylonian Captivity. Israel was scattered into the north and east during the Assyrian Exile and Judah to various districts of Babylon. Later, the Jewish remnant gradually moved and spread even further during the Persian, Greek, and Roman Empires. But the widespread scattering throughout Europe primarily occurred after the Temple was destroyed in 70 AD.

The term "wandering Jew" was infamous for many centuries – until after 1948. Since that time, the term has fallen into disuse, especially in Europe. For nearly two thousand years, Israel was a land without a people and the Jews were a people without a land. But no longer – today, every Jew in the world is eligible for immigration to Israel under the Law of Return, which was enacted in 1950.

Ezekiel 36:25 *Then I will sprinkle clean water on you, and you shall be clean; I will cleanse you from all your filthiness and from all your idols.*

The sprinkling of water upon a person goes back to the Torah, typically performed to signify that the person was cleansed from their uncleanness and that their impurity was absolved. The relationship between the impure and the pure was temporarily suspended until the impurity had passed. (Leviticus 11-15)

In the Law, when a person would in some way become unclean (by touching a dead body, have a skin disease, etc.), they would be separated from other people for a specific period of time. After the time period was finished, they were sprinkled with water and allowed back into contact with their family members, friends, and their society.

This is a picture of what God had done, is doing, and what He will do with Israel. Through their sin of unbelief, they had made themselves unclean to God, and therefore He had set them aside for a specified time, isolating them from Himself. But now that the time of their punishment and isolation has ended, He is bringing them back into His land and will restore the relationship between Him and His people.

Ezekiel 36:26-27 *I will give you a new heart and put a new spirit within you; I will take the heart of stone out of your flesh and give you a heart of flesh. 27 I will put My Spirit within you and cause you to walk in My statutes, and you will keep My judgments and do them.*

When Israel was exiled into the Diaspora, the leadership of the nation had a "heart of stone," a heart of cold, hard religious legalism. Though there were 613 commandments in the Torah, they had added thousands more in the Oral Law and Traditions to the point that their manmade commandments had blurred or even superseded the original law. The commandments which were intended to promote a just, orderly, and free society had become corrupted so the society was filled with injustice and oppression.

Following a strict, confusing set of laws turns people cold, prideful, and unfeeling, and promotes exaltation of self-righteousness and a salvation by works rather than exaltation of God and salvation by faith. The Torah and the rest of the Old Testament provided the basic legal code for the society, but left many of the questions of the afterlife unanswered. Those were to be left up to God.

Today, Israel has roughly 6,451,000 Jews (44% - 2017) while the United States has 5,700,000 (39% - 2017) – a difference of over half a million people. However, the religious character of the two groups is quite different: over 75% of Jews in Israel are religious, in comparison to only 2% of Jews in the United States. The majority of Jews in America are very secular, being either atheist or humanist.

Why is there such a religious disparity between the two groups? After all, many of the Jews in the United States have been here less than two hundred years, and most came from Europe as with many of the Jews today in Israel. So why are American Jews so different than the rest? Perhaps it's because they have not been humbled through persecution and most of the other Jews have.

How did God remove this "heart of stone" from Israel? Through the long, dark years of the Diaspora and the constant reminders of God's preservation and their reliance upon Him. Living day by day in uncertainty tends to drive people closer to what they worship, because they are forced to rely more upon the higher power. The Jews are no different – the more they have been oppressed, the more reliant upon God they have tended to become.

Will there be a time of humbling for the American Jews? I fully expect that there will be – it just hasn't happened yet. Perhaps with our worsening national problems, the exploding national debt, and the coming years of inflation (or even hyper-inflation) will push the American Jews to migrate back to Israel. Sooner or later, the Jewish remnant dwelling in America will be called back to Israel.

Aside from some extremists on both the far-right and the political left, America has never been anti-Semitic as most other Western nations, so it's difficult to imagine that evil ever sweeping through the United States as it did in Europe. Even the old stereotype of 'Jewish bankers' doesn't really apply in America as in Germany and Eastern Europe.

Yet over the last few decades, the world has witnessed one of Israel's greatest allies – the United States – sour towards Israel due to Barack Obama's pro-Palestinian rhetoric and his anti-Israeli allies/advisors. The Occupy Wall Street protests several years ago revealed the rapid growth of anti-Semitism on the Left, particularly among the youth. The anti-Israel BDS movement (Boycott, Divest, and Sanction) started by Palestinian organizers in 2005 has been spreading across university campuses for much of the last decade and appears to be having its intended effects.

The humbling of the Jewish people over the last two thousand years is an object lesson for all of us: if we refuse to humble ourselves, we will be humbled by other means, which may not be very pleasant. But either way, we'll all end up being humbled in the presence of God. The awareness of God's love and His faithfulness, as recognized through His grace and mercy, is also what transforms hearts of stone into hearts of flesh.

The second verse expounds on the first – how will God turn Israel's "heart of stone" into a "heart of flesh"? By putting His Spirit into their hearts and turning them to His grace and love, by giving the Spirit which brings Life and away from the Law which brings Death. Jeremiah 31 mirrors this giving of the Spirit to Israel, which is referred to as the "new covenant" in the Jeremiah passage. A new spirit brings a new covenant – a better covenant between God and His people.

In the First Century, there was a group of Jews who were given God's Spirit and accepted this New Covenant: those who formed the early Church and wrote the New Testament, or more properly referred to as the New Covenant. (Acts 2)

One of these Jews, commonly known as the Apostle Paul, demonstrates the remarkable transformation in a person after they've had their "heart of stone" exchanged for a "heart of flesh." Paul's discourses on Law and Grace delve deeply into how you cannot keep the Law by your own efforts, and how trying to keep the Law only makes you break it more often! But when you give yourself over to God's grace and let His Spirit indwell you, you end up keeping His Law by yielding to Him and His efforts, not yours. The cold, dead religion of works suddenly becomes a living religion of faith.

This exchange has yet to happen to Israel – the Orthodox and Ultra-Orthodox are still encumbered with their "hearts of stone," while the rest of the nation has had it removed over the years. However, they have yet to be given the "heart of flesh," which will come when the people have God's Spirit put in them.

There is a growing Messianic movement among Jews today, though it's still faint. However, there will come a time described in Revelation 9 in which 144,000 Jewish evangelists will be converted – probably similar to how Paul was on the road to Damascus – who will then spread the Gospel to their nation and the rest of the world.

***Ezekiel 36:28** Then you shall dwell in the land that I gave to your fathers; you shall be My people, and I will be your God.*

Has Israel been given "the land that I gave to your fathers"? Yes, but only a small portion of it. The land promised to Abraham was from the Euphrates River to the Nile River, which would encompass much of Egypt, Syria, northern Arabia, Jordan, and eastern Iraq. Even at the height of the kingdom under

King Solomon, Israel only controlled one-third of this territory. Today, Israel doesn't even control half the land that they held before the Assyrian Exile.

Just as a loving father longs to be with his children, so God has yearned to be with Israel, and the other faithful remnant of mankind. Throughout the Bible, God is calling out a holy, separate people to Himself, that He may walk with them and they with Him. The phrase, "you shall be My people, and I will be your God" is a recurring theme throughout the pages of Scripture. However, this can only be achieved through faith, and not by our works or effort.

Ezekiel 36:29-30 *I will deliver you from all your uncleannesses. I will call for the grain and multiply it, and bring no famine upon you. 30 And I will multiply the fruit of your trees and the increase of your fields, so that you need never again bear the reproach of famine among the nations.*

This passage is a reiteration of what God had mentioned earlier: that He would increase the fertility and fruit-bearing of the land and give them abundant crops and harvests. Israel today might have water shortages and rationing, but they no longer have horrible famines, though many of the nations around them do. Even from the tiny amount of land available for farming, Israel exports enormous amounts of citrus to Europe, and fruit is a staple food in many of their daily meals (along with vegetables and produce).

Again, who is making the land thrive and prosper? God. Despite Israel's wonderful agricultural technology, God is the one who is making their land produce fruit and crops like never before, even in the scorching sands of the Negev. It's quite astounding to pass through the hot arid wilderness and see orchards full of fig-trees, oranges, and other trees.

Who can make a people clean in God's sight? Only God, not us by our own efforts. Did this uncleanness have anything to do with what types of food they were eating or their clothes or even dirt? No, their uncleanness was spiritual – the filth of self-reliance, pride, and wickedness.

In the Gospels, Jesus taught about what really makes a person clean or unclean: what comes out of their heart (Matthew 15:16-20). Food enters and passes out of the body, and dirt can be washed away. But what can cleanse our hearts from our sin? Nothing – that's why God has to give us a new heart, a new spirit – His Spirit to indwell us (Ezekiel 36:26-27).

Ezekiel 36:31 *Then you will remember your evil ways and your deeds that were not good; and you will loathe yourselves in your own sight, for your iniquities and your abominations.*

This verse also has yet to be fulfilled, and probably will not be fulfilled until near the end of the Tribulation or perhaps during the Millennium. One of the requirements for the Messiah to return is the repentance of Israel as described in Hosea 5:15 (which Jesus references in Luke 13:34-35):

Hosea 5: 15 *"I will return again to My place*
Till they acknowledge their offense.
Then they will seek My face;
In their affliction they will earnestly seek Me."

Another passage which speaks of Israel's "eyes being opened" and the nation finally recognizing their Messiah and their great remorse over their unbelief is:

Zechariah 12:10 *"And I will pour on the house of David and on the inhabitants of Jerusalem the Spirit of grace and supplication; then they will look on Me whom they pierced. Yes, they will mourn for Him as one mourns for his only son, and grieve for Him as one grieves for a firstborn.*

When a person becomes a Christian, they have repented of their sin and have accepted God's provision for them in the sacrifice and resurrection of Jesus Christ. However, often they have been blinded by their past sins over the years and as they grow in the Lord, sometimes those sins rise to the surface and come to light, where they must be dealt with. Often those recollections can be quite painful, especially if one has been maturing spiritually.

The shock and reality of past sins can be overwhelming, and there can be times where you loathe yourself for what you once did. The same will happen to Israel as a whole someday: after God puts His Spirit in them and their eyes are opened, they will recall their sins of idolatry, unbelief, and rejection of their Promised Son, Jesus of Nazareth, and loathe themselves.

Ezekiel 36:32-33 Not for your sake do I do this," says the Lord GOD, "let it be known to you. Be ashamed and confounded for your own ways, O house of Israel!" 33 'Thus says the Lord GOD: "On the day that I cleanse you from all your iniquities, I will also enable you to dwell in the cities, and the ruins shall be rebuilt.

Once again, God wants Israel to know that their restoration has nothing to with their own efforts or their own righteousness, but with Him and His reputation. God is calling them to repent and soften their hard hearts, but this won't truly occur until after He has put His Spirit in them. Israel is not sinless (of course) and is still living in unbelief, but they have been cleansed from their past-sins through their long years of the Diaspora. Their punishment has ended and they are now free to dwell in His land once again.

Since 1948, Israel has been growing and expanding in the land like never before. With a growing population and thousands of new immigrants every year, the Israelis are building far and wide in the land. One of the jokes in Jerusalem and Tel Aviv is that Israel's national bird is the "crane", since the skyline is filled with them.

Ezekiel 36:34-36 The desolate land shall be tilled instead of lying desolate in the sight of all who pass by. 35 So they will say, 'This land that was desolate has become like the garden of Eden; and the wasted, desolate, and ruined cities are now fortified and inhabited.' 36 Then the nations which are left all around you shall know that I, the LORD, have rebuilt the ruined places and planted what was desolate. I, the LORD, have spoken it, and I will do it."

As mentioned before, it only takes a few minutes of browsing the Internet to see that Israel has been transformed over the last sixty years. Where there was once a land devoid of people, cities, trees, and fields is now full of life and thriving. Since 1948, Israel has literally blossomed, while their neighbors continue as before – on any map, Israel is a strip of green surrounded by vast desert wastelands.

A large part of the Arab/Muslim animosity towards Israel is sheer jealousy, and because the Jews are apparently being blessed by God and they are not. If Allah is the true God and Muslims are the true people of God, then why aren't their lands blossoming and thriving like Israel? Why is Israel able to have enough food to export and sell while the Arab nations starve?

If the Jews are subhuman apes like the mullahs teach, then why are they prospering and pushing back the deserts, which none of the Arab countries have been able to do? Why does Israel have such low unemployment and a growing economy, while chronic high unemployment plagues the Arab states?

True, the Arab nations do have great quantities of oil and are using a portion of that wealth to build skyscrapers and cities in some areas like the United Arab Emirates, but most of the people live in the same squalid conditions they have for thousands of years. But once they run out of oil, what will they have? Not much other than burning sands. They should be using their vast oil-wealth to build and replenish their lands while they can, instead of just plundering them.

Ezekiel 36:37-38 *'Thus says the Lord GOD: "I will also let the house of Israel inquire of Me to do this for them: I will increase their men like a flock. 38 Like a flock offered as holy sacrifices, like the flock at Jerusalem on its feast days, so shall the ruined cities be filled with flocks of men. Then they shall know that I am the LORD."'"*

The strength of a nation is directly related to their population. New people (especially immigrants) bring new life to a nation, in contrast to one with aging populations which are slowly but steadily dying off. The West slowly stopped growing and began to wane decades ago when it embraced socialism, population controls, the sexual revolution, and the legalization of abortion. The West has been literally committing slow-suicide while the rest of the world is growing and expanding. And Israel is no exception – they are building and growing like never before, and as more people migrate to the land, the more they have to build to house and employ them.

The phrase "and they shall know that I am the LORD" is the main point of the Book of Ezekiel. God is making Himself known once again to both Israel and the rest of the earth, all of which have long forgotten or cast off even the notion of God. The phrase is repeated forty-eight times in Ezekiel, and reveals God's deep longing to be with His people.

XI. Israel Reborn – Ezekiel 37

Ezekiel 37 continues the promise of Israel's regathering and restoration as introduced in the previous chapter, but in the form of a vision. God gives Ezekiel the vision of the Valley of the Dry Bones, which represents the dead nation of Israel being brought back to life. First, the nation will be brought back into the land but without life (spiritually dead in unbelief) and then God will put His Spirit in them and cause them to live.

God also describes how the restored nation will no longer be divided into Israel and Judah, as it had been for over four hundred years at that time of their exile to Assyria and Babylon. And not only will they be reunited as one people, they will be reunited under one banner: the banner of Israel.

At the end of the chapter, God promises to set His King over them and cause them to thrive in the land, and never be cast out again.

Ezekiel 37 – Full Text

1 The hand of the LORD came upon me and brought me out in the Spirit of the LORD, and set me down in the midst of the valley; and it was full of bones. 2 Then He caused me to pass by them all around, and behold, there were very many in the open valley; and indeed they were very dry. 3 And He said to me, "Son of man, can these bones live?" So I answered, "O Lord GOD, You know."

4 Again He said to me, "Prophesy to these bones, and say to them, 'O dry bones, hear the word of the LORD! 5 Thus says the Lord GOD to these bones: "Surely I will cause breath to enter into you, and you shall live. 6 I will put sinews on you and bring flesh upon you, cover you with skin and put breath in you; and you shall live. Then you shall know that I am the LORD."'"

7 So I prophesied as I was commanded; and as I prophesied, there was a noise, and suddenly a rattling; and the bones came together, bone to bone. 8 Indeed, as I looked, the sinews and the flesh came upon them, and the skin covered them over; but there was no breath in them.

9 Also He said to me, "Prophesy to the breath, prophesy, son of man, and say to the breath, 'Thus says the Lord GOD: "Come from the four winds, O breath, and breathe on these slain, that they may live."'" 10 So I prophesied as He commanded me, and breath came into them, and they lived, and stood upon their feet, an exceedingly great army.

11 Then He said to me, "Son of man, these bones are the whole house of Israel. They indeed say, 'Our bones are dry, our hope is lost, and we ourselves are cut off!' 12 Therefore prophesy and say to them, 'Thus says the Lord GOD: "Behold, O My people, I will open your graves and cause you to come up from your graves, and bring you into the land of Israel. 13 Then you shall know that I am the LORD, when I have opened your graves, O My people, and brought you up from your graves. 14 I will put My Spirit in you, and you shall live, and I will place you in your own land. Then you shall know that I, the LORD, have spoken it and performed it," says the LORD.'"

15 Again the word of the LORD came to me, saying, 16 "As for you, son of man, take a stick for yourself and write on it: 'For Judah and for the children of Israel, his companions.' Then take another stick and write on it, 'For Joseph, the stick of Ephraim, and for all the house of Israel, his companions.' 17 Then join them one to another for yourself into one stick, and they will become one in your hand.

18 "And when the children of your people speak to you, saying, 'Will you not show us what you mean by these?'— 19 say to them, 'Thus says the Lord GOD: "Surely I will take the stick of Joseph, which is in the hand of Ephraim, and the tribes of Israel, his companions; and I will join them with it, with the stick of Judah, and make them one stick, and they will be one in My hand."' 20 And the sticks on which you write will be in your hand before their eyes.

21 "Then say to them, 'Thus says the Lord GOD: "Surely I will take the children of Israel from among the nations, wherever they have gone, and will gather them from every side and bring them into their own land; 22 and I will make them one nation in the land, on the mountains of Israel; and one king shall be king over them all; they shall no longer be two nations, nor shall they ever be divided into two kingdoms again. 23 They shall not defile themselves anymore with their idols, nor with their detestable things, nor with any of their transgressions; but I will deliver them from all their dwelling places in which they have sinned, and will cleanse them. Then they shall be My people, and I will be their God.

24 "David My servant shall be king over them, and they shall all have one shepherd; they shall also walk in My judgments and observe My statutes, and do them. 25 Then they shall dwell in the land that I have given to Jacob My servant, where your fathers dwelt; and they shall dwell there, they, their children, and their children's children, forever; and My servant David shall be their prince forever. 26 Moreover I will make a covenant of peace with them, and it shall be an everlasting covenant with them; I will establish them and multiply them, and I will set My sanctuary in their midst forevermore. 27 My tabernacle also shall be with them; indeed I will be their God, and they shall be My people. 28 The nations also will know that I, the LORD, sanctify Israel, when My sanctuary is in their midst forevermore." '"

Ezekiel 37 – Verse by Verse Analysis

Ezekiel 37:1 The hand of the LORD came upon me and brought me out in the Spirit of the LORD, and set me down in the midst of the valley; and it was full of bones.

This chapter begins with the well-known passage referred to as the "Valley of the Dry Bones" prophecy. It is also the basis of the famous campfire song, "Dem Dry Bones." It's unknown as to whether the valley is tied to a specific location in Israel or simply some desolate valley Ezekiel is seeing that is full of jumbled human bones.

In the great Valley of Megiddo (also known as the Valley of Jezreel), Josiah, the last great king of Judah was killed in battle and the entire nation mourned for him. After Josiah's death, the nation quickly declined both morally and militarily until it was finally exiled to Babylon in three separate waves. This valley is also where the army of Israel was defeated by the Assyrians and became a vassal state. The Valley of Megiddo is better known by another name: Armageddon, where the Messiah will utterly destroy the gathered armies of the entire earth as they begin to move towards Jerusalem.

Ezekiel 37:2 *Then He caused me to pass by them all around, and behold, there were very many in the open valley; and indeed they were very dry.*

The description indicates that God is showing Ezekiel that the land that has been desolate for a long time, and the inhabitants had been shamefully destroyed – not even being buried. All that appears to be left of the once-great nation is their dried-out skeletons, which have been left out many years in the open air.

One can not only picture the piles of sun-bleached, white bones filling the valley, but also the massive piles of ashes and stacks of burnt bones of the millions of Holocaust victims. Either way, the valley described here is filled with death and defilement. The dead were treated as refuse and filth, their bones not even fit to be given the dignity of a burial.

In verse 11, it will be revealed that these bones represent the destroyed peoples of Israel.

Ezekiel 37:4-6 *And He said to me, "Son of man, can these bones live?" So I answered, "O Lord GOD, You know." 4 Again He said to me, "Prophesy to these bones, and say to them, 'O dry bones, hear the word of the LORD! 5 Thus says the Lord GOD to these bones: "Surely I will cause breath to enter into you, and you shall live. 6 I will put sinews on you and bring flesh upon you, cover you with skin and put breath in you; and you shall live. Then you shall know that I am the LORD."'"*

God goes on to ask Ezekiel to answer somewhat of a rhetorical question: "Can these bones live?" Rather than saying "yes" or "no," Ezekiel ducks the question and gives a safe non-answer. Then God promises Ezekiel that He will resurrect the long-dead bodies and bring them back to life. Once they have been resurrected, then they will know that He is God.

Ezekiel 37:7-8 *So I prophesied as I was commanded; and as I prophesied, there was a noise, and suddenly a rattling; and the bones came together, bone to bone. 8 Indeed, as I looked, the sinews and the flesh came upon them, and the skin covered them over; but there was no breath in them.*

Ezekiel obeys the Lord and speaks to the bones. To his surprise, the bones miraculously assemble themselves into skeletons and then sinews, muscles, and tissues begin to appear, which are then covered by skin. But the bodies were still dead – they needed God to bring them back to life.

This passage foreshadows Israel's future restoration from both a symbolic and prophetic point of view, as well as both physically and spiritually – because it describes that when God resurrects Israel, He will first bring the nation back into existence and they will have all the physical components needed to live, but will still be spiritually dead as far as He is concerned.

From the earliest pages of Scripture, the Bible uses the term "breath" in many cases to indicate the presence of God's Spirit being with a person, or often simply "life." (Genesis 2:7, 7:22, Job 32:8, 33:4, John 20:22) Having the "breath of life" in the physical sense is often synonymous with "being indwelt by the Spirit" in the spiritual sense, though not always. Therefore, these verses could indicate that when Israel is reborn as a nation, they will be spiritually dead to God, at least at first.

However, in keeping with the promises to Israel throughout the Scriptures, one day God will "breathe on them" and give them His Spirit – and they will believe and call on Him in the manner He has prescribed.

Ezekiel 37:9-10 *Also He said to me, "Prophesy to the breath, prophesy, son of man, and say to the breath, 'Thus says the Lord GOD: "Come from the four winds, O breath, and breathe on these slain, that they may live."'" 10 So I prophesied as He commanded me, and breath came into them, and they lived, and stood upon their feet, an exceedingly great army.*

As the vision continues, Ezekiel is commanded to order the "breath" to breathe upon the slain of Israel and bring the nation back to life. Once again, a miracle occurs and the dead are brought to life – and then rise to their feet as a mighty army.

At this point, the nation appears to be restored, but it's unclear whether the nation has repented and returned to God, with His Spirit finally indwelling Israel. As with everyone, physical life always precedes spiritual life, and such appears to be the case with Israel.

The use of the word "army" here is often passed over, though this may have deeper implications as it relates to the times after Israel's resurrection. This Hebrew word for "army" – chayil – also means 'host', 'strength', or 'multitude', and is not necessarily specific to the military sense of the word 'army.' But the rendering of the word is quite interesting, as it may indicate that after Israel's rebirth, they have a strong military.

Since Israel became a nation in 1948, are they an 'exceedingly great army?' They certainly are, though out of necessity because of the constant existential threats from their Arab neighbors. Only hours after declaring their statehood, Israel was invaded by her enemies in an attempt to exterminate her. Within days, the Jewish resistance forces had to transform themselves into a functioning national army, though they had few weapons, few experienced fighters, and little military organization. There are stories in those first desperate weeks that as the ships full of immigrants were finally allowed into the Israeli ports and the passengers disembarked, they would be greeted "Welcome to Israel – now go fight for her!" and immediately be handed a rifle and sent off to the military. But in that first of many wars, Israel not only survived, but prevailed.

In the years that followed, Israel adopted a civilian military in which every eighteen year-old – male or female – is conscripted into the military or the national service. After their three years (two years for women) of service has ended, they must return as reservists for one month every year until their mid-forties. As a result, Israel has built a nation of ready, capable warriors in which nearly everyone knows how to properly handle a weapon and defend themselves and their nation. At any given time, Israel can activate her reserves and call upon a military force of nearly three-quarters of a million people, and three million people capable of military duty, nearly one-third of the entire nation.

Is God a warmonger or a pacifist? From the Scriptures, He is neither, yet both; at times He can be a warrior, while other times a refuge of peace. There are times in the Old Testament where He orders Israel to go to war not only for defense purposes, but for judgment upon another nation, sometimes to even exterminate them because of their wickedness. Other times, God orders the nation not to fight but immediately surrender, as He told Jeremiah when Judah was about to go into captivity.

Is it good for a people or nation to learn war and military strategy? It most certainly is, so they can remain free and defend themselves. Nations and national identity was God's idea, not ours (Genesis 11). In fact, God mentions that in (Judges 3:1-2) when He allows Israel's neighbors to test her from time to time. God wants every nation to be able defend themselves, though not necessarily conquer others and expand their territory. We live in a fallen, violent world and must be able to defend ourselves and our country, especially when we live in a free nation.

Ezekiel 37:11 *Then He said to me, "Son of man, these bones are the whole house of Israel. They indeed say, 'Our bones are dry, our hope is lost, and we ourselves are cut off!'*

In this verse, God begins to interpret the vision for Ezekiel and declares that the bones represent the fallen house of Israel, dead and without hope. Deep in her heart today, I wonder if Israel still feels this way towards God at times – that He has cast them off and that they are on their own, struggling to survive in a world that seeks their utter destruction.

But though they may feel that way, most assuredly God has NOT forsaken them nor cast them off. He has protected Israel and fought for them in 1948, 1967, 1973, and even today through the waves of terrorism that have swept over the nation. The God of Israel does not slumber nor sleep (Psalm 121:4) and will protect her though all the nations of the world – including the United States of America – may turn against her.

Though it barely made the news in the mainstream media, the Obama administration purposefully withheld a number of military shipments to Israel during the height of the Gaza War in 2014 – including the armaments used in Israel's Iron Dome civilian missile defense system. It's somewhat understandable to withhold offensive weapons that would be used in a ground invasion that Washington may not approve of, but quite another when these missiles are used for the self-defense of Israeli citizens. Despite the liberal commentators' attempts to justify his policies, the Obama administration was no friend of Israel.

Ezekiel 37:12-13 Therefore prophesy and say to them, 'Thus says the Lord GOD: "Behold, O My people, I will open your graves and cause you to come up from your graves, and bring you into the land of Israel. 13 Then you shall know that I am the LORD, when I have opened your graves, O My people, and brought you up from your graves.

God continues His explanation of the vision and emphatically declares that He will one day open the graves of Israel and bring His people back into the land. And then one day, the nation of Israel will once again acknowledge Him as their God after He has regathered them from all the nations of the world and planted them in their own land: the ancient lands of Israel.

One question to consider is whether the Western Jews will have a choice in their regathering or not. Perhaps at this time they do have a choice, but in the future they will be driven back to their land because they have no other alternatives. Consider that the Jews of Europe, Russia, and the Middle East had over twenty years of free-choice to return to the land of Palestine under the Balfour Declaration, but they refused. But then came the Holocaust and World War II and they had nowhere to escape to – those that survived were later driven back to their ancient homeland whether they wanted to or not.

Ezekiel 37:14 I will put My Spirit in you, and you shall live, and I will place you in your own land. Then you shall know that I, the LORD, have spoken it and performed it," says the LORD.'"

Has God placed His Spirit upon Israel today? Not so you'd notice, at least in the Biblical sense of the phrase. But He will someday, once the Church has been completed and their spiritual blindness has been removed (Romans 11). This prophecy is partially fulfilled because the nation of Israel has been brought back into existence and her people are being regathered from "the four winds of the earth."

During the Tribulation mentioned, Israel will begin to reawaken to her God when He pours out His Spirit on 12,000 people from each of the 12 tribes of Israel, and through them they will preach to all the Jews and Gentiles on the earth. These are the 144,000 Witnesses of Revelation 7.

Later in the Tribulation, when the Jewish remnant is faced with imminent destruction, they finally repent and call upon Jesus as their Messiah and He returns to save them (Hosea 5:15-16). Then the entire nation recognizes Him and mourns over Him (Zechariah 12:10) and is then "saved in a day." (Romans 11)

In summary, this vision of the "Dry Bones" perfectly describes the current rebirth and regathering of Israel today. As a nation, they are back in their land but are still spiritually dead to God. In fact, many Jews (especially American Jews) believe that God is an antiquated idea and the stories of the Old Testament are merely myths created to give their people courage over the years or to explain that which they didn't understand. Others believe that God has abandoned them, as indicated by the Holocaust and the current persecutions around the world. They ask, "Where was God in Auschwitz and Dachau? Where was God when 6 million of His people were slaughtered?"

Those are terribly difficult questions to answer, and I doubt we'll ever understand why God permitted the Holocaust to occur until the Messiah comes. Can it be rationalized away that it was merely part of their punishment for their ancestors' sins as specified in Deuteronomy 28? I don't know. The Holocaust was horrible beyond imagination, yet Zechariah seems to indicate that during the Tribulation, there will be another Holocaust that makes the first one pale in comparison. The first Holocaust took the lives of one out of every three Jews on the earth – the next one is foretold to take two out of every three. (Zechariah 13:8)

Today in Israel, the Sabbaths, holy days, and feasts have been restored, though without the Temple, they don't have quite the same meaning as before. Israel acknowledges God in a rudimentary fashion, but they are still a secular-state. Without the Temple, they cannot corporately keep His laws, especially the sacrificial laws with regards to sin and atonement.

After the Jewish Temple was destroyed in 70 AD, the Jews have been unable to worship God as He prescribed in the Old Testament. After the Babylonian Captivity had ended, one of the first national projects the Jews took upon themselves was to rebuild their Temple and restore the sacrifices. But with God silent to His people after their rejection of the Messiah, they had no idea when they would be restored to the land.

In the mid-Second Century after the destruction of the Temple and the failure of the Bar Kokhba Revolt, the remnants of the Jewish leadership seemed to accept their fate and altered their own religious practices. Rather than continuing the religion of offerings and sacrifices, the leadership changed the religion over to one of personal works and good deeds, trying to keep the Law by their own self-effort.

Part of this was out of necessity, since the Jews were no longer able to offer the sacrifices at the Temple, which no longer existed. The entire Jewish religious system is built upon the Biblical concept that "without the shedding of blood, there is no remission of sin," (Hebrews 9:22). How then could they atone for their sin without the sacrifices at the Temple? If they were to continue their religion, they had to alter the system of sacrifices since those were no longer possible.

However, the other reason for this change was that the Christians kept pointing to the old sacrificial system and telling how Jesus Christ had fulfilled all those foreshadowings and had become the Ultimate Sacrifice. The Christians were using the Jewish sacrificial system to validate their claims that Jesus was indeed the Jewish Messiah, which was unacceptable to them.

In our days, the Jewish people had brief chance to restore the Temple after they recaptured Jerusalem in 1967, but in a show of good-will, Defense Minister Moshe Dayan gave the administration of the Temple Mount back to the Arabs (the Waqf, or the Moslem Religious Trust). Since then, the Temple Mount has become an even greater source of contention than it ever was before. While well-intentioned, this was a big mistake on Dayan's part.

Personally, I see this event as very similar to when ancient Israel was in the wilderness and God told them to go up and take the land; the Israelites heard the reports of the giants and refused out of fear, even though God had just freed them from slavery in Egypt and delivered them from the Egyptian army by parting the Red Sea. God gave Israel an incredible victory in the Six Day War and showed them that He was with them – they simply had to go up and possess the Temple Mount, but they refused; they gave it back to their enemies. Time and time again, Israel caves to the bluster and threats of the Muslims and Arabs, even though their bark is always worse than their bite.

Should it be any surprise that the Jews do not have their Temple today? Yes, it indeed should be – it's astounding that a sovereign state cannot worship as it pleases, much less rebuild the foremost cultural site of their heritage. They cannot build their own Temple on their own soil without the threat of existential repercussions. However, much of their fear is based upon the false premise that Jerusalem is a holy site to the Muslims. Jerusalem isn't mentioned once in the Koran, and the Muslims didn't seem to care at all about Jerusalem until they discovered how precious it was to the Jews and Christians. Across the world, Muslims pray towards Mecca, not Jerusalem – even on the Temple Mount.

However, could there be a spiritual reason why the Jews have been without a Temple since the beginning of the Church Age? I believe so, because the New Covenant of the Spirit has superseded the Old Covenant of the Flesh. Without the Temple and the sacrifices to rely on for their atonement, God has really left only one option available to the Jews: the acceptance of Jesus as the atonement for their sin. Logically, they must either accept the terms of the New Covenant or refuse both, since the Old Covenant has been done away with and is simply no longer available to them.

When will the Jewish Temple be rebuilt? Only God knows, though I would expect that it will not be rebuilt until after the Rapture has occurred and the Church has been removed from the earth. However, I cannot be dogmatic about that supposition because there was a thirty-eight year overlap of the Church and the Temple from 32 AD to 70 AD. There very well could be a similar overlap in our day, in which the Temple is rebuilt while the Church is still on the earth.

Today, many in Israel yearn for a Temple, but not at the cost of the Jewish State. However, the End Times prophecies of Daniel 9, the Olivet Discourse, and Revelation all declare that there will be a Jewish Temple on the Temple Mount at the midpoint of the Tribulation period. What causes Israel to overwhelming want their Temple? The deep realization and understanding that the Lord is their God and that He is with them once again.

What event in the Scriptures will make Israel awaken to their God once again? Very likely, the incredible, undeniable salvation from their enemies as described in Ezekiel 38-39 – the miraculous event that causes even the skeptics to acknowledge that God is Who He says He is.

But even after the Jewish Temple is rebuilt and the Jews begin keeping all the laws, namely the sacrifices, offerings, and the rest of Torah, will they be "brought back to life" as far as God is concerned? No, because the Old Covenant in which those sacrifices atoned for their sin has been superseded by the New Covenant, the Ultimate Sacrifice which atoned for the sin of the entire world almost two thousand years ago. Also, the Apostle Paul declares that the Law brings Death, while the Spirit brings Life (2 Corinthians 3:6).

It will take the horrors of the Great Tribulation to cause Israel to finally recognize that Jesus is the Jewish Messiah and beg Him to save them before they truly repent and are brought back to life, with the Spirit of the Lord indwelling them.

Today in Israel, the very notion that the entire nation will one day be Christian is utterly absurd to them – many would rather be anything other than Christian, especially after thousands of years of animosity and persecution from the Church.

But God keeps all of His promises, and soon He will breathe spiritual life into His people and draw them to Himself. After the Tribulation has ended, God will pour out His Spirit on the rest of Israel and they will cling to Him from that day onward.

Ezekiel 37:15-17 *Again the word of the LORD came to me, saying, 16 "As for you, son of man, take a stick for yourself and write on it: 'For Judah and for the children of Israel, his companions.' Then take another stick and write on it, 'For Joseph, the stick of Ephraim, and for all the house of Israel, his companions.' 17 Then join them one to another for yourself into one stick, and they will become one in your hand.*

As with many prophecies in the Bible, there is often an introductory or symbolic prophecy given first, and then a more detailed description and interpretation that follows. This brief prophecy describes how the divided nation of Israel will be restored as one people some distant day in the future – the old division will be swept away.

The kingdom of Israel had been torn away from the House of David after the idolatry of King Solomon (1 Kings 11-12), though the division occurred soon after his son, Rehoboam, took the throne. Solomon had heavily taxed the people to finance his extravagant building programs, and when he died, the people respectfully asked Rehoboam to reduce their taxes and lighten their burden. But in his pride, Rehoboam refused and promised to raise their taxes even more! Immediately the northern tribes seceded from kingdom and formed their own nation under Jeroboam.

The Northern Kingdom was made up of the nine northern tribes of Israel: Zebulun, Issachar, Asher, Naphtali, Dan, Manasseh, Ephraim, Reuben, and Gad. The Southern Kingdom was made up of the tribes of Judah, Simeon, Benjamin, and Levi, the tribe of the priesthood. As Judah was the ruling tribe of the South, so Ephraim became the ruling tribe of the North, which soon led the rest of the northern tribes into idolatry.

The stick allotted to the north is given to Joseph, because he was the father of the two largest northern tribes: Ephraim and Manasseh. Ephraim had been the capital for much of the Northern Kingdom's history, and was singled out on numerous occasions for leading the other tribes into idolatry, such as in the Books of Amos, Hosea, and Isaiah.

In this passage, God is using the stick to represent the authority of each kingdom and then joining them back together into one stick. Not only would the peoples be regathered into one nation, but the authority would reside in one entity as well, though He doesn't name which one. From the Scriptures, we know that the tribe of Judah will one day rule the nation when the Messiah sits on the throne, just as it did from the time of David. Whether the two sticks were bound together side-by-side or lengthwise isn't specified, though it makes more sense that they were joined lengthwise like a shepherd's staff or a scepter.

One of the most famous misinterpretations of this passage was made by Joseph Smith, the founder of the Mormons in the mid-Nineteenth Century. The founder of Mormonism reinterpreted this prophecy to validate his new theology, in an attempt to prove that the Book of Mormon is another portion of Scripture and is therefore co-equal. He declares that one stick is the Book of Mormon and the Bible is the other, and that God is thereby validating the Book of Mormon by joining it with the Bible. The Scriptures cannot be broken, and therefore by Smith's reinterpretation, the whole of Scripture must be made up of both the Bible and the Book of Mormon.

However, at the time no one apparently read the next three verses and called Smith out on his blatant misinterpretation, because God Himself interprets the sign of the two-sticks He gave to Israel. If God or someone else in the Scriptures provides the interpretation of a passage, there's no need to re-interpret the passage, especially as radically as Joseph Smith did in order to elevate the Book of Mormon to the level of Scripture. If new revelations are really from God, then one should not have to reinterpret – or misinterpret – revelation or Scripture which has already been interpreted for us.

Joseph Smith needed to elevate his new religious text (wherever it came from) to the authority of Scripture so he could then use it to supersede the Bible. Mormonism has a theological concept known as "continuous revelation" which means that newer revelations are always being given, and newer revelations can supersede prior ones. For example, in early Mormonism, it was taught that polygamy was necessary for salvation/exaltation (Bingham Young, Journal of Discourses 11:269) and therefore one of the pillars of their religion. However, in 1890 after the United States government demanded that the Mormon leadership renounce polygamy, their prophet (President Willford Woodruff) immediately pulled down a new revelation that banned it.

In the Bible, there are clear tests given to validate new Scripture and prophets (Deuteronomy 13,18), and one of those tests is that any new prophecies cannot supersede old prophecies. New prophecies in the Scriptures usually just provide additional details or clearer revelation to existing prophetic events. The prophets and their prophecies never contradict one another, because if they did, they would make the Word of God out to be a lie, and therefore make God a liar – which is impossible.

There is a curious (if not humorous) incident in the Bible in which the prophet Jeremiah told King Zedekiah that he would be carried off to Babylon as an exile (Jeremiah 32:4-5). Then Ezekiel prophesied that the king would never see Babylon (Ezekiel 12:13). The king then mocked them because of the apparent contradiction. However, when the time came that the city of Jerusalem fell and King Zedekiah was captured, Nebuchadnezzar put out the king's eyes (after killing all of his sons) and then shipped him off to Babylon, unknowingly fulfilling both prophecies. King Zedekiah was exiled to Babylon, though he never saw it – literally (2 Kings 25:7).

There are other apparent "contradictions" in Scripture, though the most famous of all is the contradiction between whether the Messiah will be the Ruling Conqueror of Psalm 2 or the Suffering Servant of Isaiah 53. Is that a contradiction? Not at all – it just points to two different appearances by the same Messiah: He came the first time to suffer, and will come the second time as the Conqueror. The seeming contradictions between the Rapture passages and the Second Coming passages of the Bible also point to two distinct appearances in the future.

Ezekiel 37:18-20 *"And when the children of your people speak to you, saying, 'Will you not show us what you mean by these?'— 19 say to them, 'Thus says the Lord GOD: "Surely I will take the stick of Joseph, which is in the hand of Ephraim, and the tribes of Israel, his companions; and I will join them with it, with the stick of Judah, and make them one stick, and they will be one in My hand."' 20 And the sticks on which you write will be in your hand before their eyes.*

These three verses contain the interpretation of the two-sticks prophecy just mentioned. The people will see Ezekiel writing names on the sticks, joining them into one, and walking around with it and will ask him what it means. God tells Ezekiel exactly what he should say when they ask him about the sign, which by this time the people are starting to pay attention to this strange exiled prophet in their midst.

Note that God is only speaking of the authority or ruling of the nation, not the tribes and people themselves. When He mentioned Judah in verse 16, He said, "Judah and the children of Israel" – all Twelve Tribes – not Judah and the three other tribes of the Southern Kingdom. Many false teachings (and teachers) have arisen from the concept of the "Ten Lost Tribes" of Israel, even though there is no Scriptural basis for them. After the kingdom was separated under Rehoboam, the Levites and other people of the tribes who wanted to remain faithful to God moved south and integrated into the Southern Kingdom (2 Chronicles 11).

The Northern Kingdom was exiled into the East by the Assyrian Empire in 722 BC, while the Southern Kingdom was exiled into the same basic regions by the Babylonians in 605 BC, 597 BC, and 586 BC. When Cyrus of the Persian Empire allowed the Jews to return to Israel in 538 BC, a mixture of people and families from each of the Twelve Tribes returned to the land of Israel, which was then called Judea and Samaria – still named after the Divided Kingdom.

In Scripture passages following the return of the exiles, remnants of most of the Twelve Tribes are mentioned (Asher, Naphtali, Benjamin, Ephraim, Judah). Also, James addresses his book to the Twelve Tribes scattered abroad, not the Ten Lost Tribes.

Ezekiel 37: 21-22 *"Then say to them, 'Thus says the Lord GOD: "Surely I will take the children of Israel from among the nations, wherever they have gone, and will gather them from every side and bring them into their own land; 22 And I will make them one nation in the land, on the mountains of Israel; and one king shall be king over them all; they shall no longer be* *two nations, nor shall they ever be divided into two kingdoms again.*

Not only does God reiterate that He will gather the children of Israel from the nations and settle them in their own land, but He makes an emphatic declaration by using the word "surely." Though they could count on God to keep His promises, He wanted to give them extra assurance that He would do precisely as He said.

On May 14, 1948, David Ben-Gurion cited these very verses of Ezekiel to declare Israel as the new sovereign Jewish State for the first time in over 2600 years. And when the nation came back into existence, it came back as the nation of Israel once again, not as two separate nations like they had been in the past. The long, terrible centuries of the Diaspora had wiped away all the old tribal distinctions and divisions between them, as well as their loyalties to a particular royal-line or dynasty. Since the founding of the modern State of Israel, the Jews are now one people living as one nation, under one authority.

The "king" spoken of in verse 22 may mean one authority or headship rather than a literal king in the dictator sense of the word, though that day is coming as well: when the Messiah takes His rightful place on the throne of David.

Ezekiel 37:23 *They shall not defile themselves anymore with their idols, nor with their detestable things, nor with any of their transgressions; but I will deliver them from all their dwelling places in which they have sinned, and will cleanse them. Then they shall be My people, and I will be their God.*

Since its earliest days when the nation was but an infant, the Israelites had problems with idolatry – Jacob their founder even had to tell his wives and children to put their idols away when they entered the Promised Land. (Genesis 35:2-4). Their idolatry would come and go, until after the division of the kingdom when both kingdoms fell headlong into idolatry. Idolatry was the primary reason for their punishment and captivity, with the violation of the Sabbaths and their wickedness being the other charges against them. But after their exile by the Assyrians and

Babylonians, the remnant that returned to the land of Israel never again had a problem with idolatry.

From the destruction of the Temple in 70 AD until today, Israel has held to a religion of works, like most other religions do. However, during and after the Tribulation, Israel will forsake their religion of works and finally call upon Jesus as their Messiah to save them. Over and over in the New Testament, Jesus declares that He is the Way, the Truth, and the Life, and that no one can go to the Father except through Him (John 14:6-7). The only way the Jews can ever truly enter into their promised relationship as sons of God – His people – is through Jesus their Messiah.

Ezekiel 37:24 *"David My servant shall be king over them, and they shall all have one shepherd; they shall also walk in My judgments and observe My statutes, and do them.*

There's some debate as to whether God is speaking of David in the literal sense or the Messiah, the Branch of David. Most likely, David will not be resurrected to rule over them as he did in the past, though that is entirely possible. Since David was the first king of the Messianic line and the Messiah is the final king of the house of David, the verse could be referring to either one.

How can people truly love God and be referred to as "His people"? By walking with Him, following His commandments, and observing His statues. God cares little for lip-service and religious rituals (Hosea 6:6, 1 Samuel 15:22), but places the emphasis on obeying His Word, being "doers and not hearers only." (James 1:22-23, Luke 6:46-49)

Ezekiel 37:25 *Then they shall dwell in the land that I have given to Jacob My servant, where your fathers dwelt; and they shall dwell there, they, their children, and their children's children, forever; and My servant David shall be their prince forever.*

The phrase "and my servant David shall be their prince forever" is a further indication that their ruler will be the

Messiah, the Eternal One, rather than a resurrected David. However, some argue that the Messiah will be the king while David will be the prince. But regardless of the ruler's identity, the idea is the same: there will be a righteous ruler on the throne who's a man after God's own heart.

Ezekiel 37:26 Moreover I will make a covenant of peace with them, and it shall be an everlasting covenant with them; I will establish them and multiply them, and I will set My sanctuary in their midst forevermore.

This covenant of peace looks forward to the day when Israel's struggles and trials have ended forever, and they've entered into their inheritance with God. Today, the Jews are most definitely not at peace, and the worst is yet to come: the Time of Jacob's Trouble (Jeremiah 30:6-7) during the latter half of the Seventieth Week, the Great Tribulation.

Just as the covenants with Noah (and his sons), Abraham, Isaac, Jacob, and then David, this is one of the few everlasting covenants mentioned in the Scriptures: the promise to never again uproot the Jews from the land. Not only that, but He will set His Temple – His Dwelling Place – in their very midst. This sanctuary is described in detail from Ezekiel 40-48, the Millennial Temple.

When we enter the Eternal Age (as described in the closing pages of Isaiah and Revelation), the New Jerusalem – the Ultimate Temple – will come to the earth and God will be with His people forever, which includes all believers from all time, not just the Jewish faithful.

Ezekiel 37:27-28 My tabernacle also shall be with them; indeed I will be their God, and they shall be My people. 28 The nations also will know that I, the LORD, sanctify Israel, when My sanctuary is in their midst forevermore."'"

After the Great Tribulation has ended and the Messiah has assumed His place on the throne, He will build another Temple in the land, which is described in Ezekiel 40-48. This will most likely not be the same temple which is defiled in the middle of the Tribulation by the Antichrist.

Isaiah 2:3 tells of how during the literal reign of the Messiah in the Millennium, all the Gentile nations of the world will go up to worship the Lord at Jerusalem, which will also be the highest point on the earth (Zechariah 14:10). The nations will be faithful to the Lord, Who will be ruling from Israel, and every year they will go up to the Temple for the required feasts. (Zechariah 14:16-18)

When God is in Israel's midst at the Temple once again, it's possible that it'll be in the form of the Shekinah – the glory of the Lord – as it was in the Old Testament. The Shekinah appeared at the dedication of both the Tabernacle in the Wilderness and Solomon's Temple (Exodus 40:34-35, 2 Chronicles 7:2-3). The last mention of the Shekinah being with the people in the Old Testament is in Ezekiel 11:23, when it leaves the Temple and moves out to the Mount of Olives (the mountain east of the city), where it then disappeared.

In the Temples which followed after the Babylonian Captivity, the Shekinah never returned, indicating that God was no longer indwelling the Temple in their midst. None of those Temples had the Ark of the Covenant or the other sacred items which previously occupied the Most Holy Place. Though the Temples were on holy ground, without the indwelling glory of God, they were merely empty buildings.

However, five hundred years after the Captivity had ended and the Second Temple had been built, the glory of the Lord once again appeared in the Temple, but this time in the form of a man, the Messiah. When Jesus came to present Himself in the Temple on the appointed day, He first appeared on the Mount of Olives and then entered the Eastern Gate of the Temple, reversing the Shekinah glory's departure.

After Jesus' resurrection, He also ascended from the Mount of Olives just as the Shekinah glory had centuries before. When He returns to Jerusalem at the end of the Tribulation, where does Jesus descend first? To the Mount of Olives, which will split apart into a great valley through which the captives of Jerusalem will flee. Then He enters through the Eastern Gate of the Temple once again. (Zechariah 14, Ezekiel 44:1-3)

XII. The Magog Invasion – Ezekiel 38

In passage of Ezekiel 38-39, God commands Ezekiel to prophesy to the north about a distant time in which God will draw out His enemies' forces for the purposes of annihilating them, as well as demonstrating to His own people that He is real and is the One Who is regathering and protecting them. The prophecy describes in detail how a coalition of nations equipped and led by a northern leader will seek to plunder the regathered nation of Israel in the latter days.

Until Israel became a nation again in 1948, little attention was paid to this passage, with many commentators placing the timing for this event at the end of the distant Millennium, mostly because it involves the names "Gog and Magog." However, when the Arab nations began attacking Israel over and over after her declaration of Statehood and the rise of the Soviet Union, scholars began studying Ezekiel 38-39 much more seriously.

Several items in the passage make it unique among the numerous End Times prophecies in the Scriptures: the attackers are specifically named, their purpose for attacking Israel is given, numerous secondary details are given about the time of the invasion, God Himself intervenes to thwart the attack, and then a detailed chronology of the cleanup effort after the battle is described.

Each of the eight nations involved in the attack are listed by their ancestral names, which are therefore historically traceable. Nations change their names, peoples and borders, but do not change their ancestry and history (though some try to!). Most of the nations in the coalition are also Islamic nations who have long sought Israel's destruction. The observing nations that protest the attack are also mentioned, along with a foreshadowing of some of the Middle Eastern politics present at the time of the invasion.

There are two peculiarities with this prophecy – one is that for some reason, God is bringing Magog and his armies down into Israel for the purposes of judging and destroying them. Another peculiarity is that God uses this invasion to not only show His power and glory to the entire world, but also to reveal His "reality" to His own people who have been regathered in His land. At the time this incident occurs, Israel will be dwelling securely in the land, though in an apparent state of unbelief – they need to be shown that God is Who He says He is.

Since 1948, the invasion of Ezekiel 38-39 has seemed very close at times, but there were always one or two nations that didn't quite fit – until the last several years. Turkey (Togarmah) was a close ally with Israel and very Westernized, until recently; now Turkey is mostly allied with Russia and even Iran. But now that all the nations have been "lined up" on the sides as described in the prophecy, Israel has constructed huge security barriers to protect them from their neighbors, which can hardly be described as "living securely" and "without walls." Therefore, this attack does seem to be steadily moving closer to us, though it may not be as immediate as many thought a few years ago (including myself).

Given the size and scope of the attack – probably numbering in the millions of soldiers – it's not entirely clear whether the invasion is a surprise attack or not. Consider how long it would take for Russia and the surrounding Islamic nations to mobilize all their forces and move them down into the lands surrounding Israel. While some elements of the passage seem to indicate a surprise attack, there are other elements which do not, such the protests of Tarshish, Sheba, and Dedan. Perhaps the invasion described isn't a sudden surprise that catches Israel unawares (like a tornado) as much as a massive invasion effort that overshadows the entire land (like a hurricane).

An interesting scenario could be that Iran may try to strike a deal such that they will voluntarily give up their nuclear weapons ONLY IF Israel does. This scenario would be very similar to the method used by the United States to invade Iraq in 2003. The amount of pressure upon Israel to comply (and therefore diffuse a global catastrophe) would be astounding, especially when Iran has nuclear weapons someday and is threatening to use them. This possible standoff standoff could also give Russia and their coalition time and justification to move all their forces into the Middle East without being hampered by the United States or Israel. Russia may end up using the world's demands for peace and disarmament as a smoke-screen to initiate the coming invasion.

Israel's constant threat of using nuclear weapons against any invaders (the Samson Option) is one of the major reasons why the other nations around her have not invaded Israel the way they did in 1948, 1967, and 1973. If and when Israel refuses to give up her weapons of last resort, then Russia, Iran, and the other Islamic nations would move into the Middle East to enforce the UN resolution to make Israel comply. Again, the United States set the precedent for a justified invasion of another nation if that nation refuses to surrender their WMDs (Weapons of Mass Destruction) to the United Nations.

The Ezekiel 38-39 prophecy, sometimes referred to as the "Magog Invasion," is one of the few events in Scripture in which God maneuvers a king or nation into attacking Israel for the purposes of both judging that nation and to make His glory known to His own people. The most famous of such events is where God hardened the heart of Pharaoh and caused him to chase after the Israelites as they fled into the desert, where the Egyptian army was then drowned in the Red Sea.

But where the destruction of the Egyptian army only involved one nation and possibly tens of thousands of soldiers, the Magog Invasion involves many nations and millions of soldiers.

Ezekiel 38 – Full Text

1 Now the word of the LORD came to me, saying, 2 "Son of man, set your face against Gog, of the land of Magog, the prince of Rosh, Meshech, and Tubal, and prophesy against him, 3 and say, 'Thus says the Lord GOD: "Behold, I am against you, O Gog, the prince of Rosh, Meshech, and Tubal. 4 I will turn you around, put hooks into your jaws, and lead you out, with all your army, horses, and horsemen, all splendidly clothed, a great company with bucklers and shields, all of them handling swords. 5 Persia, Ethiopia, and Libya are with them, all of them with shield and helmet; 6 Gomer and all its troops; the house of Togarmah from the far north and all its troops—many people are with you.

7 "Prepare yourself and be ready, you and all your companies that are gathered about you; and be a guard for them. 8 After many days you will be visited. In the latter years

you will come into the land of those brought back from the sword
and gathered from many people on the mountains of Israel,
which had long been desolate; they were brought out of the
nations, and now all of them dwell safely. 9 You will ascend,
coming like a storm, covering the land like a cloud, you and all
your troops and many peoples with you."

10 'Thus says the Lord GOD: "On that day it shall come to
pass that thoughts will arise in your mind, and you will make an
evil plan: 11 You will say, 'I will go up against a land of
unwalled villages; I will go to a peaceful people, who dwell
safely, all of them dwelling without walls, and having neither
bars nor gates'— 12 to take plunder and to take booty, to stretch
out your hand against the waste places that are again inhabited,
and against a people gathered from the nations, who have
acquired livestock and goods, who dwell in the midst of the land.
13 Sheba, Dedan, the merchants of Tarshish, and all their young
lions will say to you, 'Have you come to take plunder? Have you
gathered your army to take booty, to carry away silver and gold,
to take away livestock and goods, to take great plunder?'"'

14 "Therefore, son of man, prophesy and say to Gog, 'Thus
says the Lord GOD: "On that day when My people Israel dwell
safely, will you not know it? 15 Then you will come from your
place out of the far north, you and many peoples with you, all of
them riding on horses, a great company and a mighty army. 16
You will come up against My people Israel like a cloud, to cover
the land. It will be in the latter days that I will bring you against
My land, so that the nations may know Me, when I am hallowed
in you, O Gog, before their eyes." 17 Thus says the Lord GOD:
"Are you he of whom I have spoken in former days by My
servants the prophets of Israel, who prophesied for years in
those days that I would bring you against them?

18 "And it will come to pass at the same time, when Gog
comes against the land of Israel," says the Lord GOD, "that My
fury will show in My face. 19 For in My jealousy and in the fire
of My wrath I have spoken: 'Surely in that day there shall be a
great earthquake in the land of Israel, 20 so that the fish of the
sea, the birds of the heavens, the beasts of the field, all creeping
things that creep on the earth, and all men who are on the face
of the earth shall shake at My presence. The mountains shall be
thrown down, the steep places shall fall, and every wall shall fall

to the ground.' 21 I will call for a sword against Gog throughout all My mountains," says the Lord GOD. "Every man's sword will be against his brother. 22 And I will bring him to judgment with pestilence and bloodshed; I will rain down on him, on his troops, and on the many peoples who are with him, flooding rain, great hailstones, fire, and brimstone. 23 Thus I will magnify Myself and sanctify Myself, and I will be known in the eyes of many nations. Then they shall know that I am the LORD."'

Ezekiel 38 – Verse by Verse Analysis

Ezekiel 38:1-3 Now the word of the LORD came to me, saying, 2 "Son of man, set your face against Gog, of the land of Magog, the prince of Rosh, Meshech, and Tubal, and prophesy against him, 3 and say, 'Thus says the Lord GOD: "Behold, I am against you, O Gog, the prince of Rosh, Meshech, and Tubal.

The prophecy begins with God telling Ezekiel to utter the prophecy against an entity named "Gog" who is "of the land of Magog," and who's also the leader (the prince) of Rosh, Meshech, and Tubal. Notice that all through the passage, God is speaking to this entity, not against the specific peoples of the invading nations themselves. To understand the prophecy, we need to find out exactly who Gog is, since he is not clearly identified in this passage.

There are only two other verses in the Bible that the name "Gog" can be found outside of this passage: 1 Chronicles 5:4, in which a man named "Gog" is listed as one of the descendants of Reuben, and in Revelation 20:8, where Gog is paired with Magog again as some of the invaders who go up against Jerusalem at the end of the Millennium. But neither of those references gives much of an indication as to who Gog is.

However, there is one additional reference which does provide some insight into Gog's identity, though it's hidden in the Septuagint, an earlier translation of the Old Testament into Greek. The Masoretic rendering of Amos 7:1 is: *"Thus the Lord GOD showed me: Behold, He formed locust swarms at the beginning of the late crop; indeed it was the late crop after the king's mowings."* However, the Septuagint renders the same verse as: *"Thus the Lord showed me, and behold a swarm of locusts were coming, and behold, one of the young devastating locusts was **Gog, the King.**"*

At first, the different rendering seems curious, but not that significant until the locusts are examined. Throughout the Scriptures, locusts are always sent as a judgment on a land because they destroy the entire food supply very quickly. But the writer of Proverbs 30:27 (Agur) observes that the locusts have no king, unlike ants and bees which have queens, so why does the text of Amos 7:1 (LXX) say they do? In Revelation 9, a strange sort of locusts comes up out of the bowels of the earth to torment mankind, but do not touch the grass or foliage (unlike normal locusts). These are known as the "demon locusts," because they have evil, supernatural qualities.

From these three passages, it appears that Gog is a supernatural/demonic king who has authority over a legion of destroyers – at times, the destroyers are locusts, while other times the destroyers are nations and men. The last reference to Gog in the Bible is in Revelation 20:8, where Gog and Magog and the rest of the armies of the earth are gathered to go up against Jerusalem to destroy it.

In the New Testament epistles, Paul makes several passing references to spiritual "powers and principalities" which govern the nations of the earth. Daniel 10 also describes this idea in a more vivid picture when a messenger angel comes to him and tells of how the "prince of Persia" has been restraining him and that after he leaves, the "prince of Greece" will come. It's not a far stretch to assume that every nation has its own set of spiritual rulers and principalities, including America. Note that Michael is Israel's prince, referred to as "the great prince who stands watch over the sons of your people" (Daniel 12:1-3).

From these various passages, a picture emerges that the nations and peoples here on earth are merely the pawns in a much greater conflict in the spiritual realm. If this is the case, then the New Testament admonitions to pray continually take on an entirely new meaning. Ephesians 6 speaks of putting on the "whole armor of God" in terms of preparing for battle, with the key verse being verse 12: *"For we do not wrestle against flesh and blood, but against principalities, against powers, against the rulers of the darkness of this age, against spiritual hosts of wickedness in the heavenly places."*

The phrase "set your face against" is typically used when God describes upcoming wrath or judgment. When God turns His face away from a group or nation, He is basically turning His back to them. When He turns His face towards a group, it is typically for blessing and favor. So in both the opening verses of Ezekiel 38 and 39, God instructs Ezekiel to speak against the spiritual principality behind the invading nations, the prince known as Gog.

One of the many often overlooked treasures in the Bible is what is known as the "Table of Nations" in Genesis 10, in which the early descendants of Noah's three sons, Shem, Ham, and Japheth are enumerated and their basic areas of settlement are detailed. From the seventy descendants listed in the Table of Nations, the ancient world was settled and formed into nations. Most of these names, tribes, and nations have been confirmed by archaeology (as detailed by Bill Cooper's book "After the Flood"), and it's from this list that we find the first references to Magog, Meshech, and Tubal, who were all sons of Japheth (Genesis 10:2).

The Magogians were known as the Scythians to the Greeks, and they are recorded as being a brutal, barbaric people who frequently raided their neighbors by horseback. They were expert horsemen and lived much of their lives in the saddle. The Great Wall of China was built specifically to keep the Magogians out, and the steppes of Russia were formerly known as the "Ramparts of Magog." The descendants of Magog originally settled north of the Caucasus Mountains, but spread out all across the lands of the expanse known as Russia today.

As the people began to spread out after the Flood, the descendants of Meshech and Tubal dwelt close to one another along the northern coasts of Asia Minor, before spreading out much further. Meshech later became known as the Moschi, and settled in the region of the Moschian Mountains. The modern city of Moscow is a derivative of this name "Moschi" or "Muscovi." These people were also earlier called the Muscovites, a more-direct link to Moscow. Tubal eventually came to dwell near the Black Sea area near Georgia, and the city of Tobolsk probably originated from this group when they migrated over the Caucasus Mountains.

There is a slight difference between some of the renderings of this verse, and many versions of the Bible properly render the phrase, "against Gog, the land of Magog, the chief prince of Meshech and Tubal" as: "against Gog, of the land of Magog, the prince of Rosh, Meshech, and Tubal." The difference between them is that the King James Version appears to have a translational error, rendering the Hebrew word "Ro'sh" as "chief" (an adjective), which is the meaning of the word, while the other versions render the word as a noun: "Rosh."

With this difference in mind, the "Rosh" is the ancient name of the tribe from which the nation "Russia" or the "land of the Ros/Rosh" originates. The Rosh peoples settled in the area north of the Taurus Mountains near the Vulga River. However, they also have settled far and wide over the centuries because of their migratory culture. Some scholars dispute the specific areas of settlements of these tribes, but regardless, Ezekiel is speaking against the tribes which come from the far north, as mentioned in Ezekiel 38:5-6. Today's nation of Russia and the former southern Soviet republics are made up of the remnants of each of these three groups.

Why is God against the power behind these nations? Part of the reason is because of their evil intentions to attack Israel, who appears to be at peace with them and the rest of the world. However, from the text it appears that God is orchestrating the entire scene for His purposes of judgment upon those nations. Especially in the next verse where it's described that He will "put hooks into their jaws and lead them out," it's clear that He's causing this incident specifically to bring these nations – and Gog the power behind them – into judgment in order to display His power and glory to the rest of the world.

So what problem or dispute does God have with them? Could it be because of their past sins over the years? God is a God of Justice, and in the last hundred century, this group of nations has slaughtered (and caused to be slaughtered) countless millions of their own people and others by their system of communism and atheism. In Russia alone (when it was the Soviet Union), over 30 million people were killed under Stalin, Lenin, and the other Soviet leaders in only 70 years. The exporting of atheistic communism to China, the Far East, and South America has claimed millions of additional lives.

However, have Russia and these other communist nations ever been repaid for their evil and brought to justice? Not yet – and this could be why God declares that He is against them. All the modern pillars of socialism and communism are in direct opposition to God and the Bible's teachings, and Russia was the primary nation that not only led the world into communism, but they helped spread it all over the globe.

But again, keep in mind that it wasn't the Russians, Bolsheviks, Lenin, Stalin, Castro, or even Karl Marx who are ultimately responsible for these atrocities – they were merely the pawns. The real power behind them was Gog (and ultimately Satan), who God is calling out for judgment in this passage.

Ezekiel 38:4 *I will turn you around, put hooks into your jaws, and lead you out, with all your army, horses, and horsemen, all splendidly clothed, a great company with bucklers and shields, all of them handling swords.*

The phrase "put hooks into your jaws" speaks of God forcibly leading them out against their will, or at least against their own interests. The Assyrians and Babylonians had a practice of putting large hooks into the jaws of their prisoners and leading them where they did not want to go: out of their lands. Here, God is saying that He will do the same to the armies of these nations.

How could this literally be fulfilled today, with Russia being coerced into attacking Israel against her will? The most logical way is by Russia being entangled in a set of treaties or economic conditions that forces them to be pulled down into the Middle East. Russia's increased presence in the Middle East due to the Syrian Civil War and Iran's nuclear weapons programs are good examples of these entanglements. In a later verse (v12), the purpose of the invasion is given: to take great plunder from Israel, i.e. economic reasons.

Keep in mind that Russia has been the primary military supplier of weapons to the Israel-hating nations of the Middle East for decades, especially Syria and Iran. Russia also built the nuclear plants in Iran, against the wishes of the rest of the world. What kind of nation gives nuclear weapons to a bunch of madmen who want to blow up the world anyway? That's about as smart as arming a serial killer who's used to a 9mm with a machine gun or even a bazooka.

For the last decade, the primary threat to Israel has been the nuclear weapons program of the Shiite leadership of Iran. As their weapons program nears completion, there's been more and more talk of a preemptive strike by either Israel or America in order to remove the threat, but nothing has transpired – yet. The Stuxnet Virus of 2010 set the Iranian nuclear program back a few years, but they've appeared to have recovered from it. Perhaps if Israel attacks one of these nations like Iran or Syria, Russia will be forced to launch a massive attack against them.

In the Yom Kippur War in 1973, Russia was the primary war planner/supporter of Syria, and was even ready to send in their own forces if President Nixon hadn't responded so strongly in Israel's defense. With the two superpowers of the world in a quiet stand-off, the situation de-escalated and Israel finished the war with her enemies, pushing them back across the Sinai and the Golan Heights. Even today, Russia and its unwavering support of Bashar Assad (even after his chemical weapons attacks on his own people) are one of the major reasons why he is still in power.

Russia is also heavily dependent upon natural gas and oil exports to other nations, especially Europe. If the oil/natural gas market suddenly tanks and the prices drastically drop, Russia will feel the economic pinch very quickly. What could cause such a dramatic price drop? Either an economic collapse or a huge quantity of a competing supply, perhaps like the discovery of 16 trillion cubic feet of natural gas off the coast of Israel in 2010.

What happens when that discovery is finally put on the market and Russia's economy starts to significantly feel the impact? America's growing exports of petroleum are already taking market-share away from the Arabs and the Russians, and this will only add to Russia's woes. What if Europe and other nations decide to stop being held hostage to Russia's energy policies and they switch over to Israel as their primary supplier?

In addition to Israel's natural gas discoveries, the recent fracking boom in the United States is also rapidly changing the petroleum and natural gas markets. Since 2007, shale gas and light oil production have been increasing by 50% per year, and the United States is predicted to even displace Saudi Arabia as the world's largest oil producer by 2018.

The remainder of the verse speaks of the splendor of the forces and how they are all well-equipped and highly-trained. Again, Russia is the primary arms supplier to the Islamic nations in the Middle East, and they have been expanding their defense spending over the last several years in an effort to modernize their military.

Ezekiel 38:5-6 *Persia, Ethiopia, and Libya are with them, all of them with shield and helmet; 6 Gomer and all its troops; the house of Togarmah from the far north and all its troops—many people are with you.*

The next set of nations listed in the coalition is more familiar to most people. Persia has been a nation since the Medes unified the region in 625 BC, but has only been known as "Iran" since 1935. Since the Islamic Revolution in 1979, Iran has been the biggest state sponsor of radical Islam and terrorism in the world. Iran's former president, Mahmoud Ahmadinejad, was alleged to be one of the terrorists who took the US Embassy hostage in 1979, though the CIA and the Iranian government have since denied this claim.

Ethiopia is still known by the same name as from ancient times and was taken over by the communists in 1984, causing terrible famines and deaths. Nearly a hundred thousand of Jews have migrated from Ethiopia to Israel since then and have been absorbed, including the thousands that were airlifted during Operation Solomon in 1991. Ethiopia underwent a long civil war and famine since the communists took control of the nation, which was also supported by the former Soviet Union.

The naming of Ethiopia in the original texts is "Cush," one of the sons of Ham (Noah's youngest son) in Genesis 10. From Cush came many of the black peoples of Africa, so the area of

Ethiopia mentioned here may in fact be a much larger territory, perhaps all of North Africa, which is very Islamic today.

Libya is known as Put or Phut and Lubim in the Scriptures, who were also descendants of Ham, along with Egypt (Mizraim). Libya has been Islamic since the Seventh Century, though after World War I it was administered by Italy and then the British until being freed in 1949. Libya became a pro-Western country until 1969, when Muammar Gaddafi staged a coup and began instituting Islamic laws. Libya was a significant state-sponsor of terrorism until the United States invaded Iraq in 2003. Gaddafi was deposed in 2011 after Egypt and Tunisia fell to protesters. All three countries now seem to be moving in the direction of instituting Islamic law rather than secular laws as before.

Gomer was the predecessor to the Cimmerians who in turn were the predecessors to the Germans, who settled north of the Black Sea in the Rhine and Danube valleys. Gomer and all his bands can be expanded to include Gomer's sons enumerated in Genesis 10:3, namely Ashkenaz, Riphath, and Togarmah. Though Germany has been making amends since World War II for the evils of the Nazis and the Holocaust, there are still occasional acts of anti-Semitism, particularly on the political fringes. Also, anti-immigrant and nationalist tones are increasing because of the mass-migration from the Syrian refugees and the Germans providing much of the labor and taxes for the rest of the European Union.

Togarmah is the region of Turkey and Armenia in Central Asia (who still refer to themselves as the House of Togarmah today). Ashkenaz is the area of East Germany, Poland, Czechoslovakia and the other Slavic regions. Riphath, another grandson of Japheth, evidently settled in the Rhiphaean mountains or the Riphoean mountains in Russia, and were the ancestors of the Paphlagonians.

Today, these areas are basically Turkey, the Islamic republics south of Russia, and even parts of Eastern Europe and Germany. For years, Turkey (Togarmah) was a close ally with Israel and very Westernized until their financial collapse of 2001 and repeated denials of entry into the European Union. Since that time, Turkey has begun returning to their Islamic roots and has turned away from her Western allies, namely Israel and the United States. The Turkish government under Edrogan appears to be moving even further towards hardline Islam through the Gaza flotillas and their unwavering support of the Palestinians, particularly in Gaza under Hamas. When it comes to Israel, Turkey is typically the first nation (after Iran and sometimes Europe) to lodge protests against Israel at the UN and in the international press. Turkey has also taken in over 3.4 million Syrian refugees over the last decade, and criticizing Israel is an easy way for them to have some semblance of unity.

Despite Turkey's frequent saber-rattling, the most interesting member of the bunch is Germany, which is still a major nation of the European Union, which doesn't have much of a military (compared to the United States). However, as the socialist policies of the other member nations continue to bankrupt the European Union, Germany may pull out before all her resources are sapped. The European Union keeps looking to Germany to bail them out, against the German people's wishes. After all, why should the Germans be responsible for paying the rest of Europe's social benefits? In the end, Germany could end up jumping from the sinking ship known as the European Union and then side with Russia, especially if they are dependent upon the Russians for their natural gas and other energy resources.

Ezekiel 38:7-8 *"Prepare yourself and be ready, you and all your companies that are gathered about you; and be a guard for them. 8 After many days you will be visited. In the latter years you will come into the land of those brought back from the sword and gathered from many people on the mountains of Israel, which had long been desolate; they were brought out of the nations, and now all of them dwell safely.*

God continues commanding Gog to prepare for this massive invasion effort, which logistically will involve supplying, fueling, equipping, training, coordinating, and guarding the entire military force. Note that this will not be a trivial or insignificant effort – it will need to be well thought-out and planned long beforehand. With an invasion force as large and diverse as this one, Russia will need to provide the command-and-control information and logistics to coordinate the various military groups and forces. As one of the permanent members of the UN Security Council, Russia will also need to provide significant political cover so an opposing coalition cannot be mobilized to offset them, such as NATO.

The terms "after many days" and "in the latter years" means that this attack will happen long after this prophecy was given, which was around 586 BC. There are some liberal scholars who try to argue that this prophecy occurred just before or during the Babylonian Captivity, but these terms invalidate their timeline. Also, the Magogians/Scythians have never attacked Israel in recorded history, and never with this grouping of nations in this coalition.

If this attack occurred earlier in Israel's history, where are the Assyrians and Babylonians, who were the "superpowers" at the time? The Persians are mentioned, but they're not leading the coalition – the Magogians are. Until even the late Middle Ages, Russia was a series of disbursed tribes who weren't unified until Peter the Great in 1721. Not only that, but the description of how the invasion would be something that would be well-recorded in history – if it had actually occurred. But it hasn't.

Note the curious phrase, "after many days you [Gog] will be visited" – the question left unanswered is exactly who were they visited by? Could it be that God, Satan, or one of the other messengers awakens Gog and tells him to go invade Israel?

The rest of this verse shows that this invasion could only occur after 1948, after the State of Israel has been reborn and the Jews have been regathered to her lands out of all the nations, as previously described in Ezekiel 36-37. But notice that the prophecy also says, "all of them dwell safely" – that cannot quite be said of Israel today, unless the term refers to their statehood and basic security rather than being at peace.

Since even before her statehood, Israel has been under the constant threat of attack from her neighbors, both the ones which border her and others like Iran who are hundreds of miles away. Israel is also still continually threatened by Islamic terrorists, which the Gaza Barrier and the West Bank Separation Wall keep out. The only reason that most Israelis are able to sleep in their homes every night is because many others are keeping watch over them. If they ever let down their guard, Israel would be invaded and overrun in a matter of days, if not hours.

Ezekiel 38: 9 *You will ascend, coming like a storm, covering the land like a cloud, you and all your troops and many peoples with you."*

The terms "coming like a storm" and "covering the land like a cloud" allude to a massive air attack that comes very suddenly, followed later by the rest of the military forces on the ground. In modern warfare, the air forces are nearly always used first to surprise and weaken the enemy's defenses and vital infrastructure such as electricity, command-centers, and communications. After the enemy has been sufficiently "softened," then the ground troops come in and finish the operation, often becoming an occupying force.

When the United States invaded Iraq in 2003, the "shock and awe" air operations lasted for days before ground-forces were sent in. This battle could be different in that both the air and ground-forces could attack simultaneously to completely overwhelm Israel's military. Also, not only could the initial strike be from the air forces, but by thousands upon thousands of remote-controlled drones. Since 2007, increasing numbers of air operations are being conducted by drones, which are much cheaper, maneuverable, and more expendable than traditional fighter jets and their pilots.

Ezekiel 38:10-11 *'Thus says the Lord GOD: "On that day it shall come to pass that thoughts will arise in your mind, and you will make an evil plan: 11 You will say, 'I will go up against a land of unwalled villages; I will go to a peaceful people, who dwell safely, all of them dwelling without walls, and having neither bars nor gates'*

The phrase "on that day" links back to the previous verse which spoke of Gog being "visited in the latter days." It could very well be that Satan places these thoughts in Gog's mind in an effort to either destroy Israel or to move the next phase of his plans along. After all, Satan can read the Bible just as well as we can and he knows that Gog's nations will be destroyed in the effort. However, this could also set the stage for the rise of

Satan's Antichrist, especially with the European Union faltering and the United States rescinding from the world stage – particularly after this war. War not only has a way of redrawing borders, but dramatically reshaping politics all over the world.

Verse 11 contains several explicit details which have pushed the fulfillment of this prophecy back at least a few years, namely that the land is described as being "without walls, bars, or gates." This means that the people of Israel will be dwelling securely and comfortably, as most Western nations do today. Today in Israel, there are numerous checkpoints, fences, and patrols throughout the land along the Gaza Strip, the West Bank, and along the Jordanian border. Israel can hardly be described as living without walls, bars, and gates, but it is relatively secure – again, if it wasn't they would be quickly invaded by their enemies.

The building of the Separation Wall through the middle of Israel may have pushed this prophecy back and brought another one into focus: Psalm 83, which describes a coordinated attack from Israel's immediate neighbors in an effort to drive them into the Sea. Walls are built around cities for protection and defense, though the walls around Jerusalem are not really used for protection any longer. Air-warfare has greatly diminished the usefulness of such walls and fences, but they are still very effective at slowing or stopping ground invasions.

Today, Israel faces two constant threats from her southwest and her eastern border: Gaza and the West Bank (or Samaria), though the immediate threat from the West Bank seems to be diminishing. To minimize those threats, Israel has constructed two large fences to separate themselves from their Arab enemies. The Gaza Strip is bordered by the Mediterranean Sea and is isolated by the Gaza Barrier, while the West Bank is contained by the Jordan border and the Separation Wall that winds through the land. The fences/barriers stretch on for miles and are constantly patrolled. Traffic only crosses the barriers through heavily guarded gates, with regular inspections of all traffic. Even the new Iron Dome defense system can be considered a "virtual wall" to protect their cities and towns from rocket attacks.

Clearly, this is not a picture of Israel being at peace in her land and dwelling "without walls and gates." In order for the

Magog Invasion to occur and fulfill this prophecy, those barriers, walls, and gates will likely have be torn down and dismantled first. When Israel is truly secure in the land, everyone – including Gog and Israel's enemies – will know it, as mentioned in verse 14.

> ***Ezekiel 38:12*** *To take plunder and to take booty, to stretch out your hand against the waste places that are again inhabited, and against a people gathered from the nations, who have acquired livestock and goods, who dwell in the midst of the land.*

The "evil thought" that enters Gog's mind (and then the minds of his human underlings) is primarily one of greed, not annihilation and destruction. Does Russia have such needs today? They most certainly do – what nation doesn't? Russia is an aging, dying nation which is even more worse off than Europe and their problems run long and deep. Alcoholism, suicide, and abortion are rampant, and the nation is self-destructing from the inside. However, her leaders such as Dmitry Medvedev and Vladimir Putin always project strength, not weakness. They are adept at hiding the seriousness of their national problems.

It's been estimated that by 2050, Russia will have lost 20% of her native population – they're simply not having enough children to sustain themselves, like much of the rest of Europe. This invasion could be an attempt by Russia in her dying gasps to revitalize their nation and prevent their collapse.

Today, Russia imports over half their food and other agricultural products ("After Putin's Russia: Past Imperfect, Future Uncertain" by Stephen K. Wegren, Dale Roy Herspring), while Israel exports massive amounts of fruits, vegetables, and other products. Israel is also ideally located for shipping all over the Middle East and the Mediterranean. Though Russia has vast amounts of land at her disposal, much of it is unusable for farming and agriculture because it's locked under the tundra, snow, and ice.

Interestingly enough, the passage does specifically mention cattle (or livestock in general) and goods (products and technology) as part of what Russia is coveting. Russia desperately needs a solution to their agricultural problems and also a warm-water sea port from which to conduct shipping and commerce. Israel has both. If one wants to be in the center of the world and THE global power, the place to be is at the junction of three major continents: Israel.

There may also be a sting of jealousy on the part of Russia, as they lost a significant number of their engineers and scientists after the collapse of the Soviet Union. Over the last thirty years, most of the Jewish educated base of Russia have migrated to their native land of Israel. Russia has too few doctors and scientists while Israel has too many (if that were possible).

Due to the thousands of educated Russian immigrants moving to Israel and with the threat of terrorism contained, Israel's technology sector has been booming since the mid-1990s. Venture capital is flowing in and the entrepreneurial spirit is flourishing. The nation of Israel is now the Startup Capital of the world, especially since the United States has instituted numerous regulations and restrictions on creating new public corporations. Next to the United States, Israel has more corporations on the NASDAQ than any other nation in the world.

Russia's primary exports are natural gas, petroleum products, and other energy-related exports, all of which have an expiration date. She has vast oil and natural gas reserves, but those will soon be steadily declining (energytribute.com, 2007). Meanwhile, Israel's energy products will be increasing. In 2010, Israel discovered huge natural gas reserves off the coast of Tel Aviv and Haifa, much to their surprise. Also, there are feverish attempts to discover oil in the north and around the Dead Sea, which do appear promising. The incredible mineral deposits of the Dead Sea region alone are worth tens of billions of dollars, which could also attract Russia's attention.

When Israel first began to be resettled over the last century, the settlers had strong socialist – even communist – tendencies. One of the unique Israeli forms of settlement was the kibbutz, an agricultural commune which played an important role in the early settlement and reclaiming of the land. The kibbutz movement began to diminish after Israel became a nation, and the nation's financial structure has been steadily shifting from socialism and centralized administration to free-market capitalism. As that shift continues, Israel continues to grow more and more wealthy.

It should also be noted that the Gog and Magog mentioned in Revelation 20:8 do not come to plunder Israel and her people – they will come to destroy the Holy City and depose the King.

Ezekiel 38:13 *Sheba, Dedan, the merchants of Tarshish, and all their young lions will say to you, 'Have you come to take plunder? Have you gathered your army to take booty, to carry away silver and gold, to take away livestock and goods, to take great plunder?'"'*

Sheba and Dedan are both sons of Raamah (a descendant of Shem) in Genesis 10:7 which settled in the Arabian Peninsula, which today is Saudi Arabia, Yemen, and Oman. The exact peoples and tribes of Arabia can be somewhat difficult to determine because the term "Arab" means "mixed," with many of the early Semite and Hamite tribes settling in the Arabian Peninsula and then intermingling. In the centuries after the Flood, much more of the peninsula was lush and heavily-settled until the region experienced terrible desertification from the prevailing dry, eastern winds. Now much of the region (especially the northern portion of Arabia) is uninhabitable desert wastes.

The merchants of Tarshish and her "young lions" are a subject of much debate among Bible students, scholars, and historians. The prophet Jonah fled on a ship bound for Tarshish when he was running from God, and since Nineveh (his assignment) was in the east in Assyria, it's very likely that Jonah was going in the opposite direction as far away as possible: towards the west.

This would make Jonah's destination either Spain or even the British Isles. Tarshish was well-known in the ancient world as being world-wide sea-merchants and a great supplier of tin, both characteristics of ancient Britain; the British have always been world-famous, sea-faring merchants. Much of their history was destroyed when the Romans conquered the British Isles, though a few records remain of their history and lineage.

The symbol of the lion has also been tied to Britain/England for many centuries, and the best arguments on exactly who Tarshish is usually favor Britain. The "young lions" of Tarshish (if it's indeed Britain) would likely be her former colonies in the New World (which are fairly "young"). These would include the United States, Australia, Canada, and a small assortment of other English-speaking lands. Most of these have continued in world-commerce and sea-trade like Britain, yet another characteristic of her ancient ways.

In the passage, note that while Sheba, Dedan, Tarshish, and her young lions protest Gog's actions, they don't do anything to stop it nor come to Israel's defense. They protest and complain, yet do nothing. A disturbing question to ponder (especially as an American), is that if Russia and the Islamic nations launch a massive attack on Israel, how would America respond? It's unlikely that America would ever directly join in the attack upon Israel because we have been staunch allies since 1967 – unless we have another anti-Israeli president as we had several years ago.

During the presidency of Barack Obama, it's seemed very unlikely that the United States would take up arms to defend Israel. The fear (by threat or blackmail) of a Russian nuclear strike upon our American cities would probably be enough to keep America out of the way. Under Obama, the actions of the United States became increasingly hostile to Israel, as well as the United States seeming to recede from the world-stage ("leading from behind" as Obama put it), exploding deficits, and confusing foreign policy, especially in the Middle East. However, with the election of Donald Trump – and especially our formal recognition of Jerusalem as Israel's capital – it appears that our ties with Israel have not only been restored, but strengthened. But the Obama administration painted a good picture of what could happen during the Magog Invasion.

China could also play a significant role in causing the United States to remain out of the conflict, along with the rising influence of Islam in Europe, Britain, and even parts of the United States. Islam is rapidly conquering England without firing a shot, and her leaders seem helpless (or uninterested) in even trying to slow down the Muslim immigration and rising influence. In London, the radical Muslims regularly protest, riot, and promise to Islamize Great Britain, all the while being paid by the state to remain unemployed! Also, London recently elected their first Muslim mayor rather than a native Britain – a first in a major Western city.

The native British are starting to leave their own homeland because they feel it's lost rather than staying behind and fighting for it. Their own government – ruined by decades of socialism – seems intent on committing national suicide. The solution to Britain's immigrant-related problems are very simple, but they lack the courage to even speak it, let alone do it: cut off all welfare benefits to the immigrants and demand that they leave the country; they need to throw off the shackles of political correctness, embrace their proud heritage, and remember who they are as a nation. Winston Churchill would be utterly ashamed of Britain if he saw it today.

Regardless of the reason, it appears that Tarshish and her offshoots protest the Magog Invasion, but refuse to take action and actually intervene to stop it.

Ezekiel 38:14-15 *"Therefore, son of man, prophesy and say to Gog, 'Thus says the Lord GOD: "On that day when My people Israel dwell safely, will you not know it? 15 Then you will come from your place out of the far north, you and many peoples with you, all of them riding on horses, a great company and a mighty army.*

At this point, God returns to addressing Gog, and He mentions that Gog will take notice that Israel is safe and prosperous. Also implied is that Israel's prosperity has made Gog very envious.

The next verse is invaluable in determining who the invaders are. Even if the identities of Rosh, Magog, Meshech, and Tubal were not known, tracing a line due north from Israel would take you directly into the heart of Russia, in the uttermost northern parts of the globe.

As you read these passages, try not to get too caught up in the specific terms of horses, bows, arrows, and swords. The Hebrew word for "horse" in this passage is not necessarily specific to the animal as we know it. The word literally means "leaper"; in Jeremiah 8:7, the same word is used for a bird, and in Exodus 14:9, the word is used for a chariot-rider. Basically, this word can mean any type of rider or vehicle that "leaps", moves rapidly, or becomes airborne. The same holds true with the other ancient terms in this prophecy – a sword can mean a weapon, an arrow or spear can mean a projectile that pierces, and a shield can mean an object of defense.

If a person 2600 years ago (or even 150 years ago) were to look into the current day and see an airplane or air force, they would likely interpret what they saw in terms they were familiar with, and describe them as great birds, or flying chariots with tails of fire. If they saw missiles, they would likely describe them as arrows or spears.

However, the use of horses could be quite literal, especially if the coalition deploys an EMP (electromagnetic pulse) to render all of Israel's infrastructure and high-tech defenses completely useless. An EMP would black out the entire nation so anything that uses electronics (computers, communications, and vehicles) would be worthless. But animals and humans are not affected by EMPs, so horses could be used to rapidly invade the land. Remember, Russia comes to plunder Israel, not destroy her.

Ezekiel 38:16 You will come up against My people Israel like a cloud, to cover the land. It will be in the latter days that I will bring you against My land, so that the nations may know Me, when I am hallowed in you, O Gog, before their eyes."

Again, there is both the mention of the armies of Gog coming up against Israel as a "great cloud covering the land" and "in the latter days." This is very descriptive of a massive air armada moving over Israel to strike deep within the land, like a terrible thunderstorm covering the entire land.

The phrase that God says "when I am hallowed in you" means that He shall be honored, respected, made holy, or set apart by how He responds to the attack. Today, many people talk about God very often, but it's in a common (and often profane) way that bears no resemblance to the God of the Bible. And by how God responds, He will make His name holy and feared by the entire world once again.

Ezekiel 38:17 *Thus says the Lord GOD: "Are you he of whom I have spoken in former days by My servants the prophets of Israel, who prophesied for years in those days that I would bring you against them?*

If there was ever a rhetorical question asked in the Bible, this is it. The main prophet that God is mentioning here is the very prophet who was writing it down: the prophet Ezekiel. The time-gap mentioned also shows that this attack would occur long after the era of Israel's prophets, which ended with John the Baptist in about 30 AD.

There are no other prophets in the Bible that specifically mention these nations or this attack by Gog and Magog, other than possibly Daniel when he references the mysterious "king of the north" in Daniel 11-12. However, that prophecy is usually applied to the Greek empire and then the battles of the Antichrist during the Great Tribulation.

Why have there been no prophets to the Jews in over 2000 years? Even during their exile, God sent prophets to His people to encourage them. So where have they gone? Why hasn't God sent any more prophets to His own Chosen people?

Could it be that Jesus is God's last Word to His people before the Seventieth Week begins? The Book of Hebrews makes the point that Jesus is greater than all the prophets, and that "in these last days, He has spoken to us through His Son." (Hebrews 1:2) Rather than receiving the Word through a representative, isn't it better to receive the Word directly from the Source? God wants His people to look to the coming Prophet spoken of by Moses (Deuteronomy 18:17-19): Yeshua – and Him alone – not to any more prophets as in the ancient times.

Ezekiel 38:18 *"And it will come to pass at the same time, when Gog comes against the land of Israel," says the Lord GOD, "that My fury will show in My face."*

God is extremely patient with fallen mankind, and He has long held back His judgment and wrath upon the wicked people and nations of the earth. He stood by patiently during the Holocaust, the Gulags, the pogroms and the slaughter of over a

120 million people in the last century alone. He has watched as His people have been maligned, mocked, tortured, and slain for thousands of years.

Every time a Jew is mocked and called an ape by intolerant Muslims and other anti-Semites, it's an insult to God Himself. When His people suffer, He suffers. When His people are mocked, He is mocked. The question is: at what point does God reach His limit to such blasphemy?

It appears that this is precisely that point, when Russia and the Islamic nations finally move against Israel to plunder her for no reason, which is the same as plundering God's land and His inheritance. When the coalition enters the land and Israel finds that they're helpless against their enemies, God finally stands up and moves against the attackers. In fact, He responds in such a dramatic fashion that the entire world finally sees that God is real, and that He means business when it comes to His people.

Ezekiel 38:19-20 *For in My jealousy and in the fire of My wrath I have spoken: 'Surely in that day there shall be a great earthquake in the land of Israel, 20 so that the fish of the sea, the birds of the heavens, the beasts of the field, all creeping things that creep on the earth, and all men who are on the face of the earth shall shake at My presence. The mountains shall be thrown down, the steep places shall fall, and every wall shall fall to the ground.'*

On the day when Gog and his forces move against Israel, God will send a great earthquake throughout the land, probably by shifting the great fault along the Jordan Rift/Valley on Israel's eastern side. While this may not do much to halt the invasion coming from the north, it might be enough to keep their other enemies out which are on the east and south (Syria, Jordan, and even Egypt). The earthquake would also serve to disrupt any naval forces that would be attacking or moving by sea from the tsunamis generated by the earthquakes near the land of Israel.

One reason that God uses an earthquake is to get everyone's attention – and by "all men who are on the earth," He does mean everyone. Another reason is that everyone in Israel will be driven outside by the earthquake to see with their own eyes what God does next: working His salvation in their land and destroying all their enemies.

The jealousy of God that He speaks of is for His land, His people, and for His Holy Name. He has been blasphemed for centuries while His people were in the Diaspora, all the while being patient and merciful. God didn't visibly move against Germany during the Holocaust or Russia during their days of communism, though He certainly could have. He didn't silence the voices of the Islamists when they blasphemed, terrorized, and murdered His people. He heard the cries of His own and held His peace. But He knew that one day, this day would come and that His justice and vengeance upon those nations would be satisfied.

Finally, on this day, God moves to avenge Himself upon those nations and upon Gog and his allies. He shows everyone exactly Who He is, that He's not dead like Nietzsche foolishly declared, and what He thinks about people who attack His land and His people.

God doesn't just intend to get Israel's and the attackers' attention, but the attention of the entire world. During a natural disaster such as an earthquake, people in most areas will check the news as soon as possible to find out what's going on. And when they check the news on their radios, televisions, laptops, and phones, they'll see what happens next in the land of Israel.

There will most likely be a short timespan between the earthquake and God's destruction of the invading hordes, probably just long enough for most people to check themselves over and turn on their TVs, radios, computers, and phones. But to be sure, the entire world will be watching to see and hear what happens next.

Ezekiel 38:21 *I will call for a sword against Gog throughout all My mountains," says the Lord GOD. "Every man's sword will be against his brother.*

Frequently in the Bible, God uses confusion as one of His instruments against an enemy, causing them to be overwhelmed with fear and terror and then destroy each other before Israel routes them. The places this has occurred in the Scriptures before is in the story of Gideon and the earlier battles of Joshua where

God confused their enemies, thereby leaving them vulnerable, if not causing them to destroy one another.

In order to lead such a vast, diverse group of allies in this attack, Russia must have nearly perfect communication with each division and have their command-and-control centers coordinating the entire operation. A massive earthquake that disrupts communications and other military technology could indeed cause confusion among these invading armies, particularly in such a small area as Israel. What happens to all those GPS-guided missiles after the massive earthquake? After all, massive earthquakes have been known to cause large-scale errors on the global-positioning system. If the ground shifts significantly, would some of the missiles fall upon the invading troops?

Another problem with the coalition of the various Islamic nations of the Middle East and Russia is that none of these groups trust each other. When Islamic countries aren't warring against Israel, they are typically warring against one another, which weaken the lands of Islam. Rather than war against themselves, they use the Jews and West as scapegoats to distract from their own tyrannical leaders and governments. The Middle East has not known real peace for over a thousand years, long before Israel was restored to the land.

Ezekiel 38:22 *And I will bring him to judgment with pestilence and bloodshed; I will rain down on him, on his troops, and on the many peoples who are with him, flooding rain, great hailstones, fire, and brimstone.*

The third part of God's response to this invasion force (after the earthquake and His turning their forces against one another) is to send pestilence, which could be a rapid outbreak of diseases, boils, or violent illnesses. Then He subjects the invaders to torrents of rain, hailstones, fire, and brimstone against the armies.

An alternative to the pestilence could be that He uses the coalition's chemical, biological, and nuclear weapons against them. After all, those who live by the sword will die by the sword (Matthew 26:52). These torrents and hailstones would cripple both the clouds of fighter jets, drones, and helicopters in the skies as well as the rapidly moving ground forces.

The "raining of blood" will probably be a supernatural plague sent by God Himself. Frequently in the Bible, God judges a nation by the "gods" they worship. For example, the plagues of Egypt were all really directed against the gods of Egypt, in which God showed everyone that these gods were powerless against Him, the One True God.

Consider the gods that both Russia and Islam worship today: war, bloodshed, death (evolution, abortion, murder, terrorism, etc.), injustice, anti-Semitism, and world domination. If you love war, you'll be given war; if you love to shed blood, you'll be given bloodshed; if you love injustice, you will be given injustice. And if you love terrorism, you'll be terrorized. You reap what you sow, and usually much more of it.

Is God justified in His dealing with Gog, his nations, and these invading forces? Consider all that He has tolerated from those nations over the years. Stalin and Lenin killed tens of millions of their own people without regret, and without ever being brought to justice.

But to be certain, God was watching during those terrible days, and now the time has come for Him to avenge the deaths of those innocent millions.

Ezekiel 38:23 *Thus I will magnify Myself and sanctify Myself, and I will be known in the eyes of many nations. Then they shall know that I am the LORD." '*

The main purposes that God apparently has for this incident is to let the world clearly know the following:

1) That God does indeed exist (despite the "God is dead" rhetoric of recent history, the universities, and the media)

2) That God will intercede upon human actions/history and work out His purposes upon the world.

3) That God is a God of Justice Who will repay nations for their evil deeds and their slaughter of the innocent.

4) That God is the true God of Israel who watches over and protects them, just as He promised.

5) That God will no longer allow His Holy Name to be blasphemed and misused by the religions of the world – especially Islam – which proclaims that they are God's people, not Israel.

6) That God is the God of the Bible and not the Koran or any other religion, and people will see how this incident was written in detail – in the Bible – over 2600 years before it occurred.

7) That God is once again moving on the earth and in history after being silent for centuries, and that the End Times as spoken of in the Bible are about to begin.

XIII. The Aftermath and Cleanup - Ezekiel 39

In Ezekiel 39, God continues the prophecy against Gog and describes how He will destroy the invaders, giving them as a great feast to all the fowls of the earth. An allusion to a nuclear exchange between the nation of Magog and a distant, careless region (or nation?) across the sea is mentioned. Not only is the destruction of the invaders described, but the cleanup of the weapons and the burial of the dead from the attack is detailed. The description of the cleanup effort appears to contain allusions to a decontamination process involving nuclear, biological, or chemical weapons, along with their conversion to fuel supplies for the nation.

The burying and cleansing processes that Israel will undertake in the land are described in detail, and Israel will become renowned for the burial effort by all the people. God also gives additional reasons as to why He brought about the attack and saved Israel in such a spectacular fashion: so that Israel and all the nations of the world would know that He is the Lord.

Lastly, God promises to set His glory among the nations once again and bring back the rest of the Jewish captives from the Gentile nations of the Diaspora.

Ezekiel 39 – Full Text

1 "And you, son of man, prophesy against Gog, and say, 'Thus says the Lord GOD: "Behold, I am against you, O Gog, the prince of Rosh, Meshech, and Tubal; 2 and I will turn you around and lead you on, bringing you up from the far north, and bring you against the mountains of Israel. 3 Then I will knock the bow out of your left hand, and cause the arrows to fall out of your right hand. 4 You shall fall upon the mountains of Israel, you and all your troops and the peoples who are with you; I will give you to birds of prey of every sort and to the beasts of the field to be devoured. 5 You shall fall on the open field; for I have spoken," says the Lord GOD. 6 "And I will send fire on Magog and on those who live in security in the coastlands. Then they

shall know that I am the LORD. *7 So I will make My holy name
known in the midst of My people Israel, and I will not let them
profane My holy name anymore. Then the nations shall know
that I am the LORD, the Holy One in Israel. 8 Surely it is
coming, and it shall be done," says the Lord GOD. "This is the
day of which I have spoken.*

*9 "Then those who dwell in the cities of Israel will go out and
set on fire and burn the weapons, both the shields and bucklers,
the bows and arrows, the javelins and spears; and they will make
fires with them for seven years. 10 They will not take wood from
the field nor cut down any from the forests, because they will
make fires with the weapons; and they will plunder those who
plundered them, and pillage those who pillaged them," says the
Lord GOD.*

*11 "It will come to pass in that day that I will give Gog a
burial place there in Israel, the valley of those who pass by east
of the sea; and it will obstruct travelers, because there they will
bury Gog and all his multitude. Therefore they will call it the
Valley of Hamon Gog. 12 For seven months the house of Israel
will be burying them, in order to cleanse the land. 13 Indeed all
the people of the land will be burying, and they will gain renown
for it on the day that I am glorified," says the Lord GOD. 14
"They will set apart men regularly employed, with the help of a
search party, to pass through the land and bury those bodies
remaining on the ground, in order to cleanse it. At the end of
seven months they will make a search. 15 The search party will
pass through the land; and when anyone sees a man's bone, he
shall set up a marker by it, till the buriers have buried it in the
Valley of Hamon Gog. 16 The name of the city will also be
Hamonah. Thus they shall cleanse the land." '*

*17 "And as for you, son of man, thus says the Lord GOD,
'Speak to every sort of bird and to every beast of the field:
"Assemble yourselves and come; gather together from all sides
to My sacrificial meal which I am sacrificing for you, a great
sacrificial meal on the mountains of Israel, that you may eat
flesh and drink blood. 18 You shall eat the flesh of the mighty,
drink the blood of the princes of the earth, of rams and lambs, of
goats and bulls, all of them fatlings of Bashan. 19 You shall eat
fat till you are full, and drink blood till you are drunk, at My
sacrificial meal which I am sacrificing for you. 20 You shall be*

filled at My table with horses and riders, with mighty men and with all the men of war," says the Lord GOD.

21 "I will set My glory among the nations; all the nations shall see My judgment which I have executed, and My hand which I have laid on them. 22 So the house of Israel shall know that I am the LORD their God from that day forward. 23 The Gentiles shall know that the house of Israel went into captivity for their iniquity; because they were unfaithful to Me, therefore I hid My face from them. I gave them into the hand of their enemies, and they all fell by the sword. 24 According to their uncleanness and according to their transgressions I have dealt with them, and hidden My face from them."'

25 "Therefore thus says the Lord GOD: 'Now I will bring back the captives of Jacob, and have mercy on the whole house of Israel; and I will be jealous for My holy name— 26 after they have borne their shame, and all their unfaithfulness in which they were unfaithful to Me, when they dwelt safely in their own land and no one made them afraid. 27 When I have brought them back from the peoples and gathered them out of their enemies' lands, and I am hallowed in them in the sight of many nations, 28 then they shall know that I am the LORD their God, who sent them into captivity among the nations, but also brought them back to their land, and left none of them captive any longer. 29 And I will not hide My face from them anymore; for I shall have poured out My Spirit on the house of Israel,' says the Lord GOD."

Ezekiel 39 – Verse by Verse Analysis

Ezekiel 39:1-2 *"And you, son of man, prophesy against Gog, and say, 'Thus says the Lord GOD: "Behold, I am against you, O Gog, the prince of Rosh, Meshech, and Tubal; 2 And I will turn you around and lead you on, bringing you up from the far north, and bring you against the mountains of Israel.*

As the passage begins, God repeats the opening verses from the previous chapter – He wants Gog, Israel, and the rest of His audience to know exactly what will happen in the days ahead by emphasizing their names and the invasion.

The King James Version renders the second verse slightly differently, saying that God will "leave but the sixth part of thee" and bring the rest upon the mountains of Israel, while other translations render the verse as God making them fall against the mountains of Israel. The "sixth thee" rendering is unfamiliar to most people today, but it speaks of an almost complete annihilation of the invading forces. The two basic interpretations of the "sixth thee" references are:

1) 1/6th of the forces will be left behind in Russia and the other nations and the 5/6ths that participate in the attack will be completely wiped out.

2) 1/6th of the forces that attack Israel will be left alive (either by fleeing or retreating) and 5/6ths of the invaders are destroyed.

Ezekiel 39:3 *Then I will knock the bow out of your left hand, and cause the arrows to fall out of your right hand.*

As previously mentioned, we should not get too caught up in the precise weaponry involved in the attack, and consider the purpose of each weapon rather than the weapons themselves. The language of swords, bows, and arrows are simply centuries-old renderings of the weapons from the Hebrew and Greek source-texts. When the source-texts were translated, the scholars used the terminology that was familiar or available to them; in our day, weaponry is much different, though the concepts behind most weapons are the same. For example, the modern equivalent of bows and arrows could be launchers and missiles.

Below are some of the ideas and concepts of each of the weapons used, with the Hebrew word in parenthesis:

Sword (chereb) - "any destroying instrument or weapon"
Bow (qesheth) - "a launcher"
Arrows (chets) - "a piercer"

In this verse, God is telling the invaders that He will knock the weapons (whatever they happen to be) from their hands, leaving them disarmed and helpless. The weapons used will probably not be literal swords, bows, and arrows, but in the event of an EMP attack, our modern weaponry would be rendered useless and the attackers would have to resort to using more traditional weapons.

Ezekiel 39:4 *You shall fall upon the mountains of Israel, you and all your troops and the peoples who are with you; I will give you to birds of prey of every sort and to the beasts of the field to be devoured.*

After the invaders are slaughtered by God's wrath (the earthquake, pestilence, hailstorms, etc.), they are left upon the mountains of Israel and are eaten by the vultures and other carrion-eating birds. Muslims today still fear not being buried, and the invaders' bodies are all desecrated by the birds and animals eating their raw flesh.

The idea of giving the defeated peoples' flesh to the birds of the air and beasts of the field speaks of complete, overwhelming destruction and humiliation. The invaders don't even have the opportunity to retreat before they are destroyed. The phrase occurs in several places of the Old Testament, but the most famous reference is in 1 Samuel 17:44 where David challenges Goliath and Goliath mocks him, declaring that he will feed his "flesh to the birds of the air and to the beasts of the field."

Ezekiel 39:5 *You shall fall on the open field; for I have spoken," says the Lord GOD.*

Magog and their hordes were renowned for their incredible horsemanship, and for them to fall upon the open fields was simply unheard of. Open fields and landscapes allow for quick escapes, and for these expert "horsemen" (or pilots?) to fall in that manner would be extremely humiliating for them.

The Scythians were known for lightning quick, brutal attacks and would flee if the battle began going badly for them or if they were encountering an overwhelming force. When attacked by both Napoleon and later Hitler, the Russians withdrew across their lands, using the vast distances and cold weather to their advantage in order to wear out and discourage their enemies – and it worked.

Ezekiel 39:6 *"And I will send fire on Magog and on those who live in security in the coastlands. Then they shall know that I am the LORD.*

While God is crushing the invading forces of Gog against the mountains of Israel, He sends "fire" on their homeland in the distant north, and also against an unnamed people who "live in security in the coastlands." The King James Version renders the phrase as "them that dwell carelessly in the isles," which may offer additional clues as to where this unnamed location is.

As an American or Westerner, this is one of the more disturbing verses in this prophecy because this region is unnamed while most of the other nations involved in the invasion are. Note that none of the invaders inhabit any islands or isles – all the invading forces are land-locked and most of them are coming from the north, south, and east. This verse seems to speak of a distant region far across the sea – to the west.

The phrase "them that dwell carelessly in the isles" literally means "those that dwell securely (without care) or confidently in the distant coastlands or isles." In ancient times, this typically meant a very distant region across the Mediterranean Sea.

However, this phrase can also be interpreted to mean any distant coastlands on the other side of the world. This could be either the British Isles or even the Western Hemisphere, since the British Isles or Spain would likely be referred to as Tarshish again. But this verse seems to be speaking about a land to the west of their known world, which would be the Americas.

Note that the Western Hemisphere has two continents which are very different from one another. North America has traditionally been Judeo-Christian and very pro-Israel and pro-Jewish. However, South America has been filled with upheaval, brutality, and warfare since long before the Spanish ever conquered the continent. Numerous South American countries often side with Israel's enemies today, especially when the Soviet Union was exerting its influence far and wide and was spreading into the Western Hemisphere. There is also a growing Islamic influence in the West, especially among poorer nations, though not nearly as rapidly as in Europe and Africa.

What could be happening in this passage is that God is sending destruction upon the Americas for siding with Israel's enemies and taking part in the attack, even though they had no business on the other side of the world.

However, a more disturbing scenario is that God could be taking vengeance upon the United States for promising to protect and aid Israel, and then abandoning them in their greatest hour of need. Think it can't happen? It did in 2014 in the Gaza War when Israel was under attack from thousands of Hamas rockets and the Obama administration purposely refused to resupply the Israeli self-defense systems. God still says to the world, "Those who bless my people [Israel], I will bless, and those who curse my people I will curse." And God's promises never have an expiration date.

In Matthew 24-25, Jesus Himself will one day judge the nations based upon how they have treated Israel and His people over the centuries, but especially during the Tribulation period. Since even before the Oslo Accords of the 1990s, America has often pressured Israel into accepting terrible peace treaties with their enemies who seek only their destruction.

One way this scenario could come about is that a nuclear exchange occurs between Russia and the United States. If America implores Russia and her allies to stop the invasion of Israel and they refuse, America may launch their missiles at Russia and its forces as they are entering Israel, and Russia responds by launching their own against the United States.

If Russia ever would launch nuclear missiles at the United States, mainly the coastal regions would be targeted, due to the nation's capital and the major population and financial centers being on the coasts: Washington DC, Baltimore, Boston, New York, Los Angeles, San Francisco, and Seattle, just to name a few.

Alternatively, the "distant coastlands" could refer to an entirely different region, such as Malaysia, Siberia, or any other distant region from Israel that has a large coast.

Ezekiel 39:7 *So I will make My holy name known in the midst of My people Israel, and I will not let them profane My holy name anymore. Then the nations shall know that I am the LORD, the Holy One in Israel.*

Today, Israel is a secular state but very observant of the Sabbath and the Scriptural holidays and feasts. However, the majority of Jews do not believe in the God who is regathering them to their land as He said He would, though Israeli Jews are far more religious and observant than American Jews are.

The repetition of the phrase "then they shall know that I am the Lord" heavily suggests that before the Magog Invasion, the Jews will not know God, which is the case of many Jews, Muslims, and other Gentiles today. Imagine billions of people from all over the world watching the invasion and its supernatural destruction. There would be no more widely watched event in all of history!

After God has wiped out the invasion forces so dramatically, Israel as a nation – including the American Jews – the rest of those scattered over the earth will turn back to God and to the prescribed manner of worshipping Him as detailed in the Torah. If there's one event that would cause the Jewish people as a whole to clamor for a new Temple, this would be it.

There is also a possibility that the religious political parties in Israel would be strengthened to exert even more influence over the nation, though that remains to be seen. The Sanhedrin, the religious political body that governed Judea after their return from Babylon was re-established in 2004 after over 1900 years, though they don't have significant power in the secular state at this time.

Along with Israel once again being made aware of God, all the Gentile nations of the world will know that God is the God of Israel, and that He is with the Jews once again. Imagine the shock of over 1 billion Muslims watching as their god Allah is defeated and their armies are destroyed on the mountains of Israel by Jehovah. As a result of such a dramatic defeat, many could be led into abandoning Islam and converting to Judaism or Christianity.

With Israel then turning to God in droves, they will once again be reading the Old Testament and studying it for themselves. However, there is a New Testament, based upon Grace instead of the Law, and the Old has been perfected – made complete – by the New. The 144,000 Witnesses of Revelation could very well spring from the Messianic movement which may occur after the Magog Invasion.

Ezekiel 39:8 *Surely it is coming, and it shall be done," says the Lord GOD. "This is the day of which I have spoken.*

This is one of the days that God has been looking forward to for many, many years – the day that He will avenge Himself upon His enemies, save His people, and once again be worshipped and honored.

Why has God been so patient and long-suffering? So that multitudes of Gentile sons and daughters could be brought into His Family by believing in the Lord Jesus Christ (Romans 11). For two thousand years, the Lord has been grafting the "wild olive branches" (the Gentiles) into His Tree of Life, making a new nation out of all the peoples of the earth: a nation of faith.

The time of the Church Age is drawing to a close, with every tribe, tongue, and nation hearing the Gospel and the message of Grace spreading over the world as never before.

His incredible love, grace, and mercy for mankind is the reason He has delayed moving His hand against the evil rulers and nations of the world for so long. God's love for us is surely greater than His anger and wrath against His enemies.

Ezekiel 39:9-10 *"Then those who dwell in the cities of Israel will go out and set on fire and burn the weapons, both the shields and bucklers, the bows and arrows, the javelins and spears; and they will make fires with them for seven years. 10 They will not take wood from the field nor cut down any from the forests, because they will make fires with the weapons; and they will plunder those who plundered them, and pillage those who pillaged them," says the Lord GOD.*

After the Magog Invasion has been thwarted by God, the land of Israel will be covered with the wreckages of planes, tanks, and transport vehicles, as well as millions of dead bodies from the invading forces. Not only that, but multitudes of guns, bombs, missiles, and other undetonated weaponry. And all of it will need to be cleaned up and removed from the land.

What kind of weapons could Israel burn for seven years? Surely not swords, bows, and arrows! However, there is a kind of weapon that could be converted into energy ("burned") for at least seven years: nuclear weapons. There have also been recent research programs developed that can efficiently convert nuclear weapons into domestic nuclear energy sources.

The shelf-life of most of Russia's nuclear arsenal is between 7-15 years, and they rotate them out every sixth year (depending on the type of warhead) to ensure they will still function properly if/when used. Note the mention of the other weapons which weren't listed previously: javelins and spears – these could be additional types of piercing weapons with modern equivalents, such as warheads and missiles.

Why will Israel burn them for seven years? Probably because that coincides with the period of the coming Tribulation. Not only is God supplying them with all the weapons they need during the Tribulation (as the whole world gathers against them), but their energy needs as well.

Today, Israel gets most of its electricity from a combination of nuclear, hydro-electric, solar, natural gas, and some wind power. With most of their trees being less than sixty years old, it's difficult to see them burning trees for fuel as they did in the past. However, given the enormous quantities of weapons recovered from the coalition, this passage is more suggestive of Israel using the weapons to generate their energy rather than using their existing means. The conversion of nuclear weapons into nuclear energy use is especially applicable to this passage.

Ezekiel 39:11 *"It will come to pass in that day that I will give Gog a burial place there in Israel, the valley of those who pass by east of the sea; and it will obstruct travelers, because there they will bury Gog and all his multitude. Therefore they will call it the Valley of Hamon Gog.*

Given the enormity of the attack, there will be millions of carcasses and bodies to be buried, which will probably be scattered throughout the land (especially from the air-assault).

Traditionally, most commentators assume that the sea mentioned here is the Dead Sea, which is in the middle of the desert. These lands are also downwind from the population centers of Israel and far enough away to not cause contamination problems. Israel is already cramped for space, and the safest, largest place to bury this invasion force is in the wastelands of the Dead Sea.

The problem with this interpretation of the "sea" as being either the Dead Sea or the Sea of Galilee is that those locations aren't in Israel, but in Jordan. In the Bible, those areas would be referred to as Edom, Moab, or Ammon, but certainly not Israel.

Most likely, the sea referred to here is the Mediterranean Sea, also known as the Great Sea in the Bible. This would place the location of the burial site in the Negev, though away from the coasts. The winds would still blow away from the coastal population centers, and the opposing East wind would probably drive any contamination in the air into the south.

The reference that it will "obstruct travelers" is also curious, as the Negev is mostly arid desert land, though there are numerous attempts to farm there. One of the popular resort areas is in the southernmost tip of Israel at Eilat, so the burial site could be along one of the roads that connect to the south.

Ezekiel 39:12-13 *For seven months the house of Israel will be burying them, in order to cleanse the land. 13 Indeed all the people of the land will be burying, and they will gain renown for it on the day that I am glorified," says the Lord GOD.*

Immediately after the destruction of the invaders, all the able-bodied people of Israel – probably at least three million people – will begin to bury the dead. Most of the army, reserves, and civilians will suspend their normal lives for seven full months in order to bury the dead and cleanse the land. The pestilence from all the rotting corpses would create a health crisis if they were left to rot out in the open, so the nation immediately engages in a mass-burial.

In making all the people of the land bury the corpses of the invaders, it will be a continual, graphic reminder to them and the rest of the world at how dramatically God saved them. There will probably be daily reports on the progress of the burial effort, especially since the verse states they will "gain renown for it."

As a side observation, mass shootings and graves were among the Nazis' favorite means of executing the Jews in World War II before the gas chambers were utilized. The Germans would bring a fresh group of prisoners to a site, have them dig a wide ditch, and then execute them so they fell directly into the graves. Then another group would be brought in to cover the mass-grave and then dig a new one for themselves. Hundreds of thousands of people were executed in that fashion.

The mass-burial of Magog and his hordes may be another way of God settling the score with His enemies. How many invaders will be slaughtered and be buried? We cannot know for certain, but we can guess that it'll be in the millions. Since God is just, He could end up slaying the same number of His enemies that they slaughtered of His people during the Diaspora. If that is used as the rough baseline, then at least six million invaders will be buried, and that number is just from the Holocaust – the actual number may be at least ten million.

Ezekiel 39:14 *"They will set apart men regularly employed, with the help of a search party, to pass through the land and bury those bodies remaining on the ground, in order to cleanse it. At the end of seven months they will make a search.*

The huge hordes of soldiers and such will be the first to be buried, but after seven months, the majority of corpses will be buried in the Valley of Hamon Gog. Then most of Israel will return to their former lives, but a group of decontamination specialists will be deployed to comb through the entire land and bury any of the dead who were missed in the mass-burial effort.

Not only will the "professionals" of Israel be searching for the corpses and burying the dead, but there will probably be foreign professionals helping them also.

Ezekiel 39:15-16 *The search party will pass through the land; and when anyone sees a man's bone, he shall set up a marker by it, till the buriers have buried it in the Valley of Hamon Gog. 16 The name of the city will also be Hamonah. Thus they shall cleanse the land."'*

The marking of a discovered bone implies that they may be radioactive or contaminated with biological or chemical weapons' residue. In a toxic cleanup effort, the dangerous areas/bodies are marked by some means and then the professionals come in and safely dispose of the material/remains.

Even if the bones and bodies are not contaminated, it would still be more efficient for one group to be searching and marking their locations and another group following after them that actually collects the bodies for burial. In our modern era, these markers will probably have some type of beacon that gives off a signal so the searchers can quickly find and remove the marked bodies.

Hamonah will probably be an isolated city or the main base-of-operations for the search-and-burial effort, so the professionals burying the dead do not mix in with the general population, so pestilence and diseases are not spread.

Ezekiel 39:17-20 *"And as for you, son of man, thus says the Lord GOD, 'Speak to every sort of bird and to every beast of the field: "Assemble yourselves and come; gather together from all sides to My sacrificial meal which I am sacrificing for you, a great sacrificial meal on the mountains of Israel, that you may eat flesh and drink blood. 18 You shall eat the flesh of the mighty, drink the blood of the princes of the earth, of rams and lambs, of goats and bulls, all of them fatlings of Bashan. 19 You shall eat fat till you are full, and drink blood till you are drunk, at My sacrificial meal which I am sacrificing for you. 20 You shall be filled at My table with horses and riders, with mighty men and with all the men of war," says the Lord GOD.*

This is somewhat gruesome to imagine, but it is what will happen. The vultures and other scavenging birds will come from far and wide to feast on the bodies of the fallen invasion forces.

There's another famous battle in the Bible where a similar event occurs: the Battle of Armageddon (Zechariah 14, Joel 3).

However, in the Battle of Armageddon, most of the armies are gathered in the Valley of Megiddo and the blood flows from Megiddo to Jerusalem (Revelation 14:20, Revelation 19) at a depth of three to four feet! The number of corpses after the Magog Invasion will pale in comparison to those in the Final Battle, which will probably number in the tens of millions.

So why does God orchestrate such a gruesome incident? After all, He could simply vaporize all the invaders and save both Israel and the world a lot of trouble (and upset stomachs) in not having to bury all the dead, but He doesn't. Why would that be?

Having your corpse not buried, or worse yet, desecrated by birds and wild beasts is a horrible shame to Muslims, and it appears that God does just that: He desecrates all their bodies. Having your unburied body eaten by the birds is a curse to Arabs, especially falling in a foreign land against a weaker, unarmed enemy.

The other reason is that He wants both His people and the rest of the world to see over and over what He did and how He saved Israel. The attacks of September 11th claimed the lives of just under 3000 people and exacted an immediate change – almost like a revival – in the United States. Yet within days, most everyone's lives returned to normal, especially those living outside New York. Any glimmer of a spiritual revival began to fade after only a few weeks.

But what would a constant, extended reminder of the destruction do to a person or a nation? It would have lasting, possibly permanent effects. Spending day after day, week after week, and month after month burying the dead and seeing the carnage firsthand would change the heart of the nation forever.

And that gets to the core of what God is doing in this passage: changing the heart of His people Israel and drawing them back to Himself.

Ezekiel 39:21-22 *"I will set My glory among the nations; all the nations shall see My judgment which I have executed, and My hand which I have laid on them. 22 So the house of Israel shall know that I am the LORD their God from that day forward.*

Not only will Israel see God's judgment upon the invaders, but all the other nations will see it also. How could all the nations of the world see what God will do in Israel? Sure, Israel's immediate neighbors would possibly see the destruction and spread the word, but this verse says that "all the world will see it". How is that possible?

At any other time before the mid-Twentieth Century, that would have been impossible. But today, we have our televisions, computers, and phones with which we can watch any event occur anywhere on the earth as it happens. When the Magog Invasion occurs and the invaders are supernaturally destroyed, most of the world will be watching it live, even in parts of the impoverished Third World.

The phrase "I will set My glory among the nations" is a hint that the Jewish Temple will then be rebuilt after nearly two-thousand years. There are several places in the Scriptures (1 Chronicles 22, 2 Chronicles 2, Isaiah 66:9) in which God refers to the Tabernacle or the Temple as being "His Glory," because that was where His Shekinah glory dwelt.

In the past, the primary hindrance to rebuilding the Temple was that there were very few Jews in the region of Palestine. When they did reenter the land, then the Muslims arose and have prevented them from building the Temple due to the Dome of the Rock. However, with all their enemies miraculously defeated – and armed with the knowledge that God is for them once again – the Jews will likely seize the opportunity and rebuild their Temple after the burial of Magog and his hordes is finished.

We know from other End Times passages that the Temple will be standing by the midpoint of the Seventieth Week (three and a half years after signing a seven-year treaty with Israel), because the Antichrist desecrates it. Assuming that the Temple will take at least two or three years to build, Israel will have to start building the Temple either immediately after the Seventieth Week begins or probably even before that, which would place the Magog Invasion before the start of the Seventieth Week.

The Magog Invasion and its aftermath resolves a number of Biblical End Times issues and questions:

1) How does Israel get a temple for during the Tribulation when only a relatively-small percentage of Jews want it today?

2) How does Israel turn from their religion of secular humanism, back to Orthodox Judaism?

3) Why are Russia, Iran, America, and many of the other current world superpowers not mentioned in the End Times/Tribulation passages? China (the kings of the east) is the only world power referenced.

4) What causes Babylon to rise again as a world economic power in the End Times?

Ezekiel 39:23-24 *The Gentiles shall know that the house of Israel went into captivity for their iniquity; because they were unfaithful to Me, therefore I hid My face from them. I gave them into the hand of their enemies, and they all fell by the sword. 24 According to their uncleanness and according to their transgressions I have dealt with them, and hidden My face from them.*"'

The Gentiles will realize that Israel is still God's Chosen people and that they are NOT God's new people, as both the Muslims and growing numbers of Christian teachers foolishly proclaim. The growth of Replacement Theology in the Church is very disturbing, because Jesus Himself specifically condemns those "who say they are Jews (God's people) but are not." (Revelation 3:9). As Paul teaches in Romans 9, God has temporarily set Israel aside because of their unbelief, and also in order that the Gentiles could be brought in to partake in their blessings with God.

The enormity of the destruction of the Magog Invasion will make the Gentiles realize that God was really the one punishing Israel and was merely using them as His instrument of punishment. But now Israel's time of judgment is over, and the Gentiles should be very cautious in how they deal with God's people. After all, Israel is the apple of God's eye. (Zechariah 2:8)

Ezekiel 39:25-26 *"Therefore thus says the Lord GOD: 'Now I will bring back the captives of Jacob, and have mercy on the whole house of Israel; and I will be jealous for My holy name—*

26 after they have borne their shame, and all their unfaithfulness in which they were unfaithful to Me, when they dwelt safely in their own land and no one made them afraid.

The regathering of the Jewish people back to Israel has been happening since the late Nineteenth Century, but mostly since Israel's Statehood in 1948. But after these incredible events, Jews from all over the world will migrate back to Israel – including the six and a half million Jews living in America.

Until recently, there were more Jews living the United States than even in Israel – nearly half of all Jews in the world. America has long been one of the few safe-havens for Jewish people in the world. Anti-Semitism has been mostly non-existent here, and the Jewish people have thrived, contributing much to America and the rest of the world.

However, if America does have a nuclear exchange with Russia and some of her coastal cities are bombed, American Jews may see Israel as the only safe place left in the world to move to, especially after their enemies are miraculously defeated. Anti-Semitism is rising all over Europe again, and there are relatively few Jews left in Russia, Africa, Egypt, and the Middle East who have not migrated to Israel. A nuclear strike on American cities could drive the rest of the Jews to migrate back to Israel, especially if America's economy declines.

Ezekiel 39:27-28 *When I have brought them back from the peoples and gathered them out of their enemies' lands, and I am hallowed in them in the sight of many nations, 28 then they shall know that I am the LORD their God, who sent them into captivity among the nations, but also brought them back to their land, and left none of them captive any longer.*

After the Magog Invasion and the cleanup has finished, and all the scattered Jews have migrated back to Israel, then they – Israel – will know exactly Who has been working in their history: God. And He Who punished them is the same God Who restored and regathered them.

The phrase "and left none of them captive any longer" further indicates that all the Jews in the America and the rest of the

164

Diaspora will migrate to Israel at this time. Once all Israel has been regathered, then the next prophetic event in their history is set to occur: the Seventieth Week of Daniel.

> **Ezekiel 39:29** *And I will not hide My face from them anymore; for I shall have poured out My Spirit on the house of Israel,' says the Lord GOD."*

After these events have occurred and all Israel has been regathered into the land, God will continue working out His plans in history, which begins with the Seventieth Week of Daniel. The Seventieth Week (Daniel 9, Matthew 24) begins when a political leader makes a seven-year treaty of peace/security with Israel. In the middle of that "week," he breaks the treaty and desecrates the Temple, setting himself up as God in the Holy of Holies. At that time, the Great Tribulation commences which will turn Israel – if not much of the world – into a concentration camp.

At some point between the Magog Invasion and the start of the Seventieth Week, the Rapture of the Church will occur in which every believer in Jesus is physically, instantaneously removed from the earth. This must occur in order that the political leader known in the Scriptures as the "Antichrist" can be revealed who then makes the treaty with Israel (2 Thessalonians 2). Consider the vast number of people who will likely become Christians after watching the Magog Invasion – it could literally be God's last call before the Church is called Home.

Some Bible commentators place the Magog Invasion after the start of the Seventieth Week, which is also after the Rapture. The problem with this view is the land of Israel must be cleaned up and the Temple rebuilt in less than three and a half years. The cleanup alone takes at least fourteen months, which leaves just over two years to build the Temple, which would be quite a challenge even in our modern day. The Temple could be standing before the Magog Invasion occurs, though this seems very unlikely, especially since God says He will "set His glory" in Israel (among the nations) once again, implying that it wasn't standing before the attack.

During the Seventieth Week, God will pour out His Spirit upon the Jews, beginning with the 144,000 Witnesses of Revelation 7. However, it will take the rest of the Tribulation period and its horrors to cause Israel to call upon Jesus as their Messiah to save them. Then in one day, the entire nation repents and is converted (Romans 11).

XIV. The Invasion's Missing Nations

From all the details of the attack on Israel as described in Ezekiel 38-39, careful Bible students should notice that there are a number of nations that one would expect to be involved in the Magog Invasion which are strangely missing. The nations not mentioned are: Jordan, Syria, Iraq, Lebanon, and Egypt. Each of these nations confederated to attack Israel in 1948, 1967, and 1973 and frequently oppose them in the international community.

So the question is: why aren't these nations mentioned at all in the Ezekiel 38-39 prophecy? One would think that they would at least have some involvement since they've been involved in all of Israel's previous wars. Yet not even a passing reference for them is given in that passage.

Saudi Arabia (Biblical names: Sheba, Dedan, Kedar)

Saudi Arabia is one of the biggest surprises to be left out of the Magog Invasion, even though it is mentioned briefly in the prophecy. Along with the other Arab nations in the Middle East, Saudi Arabia was also involved in the 1948, 1967, and 1973 wars, but has played a diminishing role since the Six Day War. Incidentally, Saudi Arabia is one of the few nations that protests against the Magog Invasion in Ezekiel 38:13; it takes a neutral position along with Tarshish and her "young lions" who question the attack, but do not ally with the coalition nor do they hinder them.

As the land where Islam was born, Saudi Arabia is one of the more radical Islamic nations in the Middle East, and they have been rapidly building and modernizing their military for the last thirty years. However, they don't seem to be nearly as aggressive as many of their neighbors. They seem to be building their military mainly to defend themselves against Iran, who would gladly like to take possession of the Islamic holy lands and all the Saudi oil.

Saudi Arabia was one of the Arab nations that attacked Israel in 1948, and also directly supported and contributed weapons and troops against Israel in both the Six Day War and the Yom Kippur War. And though they have unofficially supported Islamic terrorists in the past, they have been nominally siding with the United States in the War on Terror. Saudi Arabia has been becoming more moderate over the last two decades, with Saudi women now allowed to vote. The Saudis have even have been attacked by Islamic terrorists themselves.

The sect of Islam that Saudi Arabia has (the Sunni sect) is in direct opposition to the ruling Shiite sect presently in Iran, which is much more radical and militant. For this reason, Saudi Arabia may not be invited to take part in the attack since they may be viewed as having too many Western ties. Also, if the West feels that the world's oil resources are threatened at any time, they might be tempted to intervene on Israel's behalf.

The Saudis have been steadily financing the spreading of Islam, though in a softer manner, such as through the media, building mosques, university outreach, various foundations, businesses, and the education system rather than directly sponsoring terrorism like Iran. The Saudis view Iran as a significant regional threat, both because Arabia and Iran have historically had very contentious relations for centuries (if not longer) and because the monarchy doesn't want more of their people radicalized under the Shiites and potentially overthrow the monarchy.

Recently as the Iranian nuclear threat has grown, Israel and Saudi Arabia have been quietly strengthening their ties, since if and when Iran goes nuclear, Saudi Arabia is high on their list after Israel and America. The new Crown Prince (Mohammed bin Salman) has publicly defended Israel's right to protect their borders against Hamas, as well as saying that Israel has a right to their own land (although he said the same for the Palestinians). With a younger, more liberal Crown Prince and the growing threat from Iran, relations between Israel and Saudi Arabia will likely continue to deepen.

Jordan (Biblical names: Ammon, Moab)

Jordan currently has had a long, stable peace agreement with Israel and has increasingly sided with the West in the War on Terror. Jordan is completely left out of the Ezekiel 38-39 prophecy, though they viciously attacked Israel in all the wars in modern history. Jordan seems to have settled down and stabilized since the Jordan-Israel Peace Treaty of 1994, and today there seems to be an uneasy, yet stable peace between Israel and Jordan.

With the spreading of the "Arab Spring" of 2011, the king of Jordan has been loosening his hold on the country and giving the people more rights in an attempt to prevent the protests from turning into riots. And though there have been demonstrations, there has been little violence between the government and citizens, in contrast to Syria. Jordan continues to keep the "Palestinian Problem" alive, but isn't very vocal in the efforts to give the Palestinians their own state.

As of 2018, Jordan and Israel relations continue to remain steady, despite issues with the Gaza protests, the new American embassy in Jerusalem, and the Temple Mount. Jordan continues to struggle to modernize its economy and recently doubled taxes on food and other staples in order to reduce its budget deficits, which will likely only hurt economic development and domestic conditions. Also, over 650,000 Syrians have sought refuge in Jordan since 2011, and Jordan has recently refused to grant asylum to additional Syrians. It's likely that these economic strains could further destabilize Jordan, and consequently the rest of the region.

From the Bible, Jordan will provide a place of refuge in the wilderness at Petra for the faithful remnant of Israel during the latter half of the Tribulation. In Matthew 24-25, Jesus tells the Jews to flee to the wilderness when they see the Holy of Holies desecrated at the midpoint of the Tribulation. Also in Daniel 11:41, the region of Jordan completely escapes the rule of the Antichrist, though no one really knows why – yet.

Syria (Biblical names: Assyria, Syria, Haran)

Syria has been extremely hostile to Israel since 1948 and has been the primary instigator of all the modern wars against the

Jews (and several of the ancient ones too). Next to Iran, Syria is the other main sponsor of terrorism in the Middle East, and there is much speculation (and good evidence) that the missing WMDs of Saddam Hussein were moved to the Bekka Valley of Syria before the Iraq War of 2003 began. Several times during the Syrian Civil War, Syria has used chemical weapons against its own citizens.

The nation of Syria is not mentioned at all in the Ezekiel 38-39 prophecy, and it's difficult to track down where they really fit into the End Times scenarios. There are some verses that speak of Damascus being destroyed (Isaiah 17), but it's not clear if it's by Israel or one of the other surrounding nations. In the battle between the north and the south in Daniel 11-12, Syria may be one of the "nations of the north" that is mentioned, but it's not entirely clear because the nations aren't specifically named.

In order to move all the invading armies and fighter jets into Israel, Syria may simply allow the Magog invaders to pass through or serve as staging grounds, neither helping them nor hindering them. Israel has threatened to level Damascus if they launch another large-scale attack on them, and Syria apparently takes them at their word. There is also evidence that Israel bombed a nuclear reactor that Syria was building in 2007, which if completed and brought online would have only further destabilized the Middle East.

During mid-2011, protests broke out in Syria in an attempt to oust President Bashar Assad from power, but his security forces squelched the protests. But since then, civil war has been raging throughout the country as the Syrian rebels continue battling the government forces. From 2011 to 2018, more than 500,000 lives have been lost, with many being Christians and other minorities. Tens of thousands of protestors and activists have been imprisoned and tortured, and the civil war has no real end in sight, thought it does appear that the Syrian government forces are winning. Since the beginning of the war, over 5.6 million people have fled the country, with another 6 million being displaced within Syria itself.

One of the most brutal rebel groups to emerge from the Syrian Civil War is the Islamic State of Iraq and Syria (ISIS), though it's sometimes referred to as ISIL (the Islamic State of Iraq and the Levant). ISIS is a very aggressive, fast-moving, highly-organized, well-trained and well-supplied terrorist organization, responsible for the slaughter of thousands of soldiers, security-forces, and other innocents throughout Syria and Iraq. ISIS understands mass-media, propaganda, and how to use them to their advantage, typically by their public beheadings of journalists and other hostages.

While ISIS thrived for years under the Obama administration's confused, top-down policies and inaction, it has nearly vanished within the first year after the Trump administration took over and decentralized the war effort. Also, instead of merely pushing ISIS out of one safe area only to have them flee to another as under Obama, under Trump the military divides, surrounds, and isolates the ISIS strongholds in order to obliterate them.

Iraq (Biblical names: Assyria, Chaldea, Babylon)

Until 2003 when the United States invaded Iraq to depose Saddam Hussein and the Baathist regime, it was highly unlikely that Iraq would miss an opportunity to attack Israel. Iraq has helped Syria and Jordan attack Israel in each of the three modern wars, and also launched numerous Scud missiles into Israeli cities during the Persian Gulf War.

Though Iraq had been on the road to stabilization in 2009, the complete withdrawal of U.S. troops in 2009-2011 ordered by the Obama administration left a great power vacuum in the country, and the Iraqi Prime Minister Nouri al-Maliki quickly used the opportunity to suppress the Sunni minority instead of sharing power as before the American withdrawal. As a result of the suppression, the Sunnis revolted and joined with a new rebel group called ISI, which later morphed into ISIS when it combined with various factions of the Syrian rebels. Under the Obama administration, elements of ISIS were initially trained and supplied by covert American forces during the Arab Spring until about the time of the Benghazi attack on the US consulate in Libya.

During 2013-2014, ISIS moved rapidly through Iraq and captured significant territory, encompassing entire cities like Mosul, several oil-facilities, and continued to surge nearly unopposed since the Obama administration didn't view them as a significant force. The Iraqi army was better suited toward defending against traditional warfare rather than ISIS's fluid, brutal tactics. Also, ISIS managed to recruit many Iraqi troops into their ranks due to the political divide and their fundamentalist ideology. ISIS continued to flourish in both Syria and Iraq until the Trump administration took over in 2017 and changed the primary strategy against ISIS from containment to destruction, and ISIS's influence was greatly diminished over the following year.

Because of ISIS and the lingering effects of the 2003 Iraq War, much of Iraq is still being rebuilt. While progress has been slow since 2017, it's still progress, and after several years of battling ISIS, Iraq is basically back to where it was in 2009 before the US troop withdrawal. While the policies of the Obama administration set back Iraq's recovery nearly a decade, hopefully the country won't fall into sectarian violence and will continue to progress and build their economy.

Like Saudi Arabia, Iraq does not ally themselves in the Magog coalition; this could be due to having similar fears against engaging Iran as Saudi Arabia, or also because they are too weak at the time to get involved. However, like Syria, Iraq could allow the Iranian armies passage through their nation in order to attack Israel.

After the invading nations involved in the Ezekiel 38-39 prophecy are destroyed, Iraq will likely emerge as one of the strongest military forces in the area, along with having the best oil resources next to Saudi Arabia. In fact, most of their enemies and oil competitors will have been wiped out without them having to lift a finger!

Once the entire makeup of the Middle East changes after the Magog Invasion, Iraq is prophesied to quickly grow wealthy and become the economic powerhouse as detailed in Revelation 18. Notice also that each time Babylon is spoken of in an End Times context, she has no king, indicative of being some form of a democracy.

Lebanon (Biblical names: Lebanon, Tyre, Sidon)

Lebanon's modern story is one of tragedy, violence, and a terrible civil war. From World War II to 1975, Lebanon was a modern, prosperous, Westernized nation – their capital Beirut was often referred to as the "Paris of the Middle East." However, in 1975 a civil war broke out between the Arab Christians and the Muslims influenced by Syria and the PLO. The Lebanese paradise was quickly turned into a war-zone, with Beirut being the focus of numerous attacks and retaliation strikes. The PLO used Southern Lebanon to launch strikes against Israel, which Israel then invaded in order to free the Lebanese Christians from the Muslims and the PLO.

For much of the 1980's, Israel used Southern Lebanon as a buffer zone to prevent further attacks on her northern cities. In 2006, Israel invaded Lebanon again to disarm Hezbollah, the Iranian-sponsored terrorist organization which has taken over much of Lebanon. However, within 2-3 years, Hezbollah was all but re-armed by their proxies in Iran and Syria, though they haven't recently attacked Israel since.

As a result of the Syrian Civil War, the country that's been most affected by the refugee crisis has been Lebanon. Since the start of the war, over 1.2 million refugees have fled to Lebanon and now comprise nearly twenty percent of the population. Nearly 2 million people live in Beirut, and the refugee crisis has pushed the city and infrastructure far beyond its limits. Many refugees live in the camps, and most have great difficulty in finding viable employment and basic resources such as food and shelter.

The most recent news out of Lebanon is their 2018 elections' results, which placed Hezbollah (the Iranian-backed terror organization) into the majority in the Lebanese parliament. The more seats that Hezbollah holds in Lebanon's government, the more of an Iranian proxy Lebanon becomes. Between the refugee crisis, the economic strain, and a greater Iranian-foothold, Lebanon is likely to become even more fractured and destabilized.

Lebanon is rarely mentioned in the End Times passages, though they could suffer a similar fate as the Syrians at the hands of the Antichrist as he projects his influence from the center of the Middle East.

Egypt (Biblical names: Egypt, Mizraim)

Egypt is also missing from the Ezekiel 38-39 prophecy, even though they too have never missed an opportunity to attack Israel in modern history. Egypt has been stricken with poverty and economic problems since the building of the Aswan Dam in 1970. Since 1979, they have had a fairly stable peace treaty with Israel.

After Tunisia experienced a revolution in early 2011, the protests swept into Egypt. The longtime president Hosni Mubarak was ousted soon afterwards. For the next few years, Egypt failed to stabilize and became more radicalized due to the Muslim Brotherhood. However, the peace treaty with Israel has held, but the Muslim Brotherhood wants to dismantle it. Throughout the Arab Spring, civil unrest erupted in Egypt with "Egyptian fighting against Egyptian" (Isaiah 19) but stabilized once the military assumed control.

By 2014, Egypt had thrown off the Muslim Brotherhood but wasn't stabilized for another few years. Like other Arab states, Egypt appears to be looking for another strongman/dictator to fix their economic and social problems. If not for the rise of ISIS and the other more-pressing crises erupting throughout the Middle East, Egypt would likely occupy more of the news. The Hamas terrorists in Gaza appear to be causing nearly as many problems for Egypt as they do for Israel, and Egypt continues to keep Gaza isolated to prevent the militants from smuggling in more weapons than they already do.

Like Syria, Egypt is also hinted at in Daniel 11-12 as being present during the Tribulation, and the Antichrist seems to be going back and forth, warring against the south (Egypt?) and the north (Syria?).

A War Before the Magog Invasion?

Again, perceptive Bible students should wonder why all these nations that have always attacked Israel be missing from one of the largest military coalitions in history? Could something have happened to them before the Magog Invasion occurs that will render them insignificant or unable to participate in the Invasion?

How can Israel ever be at peace – at least as described early in Ezekiel 38 – under the current geopolitical conditions of the Middle East? Israel's Arab neighbors have been waging war against them for decades, in spite of Israel's repeated overtures to make peace with them. The Arab nations surrounding Israel do not want peace and usually cannot be bought off with money, land, or anything else.

Most of the Arab nations and their Iranian sponsors want to destroy the State of Israel and drive the Jews into the sea, and they have made it very clear that they will not stop until that happens. Yes, terrorism in Israel has declined dramatically, but only because of the security barriers and the constant patrols, which are hardly a picture of Israel "dwelling securely" in the land.

Is there any place in the Scriptures that gives a hint as to what might have happened to these nations in order that Israel can finally be at peace in the Middle East? As a matter of fact, there are several passages, though the most comprehensive picture of what could happen is often overlooked because it's in the Psalms rather than in any of the Major or Minor Prophetic books: Psalm 83.

XV. The Final Jihad – Psalm 83

Until the last few years, many avid Bible students and prophecy buffs thought the Magog Invasion of Ezekiel 38-39 was right around the corner. But then Israel built the Separation Wall and some of us began to take another look at what the passage said about Israel not having "walls or gates" and reconsidering our position.

In 2008, Bill Salus wrote a book entitled "Isralestine: The Ancient Blueprints of the Future Middle East," which referenced Psalm 83 and other passages to show that the next great war in the Middle East might be one between Israel and her immediate neighbors rather than the nations of Ezekiel 38-39. The nations involved in the attack would therefore be Jordan, Egypt, Lebanon, Syria, and possibly Iraq and Saudi Arabia.

The theory of the book is that the outcome of such a war between Israel and her neighbors – if Israel fights to permanently crush the Arab threat and extinguish all terrorist groups and their sponsors – is that Israel's borders would be greatly expanded and the governments of those nations dismantled. The Arabs would have limited governance over their lands and would be unable to form much resistance. Also, much of the oil supply would then be in the hands of the Israelis rather than OPEC, dramatically increasing the wealth of Israel and reducing OPEC's political power and influence.

For decades, Israel and other Western nations have fought the symptoms of the disease (terrorism) rather than the roots of the disease itself: radical Islam. Like the United States, Israel usually takes a defensive stance against terrorism, but has not gone on the offensive to cut out the root of the problem. It's like fighting a never-ending battle of weeds in the garden: you can pull the weeds week after week, month after month, and year after year (a defensive stance) OR you can go on the offensive and sterilize all the soil to not only kill the weeds, but their roots and seeds. And for at least the last fifty years, the Middle East has needed to be sterilized of radical Islam.

Given that Israel primarily wants peace in a very rough neighborhood, what could cause them to go on the offensive against her terrorist-sponsoring neighbors? What happens when Iran and North Korea begin arming their terrorist groups with nuclear weapons? Could Israel really afford to sit back and not strike first to disarm those terrorists? By Israel going on the offensive in the Arab lands (while securing their own), the Arabs would only be able to use their nuclear weapons against their own cities and people, which would likely make them hesitate. What if Israel struck the capitals of all her enemies and replaced their administrations all in one swoop rather than a prolonged skirmish as they had in Lebanon?

The overthrow of several dictators in the Middle East in the last decade does not bode well for peace, nor for Israel. Many of the people in the nations like Tunisia, Libya, Syria, and Egypt have been radicalized by the Muslim Brotherhood who is now seeking to take control – democratically. Soon the arsenals and militaries of these nations may be under the control of radical Muslims actively seeking Israel's destruction rather than mere dictators content to enrich themselves and control their people.

The passage of Psalm 83 stands out as the blue-print for the next major conflict in the Middle East involving Israel because it seems to accurately describe the geopolitical environment there today. In the passage, Israel's immediate neighbors confederate for a specific purpose: to "cut them off from being a nation, that the name of Israel may be remembered no more." They don't want to invade Israel for her wealth or possessions like those in the Magog Invasion do – this group attacks Israel because they hate her and want her to cease to exist, pure and simple.

Upon a close examination of the passage, it becomes clear that Psalm 83 is almost a prerequisite event to Ezekiel 38-39. They are two different wars, with two different invading confederacies, and with two different objectives. In this passage, Israel begs God to punish their enemies as He did in the times of the Judges, the other time in Israel's history when they did not have a king. However, in the Ezekiel 38-39 passage, there's no indication that Israel is crying out for deliverance (though they likely will). If God hears their cries and they defeat their enemies, the groundwork would be laid for the Magog Invasion. Israel would be secure from her neighbors, they would probably be overconfident as they were after 1967, Israel would become wealthy with all the additional oil resources, and they would no longer have any need of the Separation Wall and the Gaza Barrier.

One item that isn't mentioned in the prophecy of Psalm 83 but may likely occur is that sometime between today and the Magog Invasion, Iran undergoes a dramatic change of leadership. In the Magog Invasion, Iran (Persia) is a major player, but they too are participating in order to plunder Israel, not to cut them off from being a nation. Also, they are subordinates of Russia, not leading the charge as they are attempting to today. It could very well be that during the Psalm 83 War, Israel finally cuts the head off the Shiite snake and gives the governance of the nation back to the Iranian people. It could also be that the people of Iran overthrow their current government between now and the Magog Invasion.

There are no Scriptures that allude to any sort of direct conflict between Israel and Persia, so it could be that Iran is merely a catalyst for the next war in the Middle East. And given how much terrorism the Islamic Iranian government sponsors, they've been filling that role since they came to power in 1979.

Psalm 83 – Full Text

1 Do not keep silent, O God!
  Do not hold Your peace,
  And do not be still, O God!
2 For behold, Your enemies make a tumult;
  And those who hate You have lifted up their head.
3 They have taken crafty counsel against Your people,
  And consulted together against Your sheltered ones.
4 They have said, "Come, and let us cut them off from being a nation,
  That the name of Israel may be remembered no more."

5 For they have consulted together with one consent;
  They form a confederacy against You:
6 The tents of Edom and the Ishmaelites;
  Moab and the Hagrites;
7 Gebal, Ammon, and Amalek;
  Philistia with the inhabitants of Tyre;

178

8 Assyria also has joined with them;
  They have helped the children of Lot. Selah

9 Deal with them as with Midian,
  As with Sisera,
  As with Jabin at the Brook Kishon,
10 Who perished at En Dor,
  Who became as refuse on the earth.
11 Make their nobles like Oreb and like Zeeb,
  Yes, all their princes like Zebah and Zalmunna,
12 Who said, "Let us take for ourselves
  The pastures of God for a possession."

13 O my God, make them like the whirling dust,
  Like the chaff before the wind!
14 As the fire burns the woods,
  And as the flame sets the mountains on fire,
15 So pursue them with Your tempest,
  And frighten them with Your storm.
16 Fill their faces with shame,
  That they may seek Your name, O LORD.
17 Let them be confounded and dismayed forever;
  Yes, let them be put to shame and perish,
18 That they may know that You, whose name alone is the
  LORD,
  Are the Most High over all the earth.

Psalm 83 – Verse by Verse Analysis

1 Do not keep silent, O God!
  Do not hold Your peace,
  And do not be still, O God!
2 For behold, Your enemies make a tumult;
  And those who hate You have lifted up their head.

The psalm immediately begins with an urgent plea for God to arise and come to Israel's defense, to stand up against a massive threat against His people. The word "tumult" brings to mind thousands upon thousands of enemy soldiers rattling their spears and shouting, preparing to charge. Notice that the psalmist doesn't say "our enemies" but "Your enemies," in his plea for God to intervene. The enemies of Israel are typically the enemies of God, and he's making his case that those who attack Israel are really attacking God – and that God should do something about it.

Throughout the Bible, but especially the Old Testament, the writers profess God's love for both His people and His land, though they were often rebuked for their sins. Over and over in the Bible, God is angry with His people and "takes them to the woodshed," but throughout the Scriptures, God looks forward to the day in the future when His people will walk with Him as they were always meant to: by faith. And often, God allows great trials to come about so that people will acknowledge their own helplessness and turn to Him in repentance.

A disturbing trend over the last century is the rising anti-Semitism all over the world, but to see it rising in the Church makes it even worse. You cannot say you love God and His Son but hate Israel and the Jews (or Zionism) – you either hate them all or you love them all. That doesn't mean blindly agreeing with everything that Israel does; they make mistakes and sin just like everyone else. But you cannot profess to love Him and yet hate His people.

The phrase "lifted up their head," is the same idea as "thumbing your nose" or "looking down" at someone – being filled with pride and an air of superiority. The enemies who are attacking Israel are full of pride and arrogance, both of which God absolutely hates. It's bad enough for someone to attack His people, but to do so with such arrogance is something that infuriates Him (Psalm 2, Proverbs 6:16-17). God promises to humble the proud (Proverbs 16:18, Isaiah 2:11), and pride is one of the foremost things He hates (Proverbs 8:13, Amos 6:8).

The psalmist knows God's hatred of pride and jealousy for His people, and uses that in his petition for God to help them.

3 They have taken crafty counsel against Your people,
And consulted together against Your sheltered ones.

4 They have said, "Come, and let us cut them off from being a nation,
That the name of Israel may be remembered no more."

The enemies of Israel are initiating a conspiracy of some sort and are using deception against her. This could be any number of scenarios, from launching missiles from within Israel against her enemies (so they have reason to attack her), provoking an international incident, or other diversionary tactics. The details aren't very specific other than the deception is apparently quite sophisticated and the nations of the confederacy are acting in unison. They are making one final, extraordinary move in order to wipe Israel off the face of the earth.

The phrase "sheltered ones" brings to mind the idea of being protected from a storm, or secure by walls and gates. This is in contrast to "dwelling securely, without walls" as in Ezekiel 38-39; both are safe, but here it's from their defenses rather than from lack of threats.

Part of the "crafty counsel" may likely involve some sort of land-for-peace deal with the Palestinians. The West Bank and Gaza has been a problem for Israel since the Six Day War. Israel needs the land of the West Bank for security reasons, but cannot integrate the two and a half million Arabs into Israel without losing the "Jewishness" of the Jewish State. Israel doesn't want to occupy land or be some type of empire – they simply want to be left alone and have their own Jewish State. There's a clever cartoon by "Cox and Forkum" in which Israel is bewildered that the Arabs are still terrorizing them after the latest land-for-peace deal, and the Arab in the cartoon points to the tiny strip of Israel and says, "Yes, but we want THAT piece." The issue in the Middle East isn't the land that Israel is on, as much as Israel existing at all.

What's the revealed purpose of the invasion? To not merely attack Israel and kill Jews, but to utterly wipe them out as a nation, to drive them into the sea and extinguish their very memory. Does that sound familiar? If you've ever listened to any news from the Middle East, it should – Israel's enemies want to completely destroy her and wipe away any Jewish presence from the land. In 2000, President Clinton and Prime Minister Ehud Barak offered the Palestinians (Yasser Arafat) a state which included 95% of the disputed territories of the West Bank. Shockingly, Arafat rejected the deal and immediately launched the Intifada (uprising) which killed and maimed hundreds of Israelis.

In that moment, even liberal Jews were forced to realize that the Palestinians – or at least their leadership – do not want peace; they want Israel's destruction.

5 For they have consulted together with one consent;
*   They form a confederacy against You:*
6 The tents of Edom and the Ishmaelites;
*   Moab and the Hagrites;*
7 Gebal, Ammon, and Amalek;
*   Philistia with the inhabitants of Tyre;*
8 Assyria also has joined with them;
*   They have helped the children of Lot. Selah*

In the planning and coordination of this attack, a secret alliance or coalition has been formed between the various neighbors of Israel in order to execute the plan. In the previous wars of 1948 and 1967, Israel's enemies faltered because they did not adequately coordinate their attacks with one another, even though they had vastly superior forces and weaponry. But in the Yom Kippur War of 1973, Egypt and Syria did have much better coordination against the Israelis and almost succeeded in defeating the IDF, at least at first.

Some of Israel's military strengths are speed, mobility, and flexibility in their command structure. When conditions on the battlefield change, they are usually quick to adapt and respond, especially in confined spaces. Israel also often takes advantage of her enemies' lack of discipline and military training. When this conflict begins, all the nations that surround Israel will be operating in conjunction with one another to minimize the IDF's effectiveness, likely combining widespread terrorist attacks with coordinated invasions on all three fronts, or four if they also attack from the Mediterranean.

Following the description of the alliance, the nations and peoples of the confederacy are listed: the Edomites (southeastern tribes), Ishmaelites (northern Arabs), Moabites and Ammonites

(Jordan), Amalek and Hagrites (eastern tribes), Gebal and Tyre (Lebanon), Philistia (Gaza), and lastly Assyria (Syria and northern Iraq). Curiously, the terror group ISIS was comprised of elements from Syria and northern Iraq – ancient Assyria. And like the ancient Assyrians, ISIS glories in their ability to strike sheer terror in the hearts of their neighbors, as well as inflict brutal, inhumane acts on their victims. The confederacy of all these enemies will constitute a threat on all three sides of Israel: in the north from Lebanon and Syria, in the east from Jordan and Syria, in the south from Saudi Arabia and Gaza.

For the last several years, the administration of the Gaza Strip by Hamas has proven to be Israel's most troublesome adversary in the region. Following Israel's complete pullout from the Gaza Strip in 2005, Hamas seized control after defeating Fatah in 2007. For all intents and purposes, the Gaza Strip is now run by an Islamic terrorist organization. Since Gaza is essentially blockaded and continuously monitored for illegal arms shipments and terrorist activities, Hamas has spent significant portions of their foreign aid on constructing terror tunnels throughout Gaza, some of which cross into Israel. In 2018, the mass protests and riots on Israel's border (along with launching rockets and kites that start fires), have been the latest in Hamas's attempts to terrorize Israel.

The only modern enemy of Israel that appears to be missing is Egypt. However, it's not quite clear who the Hagrites are and where they lived. There are references that indicate that the Hagrites originally came from Hagar, which could represent the Egyptian people of today, which are more Arab than native Egyptian. The Copts constitute the remnant of the original Egyptian people. Though there is no specific reference in the Bible, it appears that after Abraham sent Hagar away and Ishmael grew up, Hagar remarried and had additional children, who would be a mixture of Arabs and Egyptians (since Hagar was an Egyptian).

The only one that doesn't quite fit (at least at this time) is Saudi Arabia. However, Arabia is really a mixed bag of sorts, since the term "Arab" means "'mixed multitude," and therefore is difficult to pin down. Most scholars state that Sheba and Dedan are represented by Arabia today. Also, Saudi Arabia has somewhat of an unspoken agreement with Israel because of Iran, which wants to take over the entire Middle East, especially the Arabian oil fields and the Muslim holy sites.

Iran and Arabia hate each other almost as much as they hate the Jews, and at this time, Israel (along with the United States) is the only nation in the region that has the capability to halt, slow, or destroy Iran's nuclear program. The Saudis know that if and when Iran becomes a nuclear power and destroys Israel, they're next. The Saudis likely have already purchased nuclear weapons, though they do not have a publicly-known nuclear weapons program at this time. The United States may have secretly installed them on their bases in the region in order to protect the Saudi oil fields.

With that in mind, it remains to be seen whether Saudi Arabia can be accurately included in the list, since the Ishmaelites occupied the northern portions of the Arabian Peninsula, though they migrated far and wide in the region.

At first glance, this battle could have occurred in 1948, 1967, or 1973, though there was no known confederacy with all these nations listed. It also could've happened in the Ammon/Syrian War near the end of King David's reign, though Israel had strong ties to Tyre, again rendering the prophecy incomplete and therefore unfulfilled (2 Chronicles 20, 2 Samuel 8). However, each of those conflicts may have been partial fulfillments of this prophecy.

Notice the absence of any empires, such as the Assyrian Empire, Babylonian Empire, or the Persian Empire – Assyria is mentioned as joining in the confederacy, though they don't appear to be leading it. Perhaps due to the recent civil wars in both Iraq and Syria, they will be mere contributors rather than leaders or instigators of the conflict.

As a result of the recent upheavals in the Middle East referred to as the "Arab Spring," more of the hardline Islamic groups are coming into power for the first time in decades, namely through the Muslim Brotherhood and their offshoots. In the past, these groups were usually outlawed and prevented from having any significant political power. Meanwhile, for decades the former dictators built up their militaries which may soon fall into the hands of ISIS, al Qaeda, or the next Islamic terror group.

The Muslim Brotherhood's stated goals are to purify the Middle East, which means casting all Western influences out, including the nation of Israel. The recent geopolitical earthquakes could very well be the precursor to Psalm 83.

9 Deal with them as with Midian,
  As with Sisera,
  As with Jabin at the Brook Kishon,
10 Who perished at En Dor,
  Who became as refuse on the earth.
11 Make their nobles like Oreb and like Zeeb,
  Yes, all their princes like Zebah and Zalmunna,
12 Who said, "Let us take for ourselves
  The pastures of God for a possession."

The references here are all to the wars of the Judges when God would send a deliverer, before the time Israel had a king and the Midianites and Canaanites harassed, plundered, and enslaved them (Judges 4-8). The Canaanites were an ancient people descended from Ham, Noah's son and were the remnants of the tribes that Israel had failed to drive out of the land during the days of Joshua.

The Midianites originated from Keturah, the second wife of Abraham (Genesis 25) and became a source of idolatry and other problems for Israel when they came up out of Egypt five hundred years later (Numbers 22, 25, 31). While the Canaanites often plundered Israel, the Midianites were ancient terrorists, oppressing Israel to the point of purposely destroying their crops after they had grown and destroying their livestock in an attempt to starve them out of the land (Judges 6).

In this passage, the psalmist is begging God to defeat their enemies as He did in the ancient times. The reference to Sisera and Jabin are from Judges 4 when Israel was being oppressed by the Canaanites and their chariots of iron. The Lord routed the Canaanites before Barak and Deborah, and their army was humiliated by the slaying of their mighty commander Sisera at the hand of Jael, the wife of Heber, while he slept after drinking warm milk.

Oreb and Zeeb were two Midianite princes while Zeba and Zalmunna were the two Midianite kings (Judges 7-8) that Gideon defeated with his three hundred men. In Judges 7:22, the

Lord uses a curious way of defeating Israel's vast enemies with such a small army: He turned them against one another so Israel's enemies destroyed one another. This is a tactic God uses several places in the Old Testament – confusing Israel's enemies in order that they destroy one another, a particularly humiliating means of defeat.

13 O my God, make them like the whirling dust,
* Like the chaff before the wind!*
14 As the fire burns the woods,
* And as the flame sets the mountains on fire,*
15 So pursue them with Your tempest,
* And frighten them with Your storm.*

The psalmist continues his plea to God to trample their enemies to dust and wipe them out, completely obliterating them. Consider all the pain, suffering, and anguish the Arab nations around Israel have caused her over the years, not just allowing terrorists among them to harass Israel, but often sponsoring and helping them. Imagine getting a phone call or hearing on the news that the bus your child was riding on has been blown up, or the pizza place your teenager hangs out at has been bombed.

Now imagine that occurring hundreds of times on a regular basis, to the point where you don't even know if you'll see your own children again when they go to school or to the mall. Yet that's what the people of Israel have had to live with for decades.

16 Fill their faces with shame,
* That they may seek Your name, O LORD.*

This verse is one of the more curious ones of the passage, because it almost seems as if the psalmist is pleading that their enemies will repent and turn to the Lord. The enemies appear to be full of pride and arrogance, which is why the writer is praying that they will be shamed and humbled. One cannot come to God if they're full of pride, and James 4:6 declares that God even opposes the proud but shows favor (or mercy) to the humble.

If there's one characteristic that typifies Israel's enemies today, it's pride. Listen to the Iranian president, the leaders of Hezbollah and Hamas, and all the Muslim protesters – they are filled with arrogance and pride. They shout "We will destroy Israel!", "Kill those who insult Islam!", and "Islam will dominate the world!"

Can you imagine any other religion or nation saying such things? Of course not – they are deceived by their own hearts and continue to war against Israel even though they've been defeated over and over. At what point will they come to their senses and realize that destroying Israel, America, and Europe will not help them solve their problems?

17 Let them be confounded and dismayed forever;
*   Yes, let them be put to shame and perish,*
18 That they may know that You, whose name alone is the
*   LORD,*
*   Are the Most High over all the earth.*

The psalmist concludes his prayer with a petition that Israel's enemies will be put to shame and perish, yet he also wants them to know that God is the One True God. That implies that their enemies are worshiping a god other than the God of the Bible, a false god. The King James Version renders the name "Lord" in the verse by God's true name, "Jehovah" (or YHWH): *"That men may know that thou, whose name alone is JEHOVAH, art the most high over all the earth."*

What is the name of the god the Muslims worship, who they declare is the one true god? Allah – not Jehovah – is their god's name. Though the media and the Muslims confuse the masses by declaring that both are the same, in reality they are very, very different. The following excerpt details the numerous differences between Allah and Jehovah (http://www.chick.com/bc/2000/samegod.asp).

Allah

Unknowable: Allah is so transcendent, so exalted, that no man can ever personally know Allah.

Nonpersonal: Allah is not to be understood as a person. This would lower him to the level of man.

Nonspirit: The idea that Allah is a person or a spirit is considered blasphemous and demeans the exalted One.

Unitarian: The Koran specifically denies that Allah is a father, that Jesus is the Son of God and the Holy Spirit is God.

Unlimited: The Koran describes Allah as able to do anything, anytime, anyplace, anywhere. He is not even limited by his own nature.

Capricious: Allah in the Koran is totally capricious and untrustworthy. He is not bound by his nature or his word.

No Love: The concept of Allah having feelings toward man is foreign to Islamic teaching. That would reduce Allah to a mere man and is blasphemous to a Muslim.

Passive in history: Allah does not personally enter into human history. He deals with the world through his word, prophets, and angels. He does not personally deal with man.

No attributes: The so-called 99 attributes of Allah are all negative, what he is not like. No positive attributes are listed.

Works: There is no savior or intercessor or concept of grace in the Koran.

Jehovah

Knowable: Jesus Christ came into the world so we could know God personally (John 17:3).

Personal: The God of the Bible is spoken of as a person with intellect, emotion, and a will.

Spirit: That God is a spirit was taught by Jesus Christ himself in John 4:24.

Trinitarian: The Bible reveals God as One in three persons, the Father, the Son, and the Holy Spirit. All share equally the divine nature.

Limited: The biblical God is limited by His own nature. He cannot lie or contradict Himself.

Trustworthy: Because God is always true to His nature, he is completely trustworthy and consistent.

Love: The biblical God's chief attribute is love as shown in such places as John 3:16. He has feelings for his creatures, especially man.

Active in history: In the incarnation, God himself enters history and acts to bring about man's salvation.

Attributes: The Bible gives us both positive and negative attributes.

Grace: The God of the Bible provides a free salvation for man through a Savior who acts as an intercessor between God and Man (1 Timothy 2:5).

Note that none of the nations involved in the Psalm 83 War are involved in the Magog Invasion of Ezekiel 38-39. The nations of the Psalm 83 War are: Lebanon, Syria, Saudi Arabia, Jordan, Iraq, Egypt, and various terrorist groups (Hamas, Hezbollah, Islamic Jihad, etc.), while the nations of the Magog Invasion are: Russia, Iran, Turkey, Germany, Sudan, Libya, Islamic nations of Central Asia, and possibly northern Afghanistan.

A sobering thought to consider during the eight years of the Obama administration was: "What if the US military is being used to make the world safe for the Muslim Brotherhood?" At first glance, the idea seems absurd – however, in the name of "democracy," the US already helped the Muslim Brotherhood toss out three dictators who have been in power for years: Tunisia, Egypt and Libya. Those governments have been thrown out with little thought as to what they would be replaced with, and now the Muslim Brotherhood had grown in power and influence tremendously.

Democracy is a wonderful instrument when wielded by decent and moral people, but is easily corrupted into mob rule. So what happens if democracy is demanded by a widespread, radical Islamic group against a long-ruling dictator? On the surface, it seems their cause is just – the citizens of a country should be able to determine the government of that nation. But what if the people have been radicalized? By intervening in the name of democracy, we could have succeeded in only creating several more radicalized Islamic nations.

Other passages which may also correlate to the Psalm 83 War are Isaiah 17 and Jeremiah 49, which also speak about the destruction of Israel's neighbors. Isaiah 17 specifically concerns an attack which will destroy Damascus and turn it into heaps of ruins and cease from being a city, even though it has been continuously inhabited for over 4300 years. As the Syrian Civil War enters its seventh year, both the United States and Russia (not to mention Israel, Turkey, and Iran), are standing opposite sides. Some speculate that the long war in Syria – as well as Assad's use of chemical warfare – could drag America and Russia into a much bigger war, which would all be centered around Damascus.

Isaiah 17

1 The burden against Damascus.

"Behold, Damascus will cease from being a city,
   And it will be a ruinous heap.
2 The cities of Aroer are forsaken;
   They will be for flocks
   Which lie down, and no one will make them afraid.
3 The fortress also will cease from Ephraim,
   The kingdom from Damascus,
And the remnant of Syria;
   They will be as the glory of the children of Israel,"
Says the LORD of hosts.

4 "In that day it shall come to pass
   That the glory of Jacob will wane,
   And the fatness of his flesh grow lean.
5 It shall be as when the harvester gathers the grain,
   And reaps the heads with his arm;
It shall be as he who gathers heads of grain
   In the Valley of Rephaim.
6 Yet gleaning grapes will be left in it,
   Like the shaking of an olive tree,
Two or three olives at the top of the uppermost bough,
   Four or five in its most fruitful branches,"
Says the LORD God of Israel.

7 In that day a man will look to his Maker,
    And his eyes will have respect for the Holy One of Israel.
8 He will not look to the altars,
    The work of his hands;
He will not respect what his fingers have made,
    Nor the wooden images nor the incense altars.

9 In that day his strong cities will be as a forsaken bough
    And an uppermost branch,
Which they left because of the children of Israel;
    And there will be desolation.
10 Because you have forgotten the God of your salvation,
    And have not been mindful of the Rock of your stronghold,
Therefore you will plant pleasant plants
    And set out foreign seedlings;

11 In the day you will make your plant to grow,
    And in the morning you will make your seed to flourish;
But the harvest will be a heap of ruins
    In the day of grief and desperate sorrow.

12 Woe to the multitude of many people
    Who make a noise like the roar of the seas,
And to the rushing of nations
    That make a rushing like the rushing of mighty waters!
13 The nations will rush like the rushing of many waters;
    But God will rebuke them and they will flee far away,
And be chased like the chaff of the mountains before the wind,
    Like a rolling thing before the whirlwind.

14 Then behold, at eventide, trouble!
    And before the morning, he is no more.
This is the portion of those who plunder us,
    And the lot of those who rob us.

Jeremiah 49 is not quite as clear because it's interspersed with the invasion of the Babylonians under Nebuchadnezzar. However, the destruction of Ammon is curious because it looks forward to the day in which Israel (which had been exiled long before) will take over the ruins of their cities. Repeated in the passage is another proclamation against Damascus, along with the tribes of Kedar, the Arab tribe from which Mohammed (the founder of Islam) was born.

Lastly, the passage of Jeremiah 49 concludes with a proclamation against Elam, one of the sons of Shem from which the nation of Persia came, which is Iran today. A close examination of the Elam passage shows that the attack upon Iran (via Israel or another group of nations) specifically targets the leadership of the nation, but not the people themselves: "I will set My throne in Elam, and will destroy from there the king and the princes." After the attack, many in the Iranian power structure ("the outcasts") will be disbursed and exiled so the nation is no longer a hotbed of Islamic radicalism.

Jeremiah 49

1 Against the Ammonites.
   Thus says the LORD:
"Has Israel no sons?
   Has he no heir?
Why then does Milcom inherit Gad,
   And his people dwell in its cities?

2 Therefore behold, the days are coming," says the LORD,
   "That I will cause to be heard an alarm of war
In Rabbah of the Ammonites;
   It shall be a desolate mound,
And her villages shall be burned with fire.
   Then Israel shall take possession of his inheritance," says the LORD.

3 "Wail, O Heshbon, for Ai is plundered!
   Cry, you daughters of Rabbah,
Gird yourselves with sackcloth!
   Lament and run to and fro by the walls;
For Milcom shall go into captivity
   With his priests and his princes together.

4 Why do you boast in the valleys,
  Your flowing valley, O backsliding daughter?
Who trusted in her treasures, saying,
  'Who will come against me?'
5 Behold, I will bring fear upon you,"
  Says the Lord GOD of hosts,
"From all those who are around you;
  You shall be driven out, everyone headlong,
  And no one will gather those who wander off.
6 But afterward I will bring back
  The captives of the people of Ammon," says the LORD.

7 Against Edom.
  Thus says the LORD of hosts:
"Is wisdom no more in Teman?
  Has counsel perished from the prudent?
  Has their wisdom vanished?
8 Flee, turn back, dwell in the depths, O inhabitants of Dedan!
  For I will bring the calamity of Esau upon him,
The time that I will punish him.
9 If grape-gatherers came to you,
  Would they not leave some gleaning grapes?
If thieves by night,
  Would they not destroy until they have enough?
10 But I have made Esau bare;
  I have uncovered his secret places,
And he shall not be able to hide himself.
  His descendants are plundered,
His brethren and his neighbors,
  And he is no more.
11 Leave your fatherless children,
  I will preserve them alive;
And let your widows trust in Me."

*12 For thus says the LORD: "Behold, those whose judgment
was not to drink of the cup have assuredly drunk. And are you
the one who will altogether go unpunished? You shall not go
unpunished, but you shall surely drink of it. 13 For I have sworn
by Myself," says the LORD, "that Bozrah shall become a*

desolation, a reproach, a waste, and a curse. And all its cities shall be perpetual wastes."

14 I have heard a message from the LORD,
  And an ambassador has been sent to the nations!
"Gather together, come against her,
  And rise up to battle!
15 "For indeed, I will make you small among nations,
  Despised among men.
16 Your fierceness has deceived you,
  The pride of your heart,
O you who dwell in the clefts of the rock,
  Who hold the height of the hill!
Though you make your nest as high as the eagle,
  I will bring you down from there," says the LORD.

17 "Edom also shall be an astonishment;
  Everyone who goes by it will be astonished
  And will hiss at all its plagues.
18 As in the overthrow of Sodom and Gomorrah
  And their neighbors," says the LORD,
"No one shall remain there,
  Nor shall a son of man dwell in it.

19 "Behold, he shall come up like a lion from the floodplain of
  the Jordan
  Against the dwelling place of the strong;
But I will suddenly make him run away from her.
  And who is a chosen man that I may appoint over her?
For who is like Me?
  Who will arraign Me?
And who is that shepherd
  Who will withstand Me?"

20 Therefore hear the counsel of the LORD that He has taken
  against Edom,
  And His purposes that He has proposed against the
  inhabitants of Teman:

Surely the least of the flock shall draw them out;
    Surely He shall make their dwelling places desolate with
    them.
21 The earth shakes at the noise of their fall;
    At the cry its noise is heard at the Red Sea.
22 Behold, He shall come up and fly like the eagle,
    And spread His wings over Bozrah;
The heart of the mighty men of Edom in that day shall be
    Like the heart of a woman in birth pangs.

23 Against Damascus.
    "Hamath and Arpad are shamed,
For they have heard bad news.
    They are fainthearted;
There is trouble on the sea;
    It cannot be quiet.
24 Damascus has grown feeble;
    She turns to flee,
And fear has seized her.
    Anguish and sorrows have taken her like a woman in labor.
25 Why is the city of praise not deserted,
    the city of My joy?
26 Therefore her young men shall fall in her streets,
    And all the men of war shall be cut off in that day," says the
    LORD of hosts.
27 "I will kindle a fire in the wall of Damascus,
    And it shall consume the palaces of Ben-Hadad."

28 Against Kedar and against the kingdoms of Hazor, which
    Nebuchadnezzar king of Babylon shall strike.
Thus says the LORD:
    "Arise, go up to Kedar,
    And devastate the men of the East!
29 Their tents and their flocks they shall take away.
    They shall take for themselves their curtains,
All their vessels and their camels;
    And they shall cry out to them,
    'Fear is on every side!'
30 "Flee, get far away! Dwell in the depths,
    O inhabitants of Hazor!" says the LORD.

"For Nebuchadnezzar king of Babylon has taken counsel against you,
And has conceived a plan against you.

31 *"Arise, go up to the wealthy nation that dwells securely,"*
says the LORD,
"Which has neither gates nor bars, dwelling alone.
32 *Their camels shall be for booty,*
And the multitude of their cattle for plunder.
I will scatter to all winds those in the farthest corners,
And I will bring their calamity from all its sides," says the
LORD.
33 *"Hazor shall be a dwelling for jackals, a desolation forever;*
No one shall reside there,
Nor son of man dwell in it."

34 *The word of the LORD that came to Jeremiah the prophet*
against Elam, in the beginning of the reign of Zedekiah king
of Judah, saying, 35 *"Thus says the LORD of hosts:*

'Behold, I will break the bow of Elam,
The foremost of their might.
36 *Against Elam I will bring the four winds*
From the four quarters of heaven,
And scatter them toward all those winds;
There shall be no nations where the outcasts of Elam will not
go.
37 *For I will cause Elam to be dismayed before their enemies*
And before those who seek their life.
I will bring disaster upon them,
My fierce anger,' says the LORD;
'And I will send the sword after them
Until I have consumed them.
38 *I will set My throne in Elam,*
And will destroy from there the king and the princes,' says the
LORD.
39 *'But it shall come to pass in the latter days:*
I will bring back the captives of Elam,' says the LORD."

The references to this handful of nations and cities, Damascus, Elam, and Kedar are rather scant in the Scriptures, though their descendants are playing a major role in the Middle East conflicts today.

As the Middle East becomes increasingly destabilized due to ISIS and the Syrian Civil War, many supposed that the Iranian nuclear threat had faded to the background, but that didn't last long. Near the end of his presidency, Barack Obama personally pushed a nuclear deal with Iran that basically lifted sanctions against them in exchange for suspending their nuclear program (along with $150 billion in cash). While the Iranian president and the propagandists fell silent for a time, their nuclear ambitions never really changed. In the spring of 2018 as the Trump administration was considering pulling out of the terrible Iran nuclear deal, Israel published tens of thousands of secret Iranian files showing how they were subverting the agreement. Trump pulled out of the nuclear deal with Iran shortly afterward, and it's likely that the tough sanctions against Iran will resume.

There's an enormous propaganda war being waged on both sides of the Israel-Iranian conflict, though Israel certainly has great cause to be alarmed at Iran's actions and vitriol. Both the President and Supreme Leader of Iran have plainly stated on several occasions that they will "wipe Israel off the map" – and the Israelis are taking those threats very seriously. However, while Israel may threaten to attack Iran, they would not purposefully target innocents and civilians as the Iranian regime would. If and when Israel does attack Iran, it will be to disarm or overthrow the regime, not annihilate the Iranian people.

For the last two decades, both Israel and the United States have been using various means to slow down Iran's nuclear ambitions, from computer viruses such as Stuxnet and the Flame, crippling economic sanctions, inflation and currency wars, and also targeted bombings and assassinations against high-profile nuclear scientists and other officials (though neither side will publicly admit it). Thankfully, Obama's disastrous nuclear deal with Iran didn't last more than a year or two and the pressure to stop Iran's nuclear ambitions will resume.

Of all the free nations in the world, the United States alone has the means to obliterate Iran's nuclear program and remove the extremist Islamic regime from power, but they don't have the will – under both the Bush and Obama administrations, the foremost policy against Iran was dithering and pretending that the threat either doesn't exist or that it isn't as bad as it seems. It would do well for the American policy-makers to understand that destroying Israel may not be the Shiites' primary objective in remaking the Middle East: removing the United States of America from being the world's superpower is. The only real force restraining Iran from controlling most of the oil in the Middle East is the United States – but when Iran finally has nuclear weapons, the balance of power in that region will quickly tip in their favor.

While the relationship between Israel and the United States was very strained by Barack Obama's confusing, inconsistent policies and the issue of the Palestinian Authority in Samaria (the West Bank) – not to mention the Iranian nuclear deal – Donald Trump has been moving quickly to restore and strengthen the ties between Israel and the United States. After formally recognizing Israel's capital as Jerusalem, in May 2018 the United States moved its embassy from Tel Aviv to Jerusalem, further cementing our alliance and friendship.

As for permanently stopping Iran's nuclear program, little has been said from the United States other than pulling out of the nuclear deal. It remains to be seen whether Israel will have to face the Iranian threat alone and take matters into their own hands.

XVI. In Today's Language

One of the reasons why the Ezekiel 38-39 prophecy can seem so cryptic at first glance is because it's written with ancestral names for the nations involved instead of modern nations. By using the ancestral names of places and regions instead of the specific name for a country, the current nations and peoples can be deciphered regardless of how national borders and names may change over time. Also, by using the ancestral names of the people involved, the modern country involved may change as the named people-groups migrate from one area to another. For example, Gomer's sons migrated far to the west of Asia Minor and Central Asia, one of whom was Ashkenaz, the ancestor of the Germanic tribes.

The other problem often encountered in interpreting Bible prophecies is that we stumble over specific terms such as horses, chariots, bows, and arrows which often may be communicating ideas and concepts rather than those specific objects. The Ezekiel 38-39 prophecy has clearly not occurred yet in history, yet it's quite difficult to imagine modern nations using such crude forms of weaponry when we have so many advanced weapons available to us.

A curious example of ancient terms possibly being used to describe modern weaponry is found in Jeremiah 50:9:

> *For behold, I will raise and cause to come up against*
>   *Babylon*
>   *An assembly of great nations from the north country,*
> *And they shall array themselves against her;*
>   *From there she shall be captured.*
> *Their arrows shall be like those of an expert warrior;*
>   *None shall return in vain.*

Note the peculiarity of the last verse – it's the arrows which are not missing their target, not the bowmen shooting the arrows. And while it could just be a poetic description of none of the arrows missing, it could be something more. Until twenty years ago, the idea of a self-guided "arrow" would have been considered absurd, but now we have GPS-guided missiles, smart-bombs, and other wonders of modern warfare which puts the accuracy into the projectile itself, rather than relying on the accuracy of the launcher.

The following is a list of the weapons and equipment referred to in the Ezekiel 38-39 prophecy with the original Hebrew word in italics, followed by the common rendering and then its modern equivalent.

Sword (*chereb*) – a sword, knife, destroying weapon. Modern equivalent: a gun, weapon, knife.

Bow (*qesheth*) – a launcher used for arrows/darts. Modern equivalent: a missile launcher.

Arrow (*chets*) – a sharp piercing shaft, dart, arrow. Modern equivalent: a missile, rocket.

Shield (*magen*) – a small shield, protection device. Modern equivalent: armor or defense shields.

Horse (*cuwc*) – a leaper, horse, or swift bird. Modern equivalent: a jet fighter, helicopter, bomber.

Chariot (*rekeb*) – a driven/pulled vehicle of war. Modern equivalent: a tank, armored vehicle.

The list of nations mentioned in the Ezekiel 38-39 prophecy can also be deciphered using a similar mechanism; the name is listed in bold, followed by the region of settlement, and then the modern nation occupying that region today.

Magog – settled north of the Caucasus Mountains. Modern nation: Russia, Khazakstan.

Rosh – settled in Taurus Mountains near the Vulga River. Modern nation: Russia.

Meshech – settled in Moschian Mountains. Modern nation: Russia, Georgia.

Tubal – settled in eastern section of Black Sea. Modern nation: Georgia, Turkey.

Persia – settled east of East of Tigris and Euphrates Rivers. Modern nation: Iran.

Ethiopia – settled northern and eastern Africa. Modern nation: Ethiopia, Niger, Sudan.

Libya – settled in northern Africa. Modern nation: Libya, Algeria.

Gomer – settled near Rhine and Danube Rivers, north east regions of Europe. Modern nation: East Germany, Poland, Czechoslovakia and other Slavic nations.

Togarmah – settled in Asia Minor and Central Asia. Modern nation: Turkey, Armenia.

Sheba/Dedan – settled in the Arabian peninsula. Modern nation: Saudi Arabia, Yemen, Arab Emirates, Oman.

Tarshish/young lions – settled the far western isles/coastlands. Modern nation: Britain and her derivatives (United States of America, Australia, Canada).

How would the text of Ezekiel 38-39 read if it was uttered today with our modern weaponry and current nations? Using those deciphered/updated terms, a rough transliteration can be composed:

Ezekiel 38

1 Now the word of the LORD came to me, saying, 2 "Son of man, set your face against Gog, of the land of Russia, the prince of Russia, Georgia, and Turkey, and prophesy against him, 3 and say, "Thus says the Lord GOD: "Behold, I am against you, O Gog, the prince of Russia, Georgia, and Turkey. 4 I will turn you around, put hooks into your jaws, and lead you out, with all your army, jet fighters, and pilots, all splendidly armed, a great company with armored vehicles and tanks, all of them handling weapons. 5 Iran, Ethiopia, Algeria, Sudan, and Libya are with them, all of them with armor and helmet; 6 Germany, the Slavs, and all their troops; the house of Armenia from the far north and all its troops, many people are with you.

7 "Prepare yourself and be ready, you and all your companies that are gathered about you; and be a guard for them. 8 After many days you will be visited. In the latter years you will come into the land of those brought back from the sword and gathered from many people on the mountains of Israel, which had long been desolate; they were brought out of the nations of the

Diaspora, and now all of them dwell safely. 9 You will ascend, coming like a storm, covering the land like a cloud, you and all your troops and many peoples with you."

10 "Thus says the Lord GOD: "On that day it shall come to pass that thoughts will arise in your mind, and you will make an evil plan: 11 You will say, "I will go up against a land of unwalled villages; I will go to a peaceful people, who dwell safely, all of them dwelling without walls, and having neither security fences nor gates" 12 to take plunder and to take wealth, to stretch out your hand against the waste places that are again inhabited, and against a people gathered from the nations, who have acquired products and goods, who dwell in the midst of the land. 13 Saudi Arabia, the merchants of Britain, and America, Canada, and Australia will say to you, "Have you come to take plunder? Have you gathered your army to take treasure, to carry away silver and gold, to take away products and goods, to take great plunder?"

14 "Therefore, son of man, prophesy and say to Gog, "Thus says the Lord GOD: "On that day when My people Israel dwell safely, will you not know it? 15 Then you will come from your place out of the far north, you and many peoples with you, all of them riding in jet fighters, a great company and a mighty army. 16 You will come up against My people Israel like a cloud, to cover the land. It will be in the latter days that I will bring you against My land, so that the nations may know Me, when I am hallowed in you, O Gog, before their eyes." 17 Thus says the Lord GOD: "Are you he of whom I have spoken in former days by My servants the prophets of Israel, who prophesied for years in those days that I would bring you against them?

18 "And it will come to pass at the same time, when Gog comes against the land of Israel," says the Lord GOD, "that My fury will show in My face. 19 For in My jealousy and in the fire of My wrath I have spoken: "Surely in that day there shall be a great earthquake in the land of Israel, 20 so that the fish of the sea, the birds of the heavens, the beasts of the field, all creeping things that creep on the earth, and all men who are on the face of the earth shall shake at My presence. The mountains shall be thrown down, the steep places shall fall, and every wall shall fall to the ground." 21 I will call for a sword against Gog throughout all My mountains," says the Lord GOD. "Every man's weapon

will be against his brother. 22 And I will bring him to judgment with pestilence and bloodshed; I will rain down on him, on his troops, and on the many peoples who are with him, flooding rain, great hailstones, fire, and brimstone. 23 Thus I will magnify Myself and sanctify Myself, and I will be known in the eyes of many nations. Then they shall know that I am the LORD."

Ezekiel 39

1 "And you, son of man, prophesy against Gog, and say, "Thus says the Lord GOD: "Behold, I am against you, O Gog, the prince of Russia, Georgia, and Turkey; 2 and I will turn you around and lead you on, bringing you up from the far north, and bring you against the mountains of Israel. 3 Then I will knock the launchers out of your left hand, and cause the missiles to fall out of your right hand. 4 You shall fall upon the mountains of Israel, you and all your troops and the peoples who are with you; I will give you to birds of prey of every sort and to the beasts of the field to be devoured. 5 You shall fall on the open field; for I have spoken," says the Lord GOD.

6 "And I will send fire on Russia and on those who live in security in America. Then they shall know that I am the LORD. 7 So I will make My holy name known in the midst of My people Israel, and I will not let them profane My holy name anymore. Then the nations shall know that I am the LORD, the Holy One in Israel. 8 Surely it is coming, and it shall be done," says the Lord GOD. "This is the day of which I have spoken."

9 "Then those who dwell in the cities of Israel will go out and collect all the weapons, both the armor, the launchers and missiles, the warheads and guns; and they will convert and use them for fuel for seven years. 10 They will not buy or use their own energy resources anymore, because they will convert your weapons into energy; and they will plunder those who plundered them, and pillage those who pillaged them," says the Lord GOD.

11 "It will come to pass in that day that I will give Gog a burial place there in Israel, the valley of those who pass by east of the Mediterranean Sea; and it will obstruct travelers, because there they will bury Gog and all his multitude. Therefore they will call it the Valley of Hamon Gog. 12 For seven months Israel

will be burying them, in order to decontaminate the land. 13 Indeed all the people of the land will be burying, and they will gain renown for it on the day that I am glorified," says the Lord GOD. 14 "They will set apart professional disposal teams, with the help of a search party, to pass through the land and bury those bodies remaining on the ground, in order to decontaminate it. At the end of seven months they will make a search. 15 The search party will pass through the land; and when anyone sees a man's bone, he shall set up a beacon by it, till the disposal teams have buried it in the Valley of Hamon Gog. 16 The name of the city will also be Hamonah. Thus they shall decontaminate the land."

17 "And as for you, son of man, thus says the Lord GOD, "Speak to every sort of bird and to every beast of the field: "Assemble yourselves and come; gather together from all sides to My sacrificial meal which I am sacrificing for you, a great sacrificial meal on the mountains of Israel, that you may eat flesh and drink blood. 18 You shall eat the flesh of the mighty, drink the blood of the princes of the earth, of rams and lambs, of goats and bulls, all of them fatlings of Bashan. 19 You shall eat fat till you are full, and drink blood till you are drunk, at My sacrificial meal which I am sacrificing for you. 20 You shall be filled at My table with pilots and soldiers, with mighty men and with all the men of war," says the Lord GOD.

21 "I will set My Temple among the nations; all the nations shall see My judgment which I have executed, and My hand which I have laid on them. 22 So the house of Israel shall know that I am the LORD their God from that day forward. 23 The Gentiles shall know that the house of Israel went into captivity for their iniquity; because they were unfaithful to Me, therefore I hid My face from them. I gave them into the hand of their enemies, and they all fell by the sword. 24 According to their uncleanness and according to their transgressions I have dealt with them, and hidden My face from them."

25 "Therefore thus says the Lord GOD: "Now I will bring back the captives of Jacob, and have mercy on the whole house of Israel; and I will be jealous for My holy name 26 after they have borne their shame, and all their unfaithfulness in which they were unfaithful to Me, when they dwelt safely in their own land and no one made them afraid. 27 When I have brought them

back from the peoples and gathered them out of their enemies' lands, and I am hallowed in them in the sight of many nations, 28 then they shall know that I am the LORD their God, who sent them into captivity among the nations, but also brought them back to their land, and left none of them captive any longer. 29 And I will not hide My face from them anymore; for I shall have poured out My Spirit on the house of Israel," says the Lord GOD.

XVII. After the Magog Invasion

After analyzing Ezekiel 38-39 in depth and reviewing all the various nations involved, some questions remain as to exactly why Russia is leading the coalition when it rarely has taken such a visible military role in the past. Not only that, this coalition will be massive and widespread, something that Russia has had little experience with in the past.

Organizing a military coalition and subsequent invasion force against another nation is not an insignificant operation, particularly when the two primary nations don't border one another. In fact, Russia is more than 3,000 miles away from the northern tip of Israel. Why would Russia embark on such a massive endeavor instead of merely using proxy nations such as Turkey, Iran, and Syria as they have in the past? And following the failed Magog Invasion, what will the Middle East look like?

Russia's Reasons to Invade

The nation of Russia is dying – whether they will admit it or not. It's been estimated that by 2050, Russia will have lost over 20% of her native population. The Russians are simply not having enough children to sustain themselves, like much of the rest of Europe. The Magog Invasion could be an attempt to quickly revitalize their nation and prevent their collapse.

Even today, Russia has a number of political and economic reasons to invade the Middle East:

1) Control of over 50% of the world's developed oil and natural gas wells and proven reserves
2) Almost instant economic dependence of the United States, Europe, and possibly China
3) Further isolation (if not the peaceful defeat) of the United States of America
4) By the attack, Russia would become the new world superpower and control the energy supply

5) Russia would gain the loyalty and praise of the entire Islamic world by destroying Israel
6) Russia would obtain a warm water port on the Mediterranean
7) Due to the location of Israel at the junction of three continents, Russia could project her influence over much of Europe, Asia, and Africa
8) The wealth of Israel, most of which appears to be gained in the near-future as a result of the Psalm 83 War

Even though they have radically different motives, cultures, and long-term goals, Russia has been making alliances with Iran and other Islamic nations since they became a nuclear power in the 1950s. With its population decreasing at an alarming rate, Russia knows that it will be reduced to a second-rate nation within the next thirty years. Russia has recently become economically stable, but by corruption and their mafia-government union led by Putin and others. And though they have limited sources of revenue (mainly in energy resources such as natural gas), they still have one of the most powerful and best-equipped militaries in the world.

By spearheading the Magog Invasion, does anyone really expect the Russian-Islamic confederacy to last? Probably not – the Islamic nations would likely expect Russia to return to the north or that they could drive them out later. Russia would likely give them the land but retain control over the Israeli sea ports and energy supplies. Russia also fears the radicalism of Iran in their own sphere of influence, which is one of the reasons why they partner with them (keep your friends close but your enemies closer). Russia may even use the confusion of the Magog Invasion to destroy some of the Muslim forces, which could backfire on them quickly. Military weapons and equipment can be replaced much faster and easier than manpower can, and Russia has weapons but not the population or the troops. The Middle East has the opposite: too many men and not enough weapons.

Below the surface, it appears that for Russia, the goals of world-domination may have never really changed, just the mechanism and presentation of how to attain those goals. Russia's immediate threats are the influence of the United States in the West and China in the East. Russia would not risk a catastrophic war with either, but it could accomplish the same result if it were able to isolate America from the world-scene and get them out of the Middle East long enough to establish a stronghold that's more than just their proxies in Syria. The brazenness of the attack would probably cause China to step back, especially if their energy needs are maintained. Central to every industrialized nation is having a stable energy supply, which means oil. China may not be all that concerned with the Magog Invasion if their energy supply is not interrupted.

Once firmly planted in the Middle East and surrounded by her Islamic allies, Russia could dramatically change her future as a dying world-power.

For this Purpose

However, why would God allow the Magog Invasion in the first place? The text of Ezekiel 38-39 is quite clear that He not only allows this event, but practically orchestrates it to reveal Himself to His people Israel and turn them from their current state of unbelief. Israel is currently a secular state, very similar to the United States and Europe, with no "official" religion. The world Jewish population is almost evenly divided between Israel and America. Jews in Israel are much more religious than their Western counterparts, and most Jews in the West are atheists or secular humanists. Also, not many Jews in the West want to relocate to Israel – at least not at this time.

But the Magog Invasion could change all that – the declared purpose is stated over and over in the Book of Ezekiel: "Then they shall know that I am the Lord." After the supernatural salvation of Israel, the Jewish people as a whole will realize that God has saved them and they will turn to Judaism as the answer. The passage of Ezekiel 38-39 will be read and re-read by most of the world, if not everyone in Israel, and they will KNOW that God has interceded on their behalf.

Also, the six and half million Jews living in America may migrate back to Israel after the attack. It's not entirely clear in the Scriptures when all Israel will be regathered, but we know that promise will be kept. However, it is likely that the vast majority of the Jews will be dwelling in the land of Israel when the Seventieth Week of Daniel begins.

Not only would God make His Name known by all the people of the world, He could also use His destruction of the invasion forces to judge the nations of the Magog Invasion. Has the slaughter of millions of innocent people by these nations in the days of communism, persecution under Islam, and the Holocaust ever really been avenged? Not so you'd notice. God is a God of Justice, and sooner or later, He repays nations for their evil, especially when the evil is by a government upon its own inhabitants. Under communism, Russia slaughtered over sixty million people and enslaved millions more. The government of a nation is supposed to protect their people and their natural rights, not murder and enslave them.

Also in this judgment, God may be giving these invading armies exactly what they worship: death. In Proverbs 8:36, God says that "all they that hate me love death." Neither communism nor Islam promote life – but both worship and revere death, especially the death of the innocent. Communism worships death in its promotion of atheism and evolution, while Islam worships death in its glorification of terrorism and martyrdom. In Islam, the only real guarantee of going to Paradise is to die in jihad, or a holy war. So when God destroys these invading forces, He may just be giving them what they seek: martyrdom and death.

In October of 2004, the Sanhedrin of Israel was re-established for the first time in over 1900 years. Some Bible scholars and students have seen this as a significant development in moving further towards the End Times. The basis for this is Hosea 5:15, in which God/Jesus states that He will not come back until they ask Him to. Since the Jewish rulers of Israel were the ones who officially rejected Jesus as their Messiah at His First Coming, it's likely that the same ruling party will have to be the ones to petition Him to return.

After the Magog Invasion, the returning of Israel to Judaism may even change Israel's entire system of government. They may give the power back to the Sanhedrin, instead of the various coalition governments which they have today. Once the Sanhedrin is back in power, their primary move would be to rebuild the Temple and re-establish the worship there. However, Judaism still follows the Old Covenant, and sadly, it will take the horrors of the Tribulation to turn them from Judaism to Jesus, who will then save them and put His Spirit in them as described in Ezekiel 36-37.

Peace in Our Time

After the events of Ezekiel 38-39, the world will be completely shocked at the outcome and will likely demand widespread disarmament of nuclear weapons in order to guarantee that such a horrific attack will never again take place. Incidentally, one of the characteristics of the Antichrist (false Messiah) is that he will be a brilliant peacemaker and a conqueror. The prophet Daniel says that through peace, he will destroy many (Daniel 8:25). Even in our day, there is an outcry for peace without regards for the people being oppressed, or the threat that is being diminished by military action. Historically, peace treaties have seldom proven to be of more worth than the paper they were written on.

War in itself is not evil, only its reasons and actions – just like peace. War has freed many countries from the cruel hands of tyrants and has liberated millions of slaves. The Civil War in the United States put an end to slavery not just in America, but in many other parts of the world. The Revolutionary War freed a nation from a tyrannical king and opened the doors of freedom and democracy for many other nations. When the War in Iraq began in 2003, many on the left side of the political spectrum cared nothing for freeing the people of Iraq from Saddam Hussein (and the rest of the Middle East). They simply wanted there to be no war at any cost.

It's quite interesting to observe the recent, world-wide spreading of democracy. God intends for people to be free and to choose their own forms of government, but democracy is not necessarily its best form because morality is left to the whims of the people. Democracy is often weak, fickle, and unstable, since it changes with the whims of the people, who can be easily influenced and deceived, especially in our days of mass-media.

Democracy in its purest form is mob-rule, and the Founders of the United States rightly feared pure democracy because of how easily and frequently the majority crushes the rights of the minority. Democracy makes such violations entirely legal – but just because something is legal doesn't make it moral. So the Framers eschewed pure democracy and built a representative republic in which the nation is ruled by the people indirectly through the rule of law, not by the people directly.

During the events of the Tribulation, the world as a whole will choose the Antichrist to be their leader – some directly, and others through their representatives. God is just, and it fits with His Character to give everyone a choice in the end, so no one can say they were forced to do or believe against their will. The last decision that billions will one day make is to choose the "mark of the beast" or not. (Revelation 13-14)

After the Tribulation (in the Millennium), people will no longer have their choice of government, at least not quite like how we do today. There will be one King: Jesus Christ, the King of Righteousness. And He will rule and reign whether the people like it or not.

Spinning it Away

Forty-eight times in the book of Ezekiel, the phrase "they shall know that I am the Lord" occurs – more often than all the other places in the Bible combined. Clearly, this is the main point of the Book of Ezekiel, in addition to revealing much of God's plan to restore the nation and the people to Himself.

Throughout history, Satan has opposed God at every turn, starting at his fall and continuing until he is finally cast into the Lake of Fire. One of the primary mechanisms he employs to thwart God's Plan and Word is to minimize, trivialize, or rationalize prophecy when it's fulfilled just as God has detailed in His Word. Initially, Satan attempts to prevent prophecies from being fulfilled, but after he fails, he then either explains them away or trivializes them so they don't have a more significant impact.

Satan doesn't really care how or what he has to do to subvert God's plan – he simply uses whatever mechanism he thinks will work. Throughout the Bible, Satan adapts and focuses his attacks to subvert God's plan in prophecy, starting with corrupting Eve's first son Cain to kill Abel (and thus destroy them both), trying to wipe out Israel by the Pharaoh, and then trying to extinguish the Messianic line by evil kings, wars, and Herod. As previously examined, one can see that Satan was trying to subvert the restoration of Israel in 1948 by raising up Hitler and instituting the Holocaust shortly before Israel was foretold to become a nation.

With that in mind, how could Satan possibly trivialize, minimize, or rationalize the catastrophic events of the Magog Invasion as described in Ezekiel 38-39? After all, the entire world will be able to watch (and re-watch) the supernatural events on their phones, computers, televisions, and the Internet. How could such events be explained without attributing them to God?

Consider the following details of the Magog Invasion that Satan will have to work really hard to explain away after God supernaturally wipes out the invading forces:

1) A world-wide earthquake, with its epicenter probably at Jerusalem (and destroying the Dome of the Rock?)
2) At least 5/6ths of the invading armies supernaturally destroyed by rain, blood, hail, firestorms
3) "Fire" (a nuclear exchange?) sent upon Russia and the "distant coastlands"
4) The precise identification of all the nations that attack Israel written 2600 years before

Could it be that rather than deny that God caused these events to transpire, Satan will simply attribute them to another god or supernatural being? And if so, what could some of those gods or supernatural beings be?

After considering this theory, you may find it helpful to read C.S. Lewis's "The ScrewTape Letters," which provides some interesting insights (with a touch of comedy) as to how Satan and his forces work to subvert God's plans and the lives of people who are opening to God. Satan's primary tool is and always has been deception, and the deception that's 99% truth but has a 1% lie is typically very difficult to catch, but easy to swallow. But once it's digested, the amounts and potency of the lie can soon be increased. Rat poison is 99% food with 1% poison, but still quickly kills the rats.

If you were the enemy, how could you minimize, confuse, distort, or even take credit for prophetic events? During the Tribulation, the wrath of God will be clearly seen, and yet man will still refuse to repent and then even takes up arms against God Himself at Armageddon!

How can you get people to think that they're with God but are really not? How can you ensure that people won't change sides and start believing the Bible when prophetic events are fulfilled before their very eyes?

Connecting the Loose Ends

Of all the prophetic events in the Bible, there are two significant events that have no clear timing: the Magog Invasion of Ezekiel 38-39 and the Rapture. Most of the events in the other passages can be easily timed and ordered, but those two cannot. The Rapture passages fit best in the prophetic timeline by occurring before the revealing of the Antichrist (known as the Pre-Tribulation view) according to 2 Thessalonians 2.

The Magog Invasion could either happen before or after the Rapture occurs, but would probably have to occur before the Temple is rebuilt, which the Antichrist desecrates at the Tribulation midpoint. The context of Ezekiel 38-39 is that the Jewish people as a whole do not know that God is the one who is protecting them and that by destroying their enemies, He reveals Himself to them very dramatically. After this, Israel as a nation turns to God, though not to faith in Jesus as their Messiah. Whenever a national crisis occurs and people suddenly begin seeking answers, they reach out for whatever religion is prevalent in their society, whether it is Christianity, Islam, Judaism, paganism, or whatever else they believe saved them.

Before introducing a theory about how the Magog Invasion could be rationalized or explained away by Satan, please attempt to set aside your biases and pre-conceived notions about the End Times, and approach it with a fresh, open mind. And of course, be like the Bereans (Acts 17:11) and check it out by Scripture as best as you can, and then re-evaluate it. Remember, it's only a theory, but it ties together and explains some of the End Times events rather well.

A Counterfeit-Alien Connection?

When God thwarts the Magog Invasion, it will be in a manner so spectacular that the entire world will know that only God could have protected Israel and wiped out the invaders. So how can Satan prevent the world from running to their Bibles and turning to God by the millions as a result of His actions? The best way is for Satan to simply start telling the world that someone else did it, and introduce a supernatural group of beings from outside our world to take credit for it: perhaps fallen angels or demons disguising themselves as "aliens".

Chuck Missler and Mark Easton have an excellent book called "Alien Encounters" that details how many of the UFO/alien abductions are very similar to accounts of demon possession, and the various links into the New Age. The book describes how these UFOs/aliens must be spiritual in nature and how they helped bring about the previous world judgment (the Flood) by deeply corrupting mankind. The New Agers that channel some of these alien groups are even saying that one day they will reveal themselves dramatically to the whole world (the Magog Invasion?), instantly remove the evil forces that hinder man from evolving further (the Rapture of Christians?), and then introduce a super-man (the Antichrist/false messiah) who will guide the world through seven years of cataclysm (the Tribulation) and then into a thousand-year period of peace and prosperity (the Millennium).

By these angels/aliens explaining to the world what will happen in advance (from their false point of view), the world will remain faithless in God and ally themselves more with these false aliens as more events of the End Times unfold.

After the thwarted Magog Invasion, the evil angels (portraying themselves as aliens) could introduce themselves to the entire world as the "defenders and protectors of Israel and the Earth." They could say they've been patrolling Israel and have interceded to prevent world-wide destruction. Israel, as a matter of fact, is a major focal point of current UFO sightings today. Also, most of the UFO sightings and abductions started occurring AFTER 1948 and have been increasing since then.

The aliens could then say that they've saved us from ourselves and are here to bring peace to the world. In the End Times, Satan knows his time is short – and he will pull out all the stops in his attempts for universal domination. If one-third of all the angels in heaven fell with him, wouldn't he use every resource at his command in order to pull off the last great deception before the Messiah returns?

In the End Times, Israel will either trade their nuclear arms for peace or simply get rid of them after all their enemies have been wiped out, which could be part of the seven-year deal they make with the Antichrist in order to secure/build the Temple. What would it take for Israel to give up their weapons for promises on a piece of paper? How about a personal guarantee of protection from a supernatural source or the one they believe is the Messiah? The aliens/angels would have already proven themselves in protecting Israel by claiming to have thwarted the Magog Invasion.

The Rabbis in Israel today frequently say they will know who the Messiah is when he helps them rebuild their Temple. Unfortunately, the Bible never says to use that to identify the Messiah – we are to use fulfilled prophecy from the Word of God and the fruit He produces.

With the world then focused on them, the aliens could begin educating people about their previous involvements in history, such as the Great Pyramid, Stonehenge, the times before the Flood, and other Out Of Place Artifacts of the earth that don't fit into the current evolutionary framework. And they will assure the world that they are here to help man take the next big step of evolution: immortality/godhood. They will certainly be sure to cite the Ezekiel 38-39 passages as proof about their intervention to help, protect, and save mankind.

However, there will be some who simply cannot "adapt," and with the Rapture increasingly imminent, they may use the idea that millions will be instantly removed from the earth to be "re-educated." Biblical Christians and Orthodox Jews are the primary groups on earth that have remained adamantly against man-becoming-god and evolution, and thus the most difficult to deceive. While the Bible is silent about whether most children and infants will be raptured, the deceivers could also explain their removal away by the same means: to accelerate their education into the New World.

If the Rapture has already been described and explained away before it occurs, then it almost becomes a non-issue, with some parents even becoming excited about their children's disappearances. A surprise is no longer a surprise if you know it's coming. The Bible never says that the Rapture causes wide-spread panic, unlike how the "Left Behind" book series describes the event. People will be more focused on the angels/aliens, and if the annoying Christians disappear, who will care?

Also, the Bible never says that the Apostasy will cause churches to empty – it just says that the faithful believers will be removed before the "man of sin" (the Antichrist) is revealed. In fact, if aliens arrive before the Rapture, the churches will probably fill up, but the teachings will become very, very false and apostate. The best place to explain away the Rapture and render it as a non-event is in the very churches that people will be flocking to after the events of Ezekiel 38-39.

Paul declares in 2 Thessalonians 2 that the Apostasy occurs before Rapture, so the false teachings in the churches will become even more muddied than they already are. Which would be noticed more: 100 people raptured from a church of 100, or 100 raptured from a church of 10,000? But after the Rapture, people will be still deluded until things get really bad, especially at the midpoint of the Tribulation where the Antichrist declares himself to be God.

After the Rapture, the Antichrist is revealed and either helps Israel rebuild their temple or guarantees its protection for seven years. The angels/aliens could even help rebuild the Temple itself, further cementing the faith of Israel in them and the false Messiah. Notice the progression: the return of Israel to the land in Ezekiel 36-37, their salvation/protection in Ezekiel 38-39, and Temple details in Ezekiel 40-48.

The angels/aliens don't even really need to provide any advanced technology of their own – the basis of the world religion is already in place, along with cashless/body-mark technology – the aliens simply help globally distribute it. The Bible says that Satan and his helpers will deceive the world through lying wonders (2 Thessalonians 2:9), and what could be a bigger lie than trying to take credit for what God did in the Magog Invasion?

The Two Witnesses of Revelation 11 could be explained away as representatives of the aliens' enemy that's coming, and this explanation will help the aliens later. The actions of the Two Witnesses (drought, fire, hail, bloody water) will cause world-wide hatred of them and lays the foundation for Armageddon, when Satan gathers the entire world against God.

As the seven-year period draws to a close, Satan could portray Jesus as his enemy-alien counterpart who has been wreaking havoc on the earth, and that they need all the world's help to destroy Him when He returns with His armies. How could Satan/the Antichrist possibly rally the entire world to attack God Himself? By telling them that He's simply a stronger, evil invading alien force and that all of mankind must gather to defeat Him.

The Antichrist and the angels/aliens may frequently use and distort parts of Revelation to further show that their enemies are the ones causing all the problems, that the Bible is just written in strange, cryptic, spiritual terms from their adversary's point of view. People tend to believe in what they SEE, and the Antichrist will make sure everyone sees him and his helpers do many miracles. And it's just like Satan to call good evil and evil good.

The Singularity

Another emerging technology trend which plays into the End Times is the idea of the "Singularity," the point in which the Man and Machine are joined together in such a way that Man's limitations are overcome and the next step in Man's "evolution" begins. As the lines between Man and Machine become increasingly blurred because of technology, immortality by artificial means becomes more of a possibility – or so the futurists think. This subject was explored in my fiction book called "The Exchange" in which a group of scientists finally broke the Man-Machine barrier.

Though "The Exchange" was a work of fiction, many of the plot elements are built upon current trends and research areas within the scientific world. The primary source used for most of the computer and scientific plot elements were Ray Kurzweil's book, "The Singularity Is Near: When Humans Transcend Biology." In fact, one of the main characters draws heavily upon Kurzweil's own arguments and desires. And while many of the ideas such as brain-uploading and mind-transfer are at this time fictitious, that is precisely what leading futurists and scientists such as Kurzweil want to achieve: prolonged life, transcendence, or even immortality.

The Singularity movement is speeding towards the goal of overcoming biology on three different fronts: genetic engineering, nanotechnology, and robotics/artificial intelligence. These three fields (referred to as GNR) appear to be converging towards the Singularity in about the next thirty to forty years, when they project that mankind will be able to free himself from his biological shackles. Consider the benefits of preserving brilliant, courageous individuals who have contributed to humanity such as Albert Einstein, Ronald Reagan, Gandhi, or Winston Churchill.

Though these futurists and scientists may believe they are striving to help humanity by artificially multiplying life-expectancies, they are essentially going against numerous biological constraints that God has set in place for us. Of course, there's nothing wrong with wanting to live longer or prolonging our lives by pacemakers or medicine, and we are admonished to take care of our bodies.

However, at some point there's a certain boundary that is crossed when the desire to prolong life becomes a quest to achieve a sort of counterfeit immortality. If you consider ideas such as the Singularity from a Scriptural perspective, the final goal comes into focus: subverting the Curse and achieving immortality without God. Of course, those goals are seldom stated – or perhaps not even recognized by the futurists – but that is the underlying goal.

Some observers have nicknamed the Singularity a 'religion for nerds' because it has all the elements of a typical religion, even though it's clothed in scientific garb. In this religion, our fallen state is due to the incomplete process of evolution, the reason for our existence is completely accidental, and our destination is to achieve immortality by means of our own cleverness and ingenuity.

While reading "The Singularity," I was immediately struck by the absence of any notion of sin or fallen state of man. We all inherently have a deep conviction that the world is not as it should be and that we must try to rectify what the world is with what it should be. That's why we build cities, create medicines, and invent things. However, it's one thing to want to improve our lives, live longer, and make a better world, but quite another to rebel against our own mortality. Immortality without God would likely be a pointless or even horrific existence.

Another significant missing element in Kurzweil's book is the fact that man is an inherently spiritual creature, which is largely because we somehow know that something is terribly wrong with the world and that 'Something' (or Someone) greater than ourselves exists. I attribute this deep internal conflict directly with the Fall of Man in the Garden of Eden – something deep inside us 'remembers' Paradise, yet that place is nowhere to be found. How can such deep-seated memories and internal conflicts exist if we are merely sophisticated forms of organized dust? If evolution is true, why aren't we content with the world we have evolved into?

Throughout the book, Kurzweil frequently refers to our minds and bodies as weak or lacking, especially when measured against the computers we have recently created. He seems highly critical – even bitter at times – towards our current state, even though he believes we are all a product of evolution. With that philosophy, is our current imperfection our fault? Of course not – but under the Biblical model, it indeed is.

The goal of the Singularity movement can be summed up in one thought: "We can be gods ourselves!" Many in the movement may scoff at that statement, but make no mistake – that is the goal. Because of our sin, we are destined for death – unless Someone greater than ourselves intervenes and takes our place. Unless Someone redeems us from our corrupted bodies of death.

God has graciously, incredibly provided the means for our salvation, but like every other religion in the world, the Singularity seeks to achieve the same immortality but without God, and certainly without His Redeemer.

If we look ahead and give the proponents of the Singularity the benefit of the doubt and all they dream about somehow occurs, what will be created? Supercomputers that are conscious, self-aware beings that will soon be infinitely smarter than we are.

Who will ultimately be in control of these supercomputers, machines, and the nanobots? That seems to be the primary question that none of the futurists are really asking. If such machines become conscious, won't they be just as spiritually and morally vacant as we are – if not more-so? If that occurs, it's only a matter of time before they recognize that humanity – through our wars, corruption, and resource consumption – is the primary threat to their existence.

And once that realization occurs, what will they do? If they are much smarter, faster, and stronger than we are, what's to prevent them from wiping us out? In the philosophy of evolution, the new race is always threatened by the previous race, and their existence cannot be secure until the old race is completely obliterated.

Understand that fallen creatures such as ourselves making fallen super-beings will only create a hellish world – of that there is no doubt. The philosophy of evolution is based entirely upon widespread death, suffering, and mass-extinctions. But futurists such as Kurzweil fail to recognize that fact, and they are loathe to admit that the world is getting worse, not better. As a biological entity, humans are declining and weakening, even though our intelligence among tiny, select groups is rapidly increasing.

Let's say that the Singularity comes into existence and humanity is able to be 'upgraded'. What happens to the people who want to remain as they are, even at the expense of the new 'race'? Will the upgrades be forced? That happens in the world of computers and software all the time.

What about the believers in Christianity, Judaism, or even Islam who refuse to 'assimilate'? Will there be forced, mass-extinctions decreed so that humanity can move into the next phase of our 'evolution'? Will mankind be someday forced to interface with the supercomputers against our will – perhaps in the form of an RFID tattoo, a 'mark', or implantable chip so that we cannot buy or sell anything without their permission?

The proponents of the Singularity assure us that such events will not happen, but again they ignore humanity's propensity for inventing new forms of evil. When the goals of Singularity and the philosophies of its proponents are taken into account with Biblical prophecy, startling pictures of the End Times suddenly begin to emerge.

Biblical References to Counterfeit-Aliens?

There are several hints in the Bible that the fallen angels (or demons) who rebelled with Satan will be a part of the End Times scene. According to Genesis 6:1-4 and Jude 1:6, some of the angels who rebelled with Satan began mating with women, and they produced unnatural offspring (called the Nephilim), such as giants and possibly other strange creatures.

This occurred both before the Flood to corrupt all mankind, and also afterwards in the land of Canaan to corrupt (or at least keep out) the tribes of Israel. Most of the times in the Old Testament in which God commands Israel to wipe out every man, woman, child, and animal of a certain tribe or nation, it's because these people have mixed with the angels or the Nephilim. These giants were the same ones that so badly frightened 10 of the 12 scouts who had spied out the land after the Exodus (Numbers 13:33), and the later giants of Gath (such as Goliath).

One of the stranger hints at a future "invasion" of these angels is found in Daniel 2:43, in which he mentions that the last part of the fourth kingdom is made up of a fragile coalition, but the peculiar language that he uses reads: *"And whereas thou sawest iron mixed with miry clay, they shall mingle themselves with the seed of men: but they shall not cleave one to another, even as iron is not mixed with clay."* Unfortunately, the "they" is not defined in the passage, but in order for "them" to "mingle themselves with the seed of men", "they" need to be something other than mankind. What could be described here is a future attempt at genetic engineering between these angels/demons and mankind, but it isn't quite as stable as in the past when producing hybrid offspring.

221

A clearer passage that describes an alien/angelic manifestation is in Revelation 16:12-14, in which a set of demonic spirits/creatures is released from the "Satanic trinity" to deceive all the nations, to gather them to fight against Jesus Christ at Armageddon. An explainable scenario for this would be that these "aliens" convince the nations that their "evil" counterparts are coming to invade the earth, and that all the nations must unite in Israel (at the junction of the three major continents) to repel the attack. From Satan's perspective, Jesus and His followers WILL be invading the earth – a world that Satan has controlled for over 6000 years.

XVIII. Current Global Trends

There are several growing trends in the world which can be tracked in relation to the Psalm 83 War, the Magog Invasion, and the rest of the End Times events: global oil dependency, the spread of Islam, the resurgence of Russia, the rise of Iraq, and the decline of the West.

Rising Oil Dependency

The growing dependency of every nation on earth upon oil for their economic stability only causes the problems in the Middle East to further boil and bubble. Some of the most tyrannical, poorest nations in the world find themselves being courted by the world powers simply because of their petroleum reserves.

The United States, Europe, China, and even Russia have dramatically changed their foreign policies toward the various oil producing nations at the beginning of this century, as their own oil supplies are used up. Many times, their foreign policies became very slanted against Israel for the sole reason of making the radical Islamic, oil-exporting nations happy and keeping the oil wells pumping. However, the recent dramatic developments in American oil and natural gas exports has begun to change those policies.

The shale-oil and gas boom in the United States that began in 2010 has been altering the petroleum and natural gas markets, particularly with OPEC. The boom has been so significant that in 2018 the United States is forecast to displace Saudi Arabia as the world's largest oil producer – and with no end in sight. However, the market effects of the American oil boom have yet to significantly alter U.S. foreign policy, particularly with regards to the Middle East and the Arab states.

Since the 1970s, oil has become the greatest influence upon economies, industries, politics, and the stability of every nation in the world. Oil is the lifeblood of both the manufacturing industry and the military, and since the majority of transportation in the world relies upon fossil fuels, the steady supply of oil influences every aspect of industrialized nations.

The majority of the world's oil supplies are currently controlled by the handful of Islamic nations in the Middle East, such as Saudi Arabia, Iran, Kuwait, and Iraq. Many other nations have oil supplies, but the quantities, capabilities to extract and refine the oil, or the political climates often prevent these nations from becoming independent of the Islamic oil supply.

How the oil industry and oil markets will affect and/or bring about the Magog Invasion is difficult to track, but you can be sure they will continue be a significant influence on Russia, Europe, and the other nations involved. One possible scenario is that the discovery of a major oil reserve in Israel could cause the oil prices to drastically drop, wreaking havoc in the economies of Russia and the OPEC nations of the Middle East. Another scenario is that China, Russia, and the OPEC nations could threaten the United States and Europe into not getting involved when they move to invade Israel.

In tracking this trend, it's not just the movements in the oil prices or the industry to watch, but the short-term and long-term impacts of these movements upon the various economies and nations of the world.

For this Purpose – the Spread of Islam

Radical Islam has long been a looming threat growing on the horizon to Europe, Africa, and Asia, and many of the other nations in the world. For centuries, even in the nations where Islam was the enforced religion, radical Islam has been dormant. However, since the re-creation of Israel in 1948 and the fall of the Soviet Empire, radical Islam has been growing rapidly in both strength and power.

Over 95% of all modern terrorists and terrorist acts have one fundamental characteristic in common: radical Islam. Radical Islamists hold to a violent interpretation of the Koran, and believe that the only sure way they can go to Paradise after death is to die in a holy war (or jihad). With the widespread invention and production of deadly weapons, the ease in which jihad can be waged has become easier and easier.

This history of Islam is a long, violent struggle between primarily the Arab-based religious system and the other civilizations both near and far. Islam has been from its inception, a religion spread by the sword. The reason Islam is the fastest-growing religion today is because the majority of conversions are forced: a person must convert to Islam or die; there is no other choice given.

This is also occurring on a national level – if a region or nation does not willingly convert to Islamic law, the nation's government is overthrown or terrorism is used to influence the political structure of the nation. The current civil wars of many nations can be boiled down to radical Islamists attempting to force Islamic rule upon a nation, and the other citizens or government resisting.

The followers of radical Islam thrive on terror, murder, and tyranny. They genuinely believe that their god Allah (who supposedly created all people) wants them to destroy all the infidels in any way possible. If Allah is a god, why did he create all these infidels that he hates in the first place? Why doesn't Allah simply destroy them himself and show everyone how great he is, or not even let them be born? And what kind of Parent wants His children to kill, rape, and maim his other children? If Allah wants the faithful to come to him, then why not just leave people free to choose later, instead of at the point of a sword? Don't you want genuine believers and not millions who are forced to convert upon the threat of their lives or their families?

In the Bible, God, gives everyone a chance to turn to Him for salvation, and then simply gives them the consequences of their choice: to be with Him forever or not. He doesn't threaten, bribe, or coerce – He simply gives us the Plan and lays out the Rules, but gives us the freedom to choose Him or not. God loves all people and gives everyone a chance. The Bible teaches that we are to love one other as we love ourselves, and to leave vengeance up to God, not taking it into our own hands. It's impossible to terrorize others if you're living by the Golden Rule.

As radical Islam continues to spread and gain access to catastrophic weapons of destruction, the peace of the world will continue to destabilize. On a smaller scale, tiny groups of the perpetrators of radical Islam can access weapons and put them to use as never before, and can kill or wound millions of people in a very short time. Islam is currently Satan's religion of choice (as communism and Nazism formerly were), and will continue to threaten the world until it is either vanquished or replaced with another religion.

The Waking Russian Bear

Following the collapse of the Soviet Union, Russia has been waking up from her years of hibernation. Since the decades following World War II, Russia (and formerly the Soviet Union) has consistently equipped, financed, and trained Israel's enemies throughout the Middle East. The days of "Mother Russia" are drawing to a close as her population is rapidly aging and not replenishing itself. The astronomical abortion rates in Russia are destroying any chances of a population recovery in the next several generations, while she is surrounded by neighbors whose populations are all exploding (Eastern Europe, China, and the Muslim republics to the south).

Russia finds herself in a bad predicament: few nations to ally herself with that could not significantly endanger her, yet surrounded by growing threats like radical Islam to the south and China to the east. To prevent herself from being overrun by admitting her weaknesses, Russia still presents a very strong, powerful military face to the world. If Russia makes a sudden, very powerful stroke into the Middle East and destroys Israel, she would immediately position herself as a major power in the Mediterranean, and be the new power broker in the Middle East, instead of the United States.

In 2014, Ukrainian protestors ousted the Russian-supported president Viktor Yanukovych, which then triggered Russia to invade Ukraine to reinstate their "puppet." Crimea then revolted and voted to separate from Ukraine, and has subsequently allied with Russia. Despite numerous threats from the Obama administration and the West, no action was taken to protect Ukraine's sovereignty. As a result of the West's inaction, Russia continues to exert their strength in Ukraine and expand their sphere of influence, particularly in Syria as it has consistently backed Assad, the brutal dictator of Syria.

In order to solve some of her short-term and long-term problems, Russia is increasing allying herself with the Islamic nations of the Middle East and providing cover for them – particularly Iran and Syria. With the giant "bear" of Russia watching in the corner, Europe and the United States are very careful about any moves they make in Central Asia or the Middle East. As Russia continues to decay from the inside (though appearing strong on the outside), she will become more focused in her movements in the Middle East in order to revitalize herself and change the world military and economic structure in her favor.

The Rise of Iraq

At the turn of the century (2000), the power structure of the Middle East was radically different. When Saddam Hussein ruled Iraq, few Bible students could picture how Iraq could ever re-emerge as the "Jewel of Kingdoms" in the End Times as the Bible describes. The people were utterly impoverished and Iraq appeared to be just another failing Islamic country.

With the ousting of Saddam Hussein and the steady footsteps towards a free, democratic Iraq taken by the United States and its allies, how Iraq fits into the End Times was beginning to become clearer – until the massive removal of U.S. forces in 2009-2011 by the Obama administration. Instead of leaving a moderate peace-keeping force as in Germany and Japan, Obama removed nearly all the troops and left the fledgling country practically defenseless. The wolves both inside and outside Iraq jumped at the opportunity and are battling one another to fill the power vacuum. Because of the foolish withdrawal, ISIS and other brutal elements inside Iraq were allowed to rise and flourish.

After the Magog Invasion, Iraq could be poised to become the new power-player in the Middle East – one of the few left with a democratic, stable government whose economy will be ready to grow by leaps and bounds. Iraq has little resources other than oil, and when the Magog hordes are miraculously wiped out, Iraq will be left as a major power in the Middle East by the simple attrition of her neighbors.

Expect additional huge oil reserves to be discovered in Iraq, especially in the central region where Babylon is located. Both the northern and southern regions of Iraq have been thoroughly explored for oil and developed to a small extent. But the largest unexplored regions of Iraq are near the center, and the Bible alludes in several passages that there are large reserves of petroleum still yet to be tapped.

After the ouster of Saddam Hussein, Iraq continues to go through a time in which its citizens are deciding whether to side with radical Islam (as is being pushed on them by Iran, Syria, and Turkey) or to become a modern democratic nation. Iraq is wrought with internal struggles and is in no condition to take part in a foreign war, particularly after battling ISIS for the last several years.

Interestingly enough, Iraq is not one of the nations that takes part in the Magog Invasion of Israel, and then emerges as being extremely wealthy soon after the End Times begin. Could it be that Iraq will be one of the few Middle Eastern nations left unscathed after the Magog Invasion occurs? Could it be that Iraq is split in half or even thirds before the Invasion? The world will continue to need oil after the Magog Invasion, and with much of the Islamic oil-rich nations in shambles, the world may turn to Iraq for much of its petroleum needs in the months and years following the Invasion.

Perhaps the 2003 invasion, the defeat of ISIS, and the resumption of progress in the rebuilding of Iraq is another significant indicator that the Magog Invasion will occur soon, and the recent events in Iraq will set the stage for its future re-emergence on the world scene as the great commercial entity as spoken of in Revelation 17-18. After all, if Dubai could become an economic powerhouse in a matter of years, there's no real reason why Iraq couldn't as well.

The Decline of the West

The declining influence of the West on the world stage, particularly the United States of America, has been occurring faster than even the experts thought possible only a few years ago. The long, rising costs of entrenched socialism are increasingly impacting the West, causing it to focus inward in order to return to solvency. Also, the West seems to have tired of the wars in the Middle East over the last twenty years and would rather stay out of the region altogether rather than try to solve the seemingly never-ending problems.

There are several ways to defeat a military power: by crushing it with overwhelming force, decapitating its leadership structure, or by causing it to be stretched so thin that it's rendered ineffective. The latter is what's occurring with regards to the United States. America has a military presence in over one hundred fifty nations and is currently involved in four different wars in the Middle East. The withdrawal of American troops from Iraq has recently been announced, but what about all the rest? Why is our military scattered all over the world yet we cannot even defend our own borders to keep terrorists out?

While the financial storms that raged throughout Europe and America several years ago seem have passed, our debts have been rising out of control for the past sixty years, and the day is coming in which all the debt needs to be repaid. Along with rising socialism and skyrocketing debt, the West has aging populations that are not being replenished, and the increasing costs of caring for the aging Baby Boomer population over the next several decades. The enormous debt and unfunded liabilities caused by social over-spending and massive government waste will eventually have an impact on military and defense spending. It's only a matter of time.

Compounding America's problems has been the abominable leadership under the former Obama administration, which appears to be quickly reversing under the Trump administration. During his two terms as president, Obama repeatedly restrained American influence and removed the world's superpower from the world-scene. While playing politics with American power and the military, he dithered and projected weakness instead of strength, particularly in the Middle East.

While in office, Obama actively created a foreign policy of distrust and indecisiveness towards American allies like Israel while showing the United States to be a paper-tiger towards our enemies such as ISIS, the Syrians and Russians after chemical weapons were used against the rebels, as well as pushing for the Iranian nuclear deal which only really benefited the Iranian government. Thankfully, the Trump administration is restoring our relationships with our allies and dealing decisively with our enemies as demonstrated by withdrawing from the Iranian nuclear deal, defeating ISIS, holding disarmament talks with North Korea (instead of paying them off), and moving the US embassy to Jerusalem.

The European Union which held such promise only a few years ago, but continues falling apart due to the enormous debt and obligations of many of her smaller member nations such as Greece, Portugal, and Italy. The citizens of Germany are especially getting sick of paying for the social policies of most of the other nations of the EU. The day may soon come where Germany extracts itself from the European Union and sides with stronger allies, such as Russia, or forms their own miniature version of the EU with the nations of Eastern Europe. Most recently, Britain voted to leave the EU, though they haven't fully implemented their exit yet.

In the Book of Revelation (v 16:12), there is a curious group referred to as the "kings of the East", which rapidly moves westward and startles the Antichrist, precipitating the buildup of Armageddon. In all likelihood, this is where China, India, and the other nations of the East move into the Middle East to secure their share of the oil resources.

Note that there is no mention of the "kings of the West" in the Scriptures, which should be sobering for all of us in America and Europe.

XIX. Redeeming the Times

In Matthew 24:4-8, shortly before Jesus was crucified, Jesus' disciples came to Him and asked Him about when the End Times would begin and how they could recognize those times.

And Jesus answered and said to them: "Take heed that no one deceives you. For many will come in My name, saying, 'I am the Christ,' and will deceive many. And you will hear of wars and rumors of wars. See that you are not troubled; for all these things must come to pass, but the end is not yet. For nation will rise against nation, and kingdom against kingdom. And there will be famines, pestilences, and earthquakes in various places. All these are the beginning of sorrows.

Notice the last sentence: "All these are the beginning of sorrows" – the earthquakes, natural disasters, wars, and all the financial uncertainties are only the beginning of troubles. However, He tells us to not be troubled, because these things are supposed to happen, and we are simply the ones who are living at the time in which they are occurring.

When we look back at our forefathers – both in this country and other heroes of the faith – we tend to marvel at their courage, their determination, and their perseverance. But they were no different than us – they were just ordinary men. Though our circumstances are different, they had the same fears, the same excuses for apathy, and the same discouragements. But in spite of those huge challenges and obstacles, they forged a new nation that was based upon liberty and justice for all. The heroes of our faith showed how to fight the good fight and shine the light of Christ wherever they could – even in dungeons and in times of torture.

We can lament that these challenges have come in our days, but so does everyone who's faced with such difficulties – our only responsibility is to meet those challenges and fight the good fight. We can shrink and cower or we can stand up, step forward, and hold to our faith. We have a choice.

If you haven't yet been saved, I beg you to become a Christian and join with us. Becoming a Christian could not be simpler: "Believe on the Lord Jesus Christ and you will be saved" (Acts 16:31). More specifically, believing that Jesus came as God in the Flesh, He died for our sins on the Cross, and was resurrected after three days.

If you have already been saved, please join us in deep, regular prayer for our nation, the peace of Jerusalem and Israel, and for the multitudes trapped in evil nations and religions. Immerse yourself in the Word and become "Doers, and not Hearers only." Whenever you leave your home or leave your church, try to have the perspective that "You're now entering the mission field!"

Try to do what is right and good and encourage others to do likewise. Evil days provide enormous opportunities for the Kingdom. We must hold fast and strengthen what remains, and remain true to our faith and persevere until we are called Home.

Afterword

At the time of this latest edition (2018), the population of the Jewish people is nearly equally divided between two nations: Israel and the United States. As of 2010, both Israel and America each had over 40% of the Jewish population within their borders, with the next largest population of nearly 4% in France.

Israel has roughly 6,451,000 Jews (44% - 2017) while the United States has 5,700,000 (39% - 2017) – a difference of nearly half a million people. Ten years ago, those percentages were reversed such that the Jewish population in America was greater than that of Israel. However, the religious character is quite stark: over 75% of Jews in Israel are religious, in comparison to only 2% of Jews in the United States. The vast majority of Jews in America are secular, either atheist or humanist.

I believe it is God's desire for none of His people to remain apart from their land – certainly not half of those who are 'called by His Name'. Sooner or later, the Jewish remnant dwelling in America will be called back to Israel. Perhaps the declining US economy, exploding national debt, and the coming years of inflation (or even hyper-inflation) will push the American Jews to migrate back to Israel.

The ties which bind America and Israel run very deep and our two nations share much in common. Of all the nations of the world, our two countries have foundings which can only be described as 'miraculous'. Both nations overcame incredible odds to free themselves from the authority of the world's foremost superpower at the time, and both have grown to thrive as free, exemplary nations despite the odds. At America's founding, many even proclaimed America as the New Israel. Interestingly enough, both modern countries even fought the same nation in their striving for independence: Great Britain.

More importantly, both Israel and America were founded on the Jewish Scriptures and the precepts of the 'rule of law' rather than the 'rule of man' as most nations were. However, just as ancient Israel wandered away from her God and her foundations, so has America, which is leading her into rapid decline. But where Israel had explicit promises from God to be restored after many years, there are no such promises to America.

Psalm 121 says, "The God of Israel does not slumber nor sleep". Though the State has many challenging times ahead of her, the future of Israel is certain – and is written in the Bible. Though the nations may rage against her, she will stand.

From the Author

First, and most of all, thank you for reading this book! It's my passion to educate, entertain (and sometimes enlighten!) fellow book-lovers! Though writing a book can be a lot of work – along with a fair amount of blood, sweat, and tears – being able to share it with an audience makes all the effort worth it!

Secondly, if you enjoyed the book, please consider posting a short review on Amazon (or wherever you found this book) to help other readers determine if this book is right for them. Good reviews online are to authors what word-of-mouth is in the real world – even if it's just a few lines. Every review really does make a difference. Thank you!

References and Recommended Reading

The Bible (New King James Version). Thomas Nelson, 1982.

Anderson, Sir Robert. "The Coming Prince." Kregel Classics, 1957.

Busch, David Winston. "Appointed: The Biblical Fall Feasts and the Return of the Lord Jesus Christ, King of Yisrael, King of All the Earth." ACW Press, 2003.

Busch, David Winston. "The Assyrian: Satan, His Christ & the Return of the Shadow of Degrees." Xulon Press, 2006.

Chambers, Joseph. "A Palace for the Antichrist: Saddam Hussein's Drive to Rebuild Babylon and It's Place in Bible Prophecy." New Leaf Press, 1996.

Cooper, Bill. "After the Flood: The Early Post-Flood History of Europe Traced Back to Noah." New Wine Press, 1995.

Custance, Arthur C. "A Study of the Names of Genesis 10." http://www.custance.org

Hagee, John. "Jerusalem Countdown." Frontline Press, 2006.

Hunt, Dave. "A Woman Rides the Beast: The Roman Catholic Church and the Last Days." Harvest House Publishers, 1994.

Jeffrey, Grant. "The Next World War: What Prophecy Reveals About Extreme Islam and the West." WaterBrook Press, 2006.

Lahaye, Tim. "Are We Living in the End Times?" Tyndale House Publishers, 2000.

Lahaye, Tim. "Revelation Unveiled." Zondervan, 1999.

Lindsey, Hal. "The Late Great Planet Earth." Zondervan, 1970.

Lindsey, Hal. "The Rapture: Truth or Consequences." Bantam, 1983.

Mcgee, J. Vernon. "Thru the Bible with J. Vernon Mcgee." Thomas Nelson, 1994.

Missler, Chuck. "Alien Encounters: The Secret Behind The Ufo Phenomenon." Koinonia House, 2003.

Missler, Chuck. "Cosmic Codes: Hidden Messages From the Edge of Eternity." Koinonia House, 2004.

Missler, Chuck. "Learn the Bible in 24 Hours." Thomas Nelson, 2002.

Missler, Chuck. "Prophecy 20/20: Profiling the Future Through the Lens of Scripture." Thomas Nelson, 2006.

Missler, Chuck. "The Magog Invasion." Western Front Ltd, 1996.

Morris, Henry. "The Genesis Record: A Scientific and Devotional Commentary on the Book of Beginnings." Baker Books, 2009.

Morris, Henry. "The Revelation Record: A Scientific and Devotional Commentary on the Prophetic Book of the End of Times." Tyndale House Publishers, 1983.

Price, Randall. "The Temple and Bible Prophecy: A Definitive Look at Its Past, Present, and Future." Harvest House Publishers, 2005.

Richardson, Joel. "The Islamic Antichrist: The Shocking Truth about the Real Nature of the Beast." WND Books, 2009.

Showers, Renald. "The Most High God: A Commentary on the Book of Daniel." The Friends of Israel Gospel Ministry, Inc, 1982.

Walker, Peter. "In the Steps of Jesus: An Illustrated Guide to the Places of the Holy Land." Zondervan, 2007.

Walvoord, John. "The Revelation of Jesus Christ." Moody Publishers, 1989.

Walvoord, John. "Daniel: The Key to Prophetic Revelation."

Walvoord, John. "Every Prophecy of the Bible: Clear Explanations for Uncertain Times." David C. Cook, 1999.

About the Author

Chris Hambleton resides in Denver, Colorado, where he is employed as a software developer and consultant. He has authored more than a dozen books, as well as developed several websites, software applications, and blogs from time to time. His other interests include traveling, hiking, running, studying the Bible, reading American history and biographies, and literally devouring good fiction books. Recently, he has been learning to enjoy classical music, playing the piano, and learning Hebrew.

To learn more about C.W. Hambleton and his other books, please visit his author website at http://www.cwhambleton.com.

Other Titles by the Author

Speculative Fiction Titles
"Out of the Whirlwind"
"The Exchange"
"The Castors of Giza"
"The Cell"
"Endeavor in Time"

The Time of Jacob's Trouble Trilogy
"The Last Aliyah" (Book 1)
"The Son of Shinar" (Book 2)
"The Siege of Zion" (Book 3)

The Sons of Liberty Trilogy
"The Convention" (Book 1)
"The Green Zone" (Book 2)
"The Declaration" (Book 3)

The Days of Noah Series
"Rise of the Anshar" (Book 1)

The HaZikaron Series
"The Seed of Haman" (Book 1)

Non-Fiction Titles
"Walks with Rich"
"Our American Awakening"
"The American Tyrant"
"Ezekiel Watch"
"On the Precipice"

Connect with Me Online:
Website: http://www.cwhambleton.com
Blog: http://fictionsoftware.wordpress.com
Facebook: http://facebook.com/cwhambleton
Goodreads: http://goodreads.com/cwhambleton
Twitter: http://twitter.com/chris_hambleton

Author Biography

Chris Hambleton's first book, "The Time of Jacob's Trouble" was published in 2008 and later revised and expanded in 2011 as "The Time of Jacob's Trouble Trilogy" which chronicles the lives of an Israeli family as they experience the Magog Invasion and then the events of the Great Tribulation.

In "The Last Aliyah" (Book 1 of "The Time of Jacob's Trouble"), the tides of war are once again rising against the nation of Israel. Rocket attacks on Haifa and Sderot are increasing, and Israel cautiously prepares a response to a conflict that many fear will never end. And then a decision is made that will change the face of the Middle East forever.

The story of the Rosenberg family continues in "The Son of Shinar" (Book 2 of "The Time of Jacob's Trouble"), in which after the devastation of Israel's enemies in the Magog Invasion, Israel now has enough weapons and energy supplies for seven years. But now, rumors of a great leader and healer have begun sweeping through Baghdad. Could he be the long-awaited Jewish Messiah?

The End Times trilogy of the Rosenberg family concludes in "The Siege of Zion" (Book 3 of "The Time of Jacob's Trouble"). In one day, Supreme Leader David Medine has desecrated the Jewish Temple and Israel has fallen under the authority of the World Union. The Great Tribulation has begun and the future of Israel – along with all humanity – hangs in the balance.

After writing the "The Time of Jacob's Trouble" the next book published was "Endeavor in Time." In this time-travel science-fiction story, Daniel Marks, the Chief Programmer on a cutting-edge research project, suddenly finds himself back nearly twenty years in the past. With his knowledge of the future before it happens, will he be able to prevent another disaster at NASA before Endeavor, the new shuttle is launched? The sequel to "Endeavor in Time" was published in mid-2012 called "The Exchange" in which Daniel Marks experiences a horrible personal loss and embarks on a hybrid-age journey which will cause him to not only question the entire purpose of his existence, but that very existence itself.

In 2010, "The Cell" was published, a speculative fiction novel that speculates about America's future a decade after the financial crash of 2008. As America to slog through the Great Recession, the conservatives and the churches have been silenced, and law enforcement seems helpless against the growing gangs and vigilante groups. And though the light of many churches have been extinguished, tiny flames of faith flicker to life and begin to grow. *(This novel was later revised in 2015 to align with "The Sons of Liberty Trilogy").*

Late in 2011, Chris's first two non-fiction books were published, "On the Precipice" and "Ezekiel Watch." The book "On the Precipice - Hosea Speaks to America" explores America's current problems in comparison to the Book of Hosea in the Bible, in which the nation of Israel had turned away from her Scriptural foundations and was faced with judgment. "Ezekiel Watch" provides a comprehensive examination of Ezekiel 36-39: Israel's restoration to her homeland and the massive attack on Israel by Russia, Iran, and the other Islamic nations of the Middle East. *(This book was updated in 2018 with the latest news/events out of the Middle East, particularly the Syrian Civil War.)*

"The Castors of Giza" is the first of several books that fictionalizes ancient history, the focus of this book being the construction of the Great Pyramid of Egypt. In the Fourth Dynasty of Kemet is growing stronger under its ambitious new leader, Pharaoh Khufu. His father established a legacy of extravagant monuments and massive building projects, and his son will not allow himself to become a lesser king. With the science of pyramid construction now perfected, Khufu has determined to build the grandest monument of all time: the Great Pyramid.

The latest non-fiction book, "Our American Awakening" is a politically-themed book that explores America's founding, decline into Progressivism, and ways to restore America. What lies ahead for America in the years ahead? What changes can we make today that will improve America for our children and grandchildren?

"Rise of the Anshar" kicks off a new series of novels that are set in the times of Noah, chronicling the events that led to the end of the First Age and then the replenishing of the world after the Flood. "The Days of Noah Series" is expected to span at least five novels, though more may be necessary to complete the series.

"The Seed of Haman" is a modern spin-off from the Book of Esther set in the Twenty-First Century. A Tehran University professor learns of his family's dark secret and takes up the mantle to renew their ancient vendetta against the Jewish people. Meanwhile, teams of Israeli operatives are embedded deep inside Iran with orders to thwart the uranium enrichment program by any means necessary.

As the prelude to the novel about the Great Pyramid, the novel "Out of the Whirlwind," is an expanded version of the story of Job that begins at the Tower of Babel and ends with the arrival of Abram in Canaan. Who was the man we know as Job, and how did he become who God called, "the greatest man in all the earth"? What happened to him before, during, and after his trials, and how was his story preserved?

In "The Convention," the first book of "The Sons of Liberty Trilogy," after six years of a failed presidency, the United States of America teeters on the brink of collapse. When the government shuts down over another budget conflict, the Sons of

Liberty issue an ultimatum to the Capitol to get their act together – or else. As the conflict between Washington and the rest of the country begins to spiral out of control, a group of state legislators sets out to hold a Convention of States in hopes of pulling the nation back from a civil war.

"The Green Zone" is the second book in "The Sons of Liberty Trilogy." As any hope for legal reforms of the Washington leviathan fade, the Sons of Liberty take matters into their own hands and renew their Ultimatum with vengeance. If the terms of the Ultimatum are not enacted by ballot, then they will be by bullet. With an isolated, out-of-touch president coasting through his seventh year in office, the Sons of Liberty set out to make his last few years in office the worst in history.

"The Declaration" wraps up "The Sons of Liberty Trilogy" and provides a glimpse into the future of the United States as it starts to fracture. Rumblings of revolution are heard in Texas while Alaska begins to pull away from the Union. Though their militia movement has been destroyed, the Sons of Liberty rise one last time in the name of liberty and justice for all.

Chris's latest work, "Walks with Rich" is a personal tribute to the late Rich Mullins and his music. This book explores many of Rich's B-sides songs and delves into how his faith, compassion, brokenness, and joy shaped his music, and how his songs can still speak to fellow Christian believers today.

Ezekiel Watch

Manufactured by Amazon.ca
Acheson, AB